Problems in Criticism
of the Arts

Science Research Associates, Inc., 259 East Erie Street, Chicago, Illinois 60611
Distributors   A Subsidiary of IBM

Problems in Criticism of the Arts

Readings Selected and Edited by

Holley Gene Duffield
Central Michigan University

Chandler Publishing Company
124 Spear Street, San Francisco, California 94105

Previously published and copyrighted materials are reprinted with the permission of authors, publishers, or copyright owners as listed below:

Aristotle, from the *Poetics.* Chapters 1–5 from *Aristotle's Theory of Poetry and the Fine Arts,* by S. H. Butcher, St. Martin's Press, 1911. Reprinted by permission of Macmillan & Company Ltd., and the Executors of the Estate of S. H. Butcher.

Clive Bell, "The Aesthetic Hypothesis": Frederick A. Stokes Co. Reprinted by permission of G. P. Putnam's Sons from *Art* by Clive Bell, Capricorn Edition.

Henri Bergson, from "Laughter": Macmillan Company, Ltd. From the book *Comedy,* copyright © 1956 by Wylie Sypher, which contains "Laughter" by Henri Bergson. Reprinted by permission of Doubleday & Company, Inc.

A. C. Bradley, "Poetry for Poetry's Sake." Reprinted from *Oxford Lectures on Poetry,* by A. C. Bradley by permission of Macmillan & Company, Ltd., and St. Martin's Press, Inc.

Manuel Bilsky, "The Significance of Locating the Art Object." Reprinted from *Philosophy and Phenomenological Research,* Vol. 13, by permission of the journal and the author.

Richard Rudner, "The Ontological Status of the Aesthetic Object." Reprinted from *Philosophy and Phenomenological Research,* Vol. 10, by permission of the author and the journal.

Paul Ziff, "The Task of Defining a Work of Art." Reprinted from *The Philosophical Review,* Vol. 62, by permission of the author and the journal.

Ruth Saw, "What Is a 'Work of Art'?" Reprinted from *Philosophy,* Vol. 36, by permission of the author and the Royal Institute of Philosophy.

Margaret Macdonald, "Art and Imagination." Reprinted from *Proceedings of the Aristotelian Society,* Vol. 53, by permission of the Editor of The Aristotelian Society.

Robert Hoffman, "Conjectures and Refutations on the Ontological Status of the Work of Art." Reprinted from *Mind,* Vol. 71, by permission of the Editor and the author.

W. B. Gallie, "Art as an Essentially Contested Concept." Reprinted from *The Philosophical Quarterly,* Vol. 6, by permission of the Editor and the author.

William E. Kennick, "Does Traditional Aesthetics Rest on a Mistake?" Reprinted from *Mind,* Vol. 67, by permission of the Editor and the author.

Morris Weitz, "The Role of Theory in Aesthetics." Reprinted from the *Journal of Aesthetics and Art Criticism,* Vol. 15, by permission of the *Journal* and the author.

Joseph Margolis, "Mr. Weitz and the Definition of Art." Reprinted from *Philosophical Studies,* Vol. 9.

Lewis K. Zerby, "A Reconsideration of the Role of Theory in Aesthetics—A Reply to Morris Weitz." Reprinted from the *Journal of Aesthetics and Art Criticism,* Vol. 16, by permission of the *Journal* and the author.

Arnold Berleant, "A Note on the Problem of Defining 'Art'." Reprinted from *Philosophy and Phenomenological Research,* Vol. 25, by permission of the author and the journal.

C. J. Ducasse, from *The Philosophy of Art.* Copyright 1929 by the Dial Press, Inc., and used with the permission of the publishers.

L. A. Reid, "Greatness." Reprinted from *A Study of Aesthetics,* copyright 1929 by George Allen & Unwin, Ltd., and used with the permission of the publishers.

Cleanth Brooks and Robert Penn Warren, "Joyce Kilmer's 'Trees'." From Cleanth Brooks and Robert Penn Warren's *Understanding Poetry,* copyright 1938, 1950, © 1960 by Holt, Rinehart and Winston, Inc. Reprinted by permission of the publishers.

Morris Weitz, "Criticism without Evaluation." Reprinted from *The Philosophical Review,* Vol. 61, by permission of the *Review* and the author.

Book designed by Joseph M. Roter

To Donna, Mark, and Matthew

Contents

Foreword

The four sections of this book are elaborations of four of the most controversial problems in criticism of the arts: the nature of art, the nature and identity of a work of art, the nature and role of aesthetic theory, and the standards of evaluation. A brief introduction and suggested additional readings accompany each section.

Because of the nature of its material, all or part of this anthology can be used in various courses, such as those in literary criticism, aesthetics, humanities, and even freshman composition.

H. G. D.

Problems in Criticism of the Arts

One

The Nature of Art

Part One. Selected Readings

Bell, Clive. "The Difference of Literature," *New Republic*, 33: 18–19 (1922).

Caudwell, Christopher. *Illusion and Reality*. London, 1947.

Collingwood, R. G. *The Principles of Art*. Oxford, 1938.

Dewey, John. *Art as Experience*. New York, 1934.

Ducasse, Curt John. *The Philosophy of Art*. New York, 1929.

———. "What Has Beauty to Do with Art?" *Journal of Philosophy*, 25: 181–185 (1928).

Duffield, Holley Gene, and Manuel Bilsky, eds. *Tolstoy and the Critics: Literature and Aesthetics*. Chicago, 1965.

Hospers, John. "The Croce-Collingwood Theory of Art," *Philosophy*, 31: 291–308 (1956).

———. "The Concept of Artistic Expression," *Proceedings of the Aristotelian Society*, 313–344 (1954–1955).

Ortega y Gasset, José. *The Dehumanization of Art*. Princeton, 1948.

Osborne, Harold. *Aesthetics and Criticism*. London, 1955.

Rader, Melvin, ed. *A Modern Book of Esthetics*. New York, 1962.

Santayana, George. *The Sense of Beauty*. New York, 1896.

Tolstoy, Leo. *What Is Art?* and *Essays on Art*. New York, 1963.

Trilling, Lionel. "Art and Neurosis," *The Liberal Imagination*. New York, 1945.

Vivas, Eliseo, and Murray Krieger, eds. *The Problems of Aesthetics*. New York, 1953.

Weitz, Morris, ed. *Problems in Aesthetics*. New York, 1959.

Introduction

The main problem this section deals with in various ways is that of isolating the feature or features of art that distinguish it from nonart. The essays fall into at least two groups: those that discuss the nature of art itself and those that discuss the nature of particular arts (such as poetry and painting). Although this arrangement of material might seem out of place in a section devoted to the nature of art, it has method. Not only can the reader study explicit statements about the nature of art, but he also can work backwards from statements about particular arts to implied ideas about the nature of art in general. For example, Véron clearly states what he believes distinguishes art from non-art, and Aristotle's theory that poetry and music are both modes of imitation (although they are different in other ways) certainly invites one to speculate about what Aristotle's theory of art might have been.

Furthermore, the reader has an opportunity to compare and contrast five essentially different theories of the nature of art and, if he desires, to try them out, even to the point of attempting to refute them.

Finally, as a supplement to his reading in Part Four, the reader ought to note the criteria writers in this section use to evaluate art. In any given theory, all art is equal, except that some is better.

Aristotle

from *Poetics*

I

I propose to treat of Poetry in itself and of its various kinds, noting the essential quality of each; to inquire into the structure of the plot as requisite to a good poem; into the number and nature of the parts of which a poem is composed; and similarly into whatever else falls within the same inquiry. Following, then, the order of nature, let us begin with the principles which come first.

Epic poetry and Tragedy, Comedy also and Dithyrambic poetry, and the music of the flute and of the lyre in most of their forms, are all in their general conception modes of imitation. They differ, however, from one another in three respects,—the medium, the objects, the manner or mode of imitation, being in each case distinct.

For as there are persons who, by conscious art or mere habit, imitate and represent various objects through the medium of colour and form, or again by the voice; so in the arts above mentioned, taken as a whole, the imitation is produced by rhythm, language, or 'harmony,' either singly or combined.

Thus in the music of the flute and of the lyre, 'harmony' and rhythm alone are employed; also in other arts, such as that of the shepherd's pipe, which are essentially similar to these. In dancing, rhythm alone is used without 'harmony'; for even dancing imitates character, emotion, and action, by rhythmical movement.

There is another art which imitates by means of language

[Reprinted from *Aristotle's Theory of Poetry and the Fine Arts*, trans. S. H. Butcher. London: Macmillan Co., Ltd., 1911. Chs. 1–5.]

5

alone, and that either in prose or verse—which verse, again, may either combine different metres or consist of but one kind—but this has hitherto been without a name. For there is no common term we could apply to the mimes of Sophron and Xenarchus and the Socratic dialogues on the one hand; and, on the other, to poetic imitations in iambic, elegiac, or any similar metre. People do, indeed, add the word 'maker' or 'poet' to the name of the metre, and speak of elegiac poets, or epic (that is, hexameter) poets, as if it were not the imitation that makes the poet, but the verse that entitles them all indiscriminately to the name. Even when a treatise on medicine or natural science is brought out in verse, the name of poet is by custom given to the author; and yet Homer and Empedocles have nothing in common but the metre, so that it would be right to call the one poet, the other physicist rather than poet. On the same principle, even if a writer in his poetic imitation were to combine all metres, as Chaeremon did in his Centaur, which is a medley composed of metres of all kinds, we should bring him too under the general term poet. So much then for these distinctions.

There are, again, some arts which employ all the means above mentioned,—namely, rhythm, tune, and metre. Such as Dithyrambic and Nomic poetry, and also Tragedy and Comedy; but between them the difference is, that in the first two cases these means are all employed in combination, in the latter, now one means is employed, now another.

Such, then, are the differences of the arts with respect to the medium of imitation.

II

Since the objects of imitation are men in action, and these men must be either of a higher or a lower type (for moral character mainly answers to these divisions, goodness and badness being the distinguishing marks of moral differences), it follows that we must represent men either as better than in real life, or as worse, or as they are. It is the same in painting. Polygnotus depicted men as nobler than they are, Pauson as less noble, Dionysius drew them true to life.

Now it is evident that each of the modes of imitation above

mentioned will exhibit these differences, and become a distinct kind in imitating objects that are thus distinct. Such diversities may be found even in dancing, flute-playing, and lyre-playing. So again in language, whether prose or verse unaccompanied by music. Homer, for example, makes men better than they are; Cleophon as they are; Hegemon the Thasian, the inventor of parodies, and Nicochares, the author of the Deiliad, worse than they are. The same thing holds good of Dithyrambs and Nomes; here too one may portray different types, as Timotheus and Philoxenus differed in representing their Cyclopes. The same distinction marks off Tragedy from Comedy; for Comedy aims at representing men as worse, Tragedy as better than in actual life.

III

There is still a third difference—the manner in which each of these objects may be imitated. For the medium being the same, and the objects the same, the poet may imitate by narration—in which case he can either take another personality as Homer does, or speak in his own person, unchanged—or he may present all his characters as living and moving before us.

These, then, as we said at the beginning, are the three differences which distinguish artistic imitation,—the medium, the objects, and the manner. So that from one point of view, Sophocles is an imitator of the same kind as Homer—for both imitate higher types of character; from another point of view, of the same kind as Aristophanes—for both imitate persons acting and doing. Hence, some say, the name of 'drama' is given to such poems, as representing action. For the same reason the Dorians claim the invention both of Tragedy and Comedy. The claim to Comedy is put forward by the Megarians,—not only by those of Greece proper, who allege that it originated under their democracy, but also by the Megarians of Sicily, for the poet Epicharmus, who is much earlier than Chionides and Magnes, belonged to that country. Tragedy too is claimed by certain Dorians of the Peloponnese. In each case they appeal to the evidence of language. The outlying villages, they say, are by them called κῶμαι, by the Athenians δῆμοι: and they assume that Comedians were so named not from κωμάζειν, 'to revel,' but because they wandered from village to village (κατά κώμας), being excluded contemptuously from the city. They add also that the Dorian word for 'doing' is δρᾶν, and the Athenian, πράττειν.

This may suffice as to the number and nature of the various modes of imitation.

IV

Poetry in general seems to have sprung from two causes, each of them lying deep in our nature. First, the instinct of imitation is implanted in man from childhood, one difference between him and other animals being that he is the most imitative of living creatures, and through imitation learns his earliest lessons; and no less universal is the pleasure felt in things imitated. We have evidence of this in the facts of experience. Objects which in themselves we view with pain, we delight to contemplate when reproduced with minute fidelity: such as the forms of the most ignoble animals and of dead bodies. The cause of this again is, that to learn gives the liveliest pleasure, not only to philosophers but to men in general; whose capacity, however, of learning is more limited. Thus the reason why men enjoy seeing a likeness is, that in contemplating it they find themselves learning or inferring, and saying perhaps, 'Ah, that is he.' For if you happen not to have seen the original, the pleasure will be due not to the imitation as such, but to the execution, the colouring, or some such other cause.

Imitation, then, is one instinct of our nature. Next, there is the instinct for 'harmony' and rhythm, metres being manifestly sections of rhythm. Persons, therefore, starting with this natural gift developed by degrees their special aptitudes, till their rude improvisations gave birth to Poetry.

Poetry now diverged in two directions, according to the individual character of the writers. The graver spirits imitated noble actions, and the actions of good men. The more trivial sort imitated the actions of meaner persons, at first composing satires, as the former did hymns to the gods and the praises of famous men. A poem of the satirical kind cannot indeed be put down to any author earlier than Homer; though many such writers probably there were. But from Homer onward, instances can be cited,

—his own Margites, for example, and other similar compositions. The appropriate metre was also here introduced; hence the measure is still called the iambic or lampooning measure, being that in which people lampooned one another. Thus the older poets were distinguished as writers of heroic or of lampooning verse.

As, in the serious style, Homer is pre-eminent among poets, for he alone combined dramatic form with excellence of imitation, so he too first laid down the main lines of Comedy, by dramatising the ludicrous instead of writing personal satire. His Margites bears the same relation to Comedy that the Iliad and Odyssey do to Tragedy. But when Tragedy and Comedy came to light, the two classes of poets still followed their natural bent: the lampooners became writers of Comedy, and the Epic poets were succeeded by Tragedians, since the drama was a larger and higher form of art.

Whether Tragedy has as yet perfected its proper types or not; and whether it is to be judged in itself, or in relation also to the audience,—this raises another question. Be that as it may, Tragedy—as also Comedy—was at first mere improvisation. The one originated with the authors of the Dithyramb, the other with those of the phallic songs, which are still in use in many of our cities. Tragedy advanced by slow degrees; each new element that showed itself was in turn developed. Having passed through many changes, it found its natural form, and there it stopped.

Aeschylus first introduced a second actor; he diminished the importance of the Chorus, and assigned the leading part to the dialogue. Sophocles raised the number of actors to three, and added scene-painting. Moreover, it was not till late that the short plot was discarded for one of greater compass, and the grotesque diction of the earlier satyric form for the stately manner of Tragedy. The iambic measure then replaced the trochaic tetrameter, which was originally employed when the poetry was of the satyric order, and had greater affinities with dancing. Once dialogue had come in, Nature herself discovered the appropriate measure. For the iambic is, of all measures, the most colloquial: we see it in the fact that conversational speech runs into iambic lines more frequently than into any other kind of verse; rarely into hexameters, and only when we drop the colloquial intonation. The additions to the number of 'episodes' or acts, and the other accessories of which tradition tells, must be taken as already described; for to discuss them in detail would, doubtless, be a large undertaking.

V

Comedy is, as we have said, an imitation of characters of a lower type,—not, however, in the full sense of the word bad, the Ludicrous being merely a subdivision of the ugly. It consists in some defect or ugliness which is not painful or destructive. To take an obvious example, the comic mask is ugly and distorted, but does not imply pain.

The successive changes through which Tragedy passed, and the authors of these changes, are well known, whereas Comedy has had no history, because it was not at first treated seriously. It was late before the Archon granted a comic chorus to a poet; the performers were till then voluntary. Comedy had already taken definite shape when comic poets, distinctively so called, are heard of. Who furnished it with masks, or prologues, or increased the number of actors,—these and other similar details remain unknown. As for the plot, it came originally from Sicily; but of Athenian writers Crates was the first who, abandoning the 'iambic' or lampooning form, generalised his themes and plots.

Epic poetry agrees with Tragedy in so far as it is an imitation in verse of characters of a higher type. They differ, in that Epic poetry admits but one kind of metre, and is narrative in form. They differ, again, in their length: for Tragedy endeavours, as far as possible, to confine itself to a single revolution of the sun, or but slightly to exceed this limit; whereas the Epic action has no limits of time. This, then, is a second point of difference; though at first the same freedom was admitted in Tragedy as in Epic poetry.

Of their constituent parts some are common to both, some peculiar to Tragedy: whoever, therefore, knows what is good or bad Tragedy, knows also about Epic poetry. All the elements of an Epic poem are found in Tragedy, but the elements of a Tragedy are not all found in the Epic poem. . . .

Eugene Véron

from *Aesthetics*

General definition of art—
Mutual relation and analysis of the different arts.

. . . art, far from being the blossom and fruit of civilization, is rather, its germ. It began to give evidence of its existence so soon as man became self-conscious, and is to be found clearly defined in his very earliest works.

By its psychologic origin it is bound up with the constituent principles of humanity. The salient and essential characteristic of man is his incessant cerebral activity, which is propagated and developed by countless acts and works of varied kind. The aim and rule of this activity is the search after *the best;* that is to say, the more and more complete satisfaction of physical and moral wants. This instinct, common to all animals, is seconded in man by an exceptionally well-developed faculty to adapt the means to the end.

The effort to satisfy physical wants has given birth to all the industries that defend, preserve, and smooth the path of life; the effort to satisfy the moral wants—of which one of the most important is the gratification of our cerebral activity itself—has created the arts, long before it could give them power sufficient for the conscious elaboration of ideas. The life of sentiment preceded the manifestations of intellectual life by many centuries.

[Reprinted from *Aesthetics,* trans. W. H. Armstrong. London: Chapman and Hall, 1879. Pp. 88–90, 105–109, 126–131, 139, 389. Footnotes have been renumbered.]

11

The gratification, *in esse* or *in posse,* of either real or imaginary wants, is the cause of happiness, joy, pleasure, and of all the feelings connected with them; the contrary is marked by grief, sadness, fear etc.: but in both cases there is emotion, whether grave or gay, and it is the nature of such emotion to give more or less lively evidence of its existence by means of exterior signs. When expressed by gesture and rhythmic movement, such motion produces the dance; when by rhythmic notes, music; when by rhythmic words, poetry.

As in another aspect man is essentially sympathetic and his joy or pain is often caused as much by the good or evil fortunes of others as by his own; as, besides, he possesses in a very high degree the faculty of combining series of fictitious facts, and of representing them in colours even more lively than those of reality: it results that the domain of art is of infinite extent for him. For the causes of emotion are multiplied for every man— not only by the number of similar beings who live around him and are attached to him by the more or less closely knit bonds of affection, alliance, similitude of situation or community of ideas and interests; but, also, by the never-ending multitude of beings and events that are able to originate or direct the imaginings of poets.

To these elements of emotion and moral enjoyment, must be added the combinations of lines, of forms and of colours, the dispositions and opposition of light and shade, etc. The instinctive search after this kind of emotion or pleasure, the special organ of which is the eye, has given birth to what are called the arts of design—sculpture, painting and architecture.

We may say then, by way of general definition, that art is the manifestation of emotion, obtaining external interpretation, now by expressive arrangements of line, form or colour, now by a series of gestures, sounds, or words governed by particular rhythmical cadence.[1]

---

[1] Thoré, in his *Salon de* 1847, speaking of Delacroix, gives a definition very like our own. "Poetry, to speak generally, is the faculty of feeling internally the essence of life (?) , and art is the faculty of expressing the same thing in external form. Artists, *littérateurs,* painters, sculptors, musicians, really invent only the form to be taken by the poetic sentiment breathed into them by

If our definition is exact, we must conclude, from it, that the merit of a work of art, whatever it may be, can be finally measured by the power with which it manifests or interprets the emotion that was its determining cause, and that, for a like reason, must constitute its innermost and supreme unity.

* * * *

Imitation is no more the aim of art, than a mere collection of letters and syllables is the aim of a writer who wishes to express his thoughts and feelings by the aid of the words which they form. The poet arranging his verses, the musician composing his airs and harmonies, are well aware that their real object lies beyond words and notes. This distinction, as we have here explained it, is perhaps less clear in matters of painting and sculpture. Some artists, and these not the least capable, are quite convinced that when they have a model before them, their one duty is to imitate it. And indeed they do nothing else; and, by virtue of such imitation they succeed in producing works of incontestable artistic value.

Here we have simply a misunderstanding. If an artist were really able to reduce himself to the condition of a copying machine; if he could so far efface and suppress himself as to confine his work to the servile reproduction of all the features and details of an object or event passing before his eyes: the only value his work would possess, would be that of a more or less exact *procès verbal,* and it would perforce remain inferior to reality. Where is the artist who would attempt to depict sunlight without taking

nature or by life. . . . Nature is the supreme artist who in her universal gallery offers to a favoured few the principles of all perfection; the object is to develop some sort of individuality, to give a second creation, with its own distinct and original signification. Art, being the form or image of a thought, or, if you will, the human interpretation of the appearances presented by nature, should be as human as possible. The more the artist has transformed external reality, the more of himself has he put into his work, the more has he raised his representation towards the ideal concealed in the heart of every man, and the farther has he penetrated into the world of poetry. On the other hand, if he has added nothing to the common physiognomy of nature, has he produced an industrial, but not an artistic work. Such work would be worthy only of a mechanic. To copy nature, as most people mean it, is folly. Take your dark room and your daguerreotype." We need not pause to consider the phraseology, which is out of date. In the main, the ideas are true.

refuge in some legerdemain, calling to his aim devices which the true sun would despise? But enough of this. Just because he is endowed with sensibility and imaginative power, the artist, in presence of the facts of nature or the events of history, finds himself, whether he will or not, in a peculiar situation. However thorough a realist he may think himself, he does not leave himself to chance. Now, choice of subject alone is enough to prove that, from the very beginning, some preference has existed, the result of a more or less predeterminate impression, and of a more or less unconscious agreement between the character of the object and that of the artist. This impression and agreement he sets to work to embody in outward form; it is the real aim of his work, and its possession gives him his claim to the name of artist. Without wishing or even knowing it, he moulds the features of nature to his dominant impression and to the idea that caused him to take pencil in hand. His work has an accidental stamp, in addition to that of the permanent genius which constitutes his individuality. Poet, musician, sculptor and architect, all pay more or less strict obedience to the same law. To it, point all those rules of artistic composition which pedantic academicism has subtly multiplied until they contradict each other.

The more of this personal character that a work possesses; the more harmonious its details and their combined expression; the more clearly each part communicates the impression of the artist, whether of grandeur, of melancholy or of joy; in fine, the more that expression of human sensation and will predominates over mere imitation: the better will be its chance of obtaining sooner or later the admiration of the world—always supposing that the sentiment expressed be a generous one, and that the execution be not of such a kind as to repel or baffle connoisseurs. It is not of course impossible, that an artist endowed with an ill-regulated or morbid imagination may place himself outside all normal conditions and condemn himself to the eternal misapprehension of the public. Impressions that are too particular, eccentric feelings, fantastic execution or processes, which do nothing to raise the intrinsic value or power of inspiration of a work, may give it so strange and ultra-individual a character, that it may become impossible for us to arrive at its real merit. The best qualities, when exaggerated, become faults; and that very personality or individuality which, when added to imitative power, results in a work of art, produces when pushed to extravagance nothing but an enigma.

We see, then, if we have succeeded in making ourselves understood, that the beautiful in art springs mainly from the intervention of the genius of man when more or less excited by special emotion.

A work is beautiful when it bears strong marks of the individuality of its author, of the permanent personality of the artist, and of the more or less accidental impression produced upon him by the sight of the object or event rendered.

In a word, it is from the worth of the artist that that of his work is derived. It is the manifestation of the faculties and qualities he possesses which attracts and fascinates us. The more sympathetic power and individuality that these faculties and qualities display, the easier is it for them to obtain our love and admiration. On the other hand, we, for a similar reason, reject and contemn bold and vulgar works that by their shortcomings demonstrate the moral and intellectual mediocrity of their authors, and prove the latter to have mistaken their vocation.

Consequently, then, beauty in art is a purely human creation. Imitation may be its means, as in sculpture and painting; or, on the other hand, it may have nothing to do with it, as in poetry and music. This beauty is of so peculiar a nature that it may exist even in ugliness itself; inasmuch as the exact reproduction of an ugly model may be a beautiful work of art, by the ensemble of qualities which the composition of it may prove are possessed by its author.

The very theory of imitation is but the incomplete and superficial statement of the ideas which we are here advocating. What is it that we admire in imitation? The resemblance? We have that much better in the object itself. But how is it that the similitude of an ugly object can be beautiful? It is obvious that between the object and its counterfeit some new element intervenes. This element is the personality, or, at least, the skill of the artist. This latter, indeed, is what they admire who will have it that beauty consists in imitation. What these applaud, in fact, is the talent of the artist. If we look below the surface and analyse their admiration we shall find that it is so; whether they mean it or not, what they praise in a work is the worker.

This was the opinion of Bürger, who, in his *Salon of* 1863, says: "In works which interest us the authors in a way substitute themselves for nature. However common or vulgar the latter may be, they have some rare and peculiar way of looking at it. It is Chardin himself whom we admire in his representation of a glass of water. We admire the genius of Rembrandt in the profound and individual character which he imparted to every head that posed before him. Thus did they seem to him, and this explains everything simple or fantastic in his expression and execution."

After all this, we need not stop to refute the theory which would found artistic beauty upon the imitation of "beautiful nature." In spite of the brilliant reputation that its triumph in three academies has given to M. Ch. Sevêyne's book upon the science of beauty, it does not seem to us to be founded upon arguments worthy of respect; it has not shown us where "beautiful nature" (*la belle nature*) is to be found in *Le Pouilleux,* in the *Raft of the Medusa,* in the *Battlefield of Eylau,* in the character of *Tartuffe,* or of *La Marneffe.*

The only beauty in a work of art is that placed there by the artist. It is both the result of his efforts and the foundation of his success. As often as he is struck by any vivid impression—whether moral, intellectual, or physical—and expresses that impression by some outward process—by poetry, music, sculpture, painting or architecture—in such a way as to cause its communication with the soul of spectator or auditor; so often does he produce a work of art the beauty of which will be in exact proportion to the intelligence and depth of the sentiment displayed, and the power shown in giving it outward form.

The union of all these conditions constitutes artistic beauty in its most complete expression.

With a few reservations, then, we may preserve the definition of æsthetics which usage has sanctified—*The Science of Beauty.* For the sake of clearness, however, and to prevent confusion, we prefer to call it the *Science of Beauty in Art.* Had not the tyranny of formulæ by custom become too strong, we would willingly refrain from using the word "beauty" at all, for it has the drawback of being too exclusively connected with the sense of seeing, and of calling up too much the idea of visible form. The employment of this word became general when *the* art *par excellence* was sculpture. To make it apply to the other arts, it was necessary to foist upon it a series of extensions which deprived it of all accuracy. Language possesses no word more vague or less precise. This absence of precision has perhaps contributed more than might at first be supposed to that confusion of ideas which can alone explain the multiplicity and absurdity of current æsthetic theories.

All these inconveniences and obscurities may be avoided by simply putting it thus:—

Æsthetics is the science whose object is the study and elucidation of the manifestations of artistic genius.

* * * *

RESUMÉ

To sum up—there are two distinct kinds of art. The one, decorative art, we understand to be that whose main object is the gratification of the eye and ear, and whose chief means perfection of form are harmony and grace of contour, diction or sound. Such art rests upon the desire for beauty, and has nothing in view beyond the peculiar delight caused by the sight of beautiful objects. It has produced admirable works in the past, and may produce them again now or in the future, on condition that its inspiration be sought in actual and existing life, and not in the imitation of works sanctified by time. We must recognize, however, that modern art has no tendency in this latter direction. Beauty no longer suffices for us. Indeed, for the last two thousand years something more has been required; for even among the chefs d'œuvre of the Greeks not a few owe their creation to a different sentiment. Some of the great artists of antiquity were certainly occupied with the interpretation of the moral life; and had not time destroyed their painted works, we should, at the present moment, probably be able to show absolute proofs of this tendency. But we may readily dispense with the confirmation

which they would have afforded to our arguments; for we find
more than sufficient evidence in the avowed character of the
music of the Greeks, in many of the most important works of
their sculptors, and in most of their great poems.

The chief characteristic of modern art—of art, that is, left to
follow its own inspiration free from academic patronage—is
power of expression. Through form this, the second kind of art,
traces the moral life, and endeavours to occupy man, body and
soul, but with no thought of sacrificing the one to the other. It is
ever becoming more imbued with the quite modern idea that the
whole being is *one,* metaphysicians notwithstanding, and that its
aim can only be complete by refusing to separate the organ from
its function. The moral life is but the general result of the
conditions of the physical. The one is bound to the other by
necessary connections which cannot be broken without destroy-
ing both. The first care of the artist should be to seek out and
grasp the methods of manifestation so as to comprehend and
master their unity.

Art, thus understood, demands from its votary an ensemble of
intellectual faculties higher and more robust than if founded
solely upon an ideal of beauty. Art founded upon the latter
notion would be sufficiently served by one possessing an acute
sense of the beautiful—the degree of his sensibility being indicated by the plastic perfection of his work. But expressive art
demands a capability of being moved by many varying sentiments, demands the power to penetrate beneath outward appearances and to seize a hidden thought, the power to grasp either the
permanent characteristic or the particular and momentary emotion; in a word, it demands that complete eloquence of representation which art might have dispensed with while it confined
itself to the investigation or delineation of a single expression,
but which became absolutely indispensable from the moment
that the interpretation of the entire man became its avowed
object.

We may say, too, that modern art is doubly expressive; because,
while the artist is indicating by form and sound the sentiments
and ideas of the personages whom he introduces, he is also by the

power and manner of such manifestation giving an unerring measure of his own sensibility, imagination, and intelligence.

Expressive art is in no way hostile to beauty; it makes use of it as one element in the subjects which require it, but its domain is not enclosed within the narrow bounds of such a conception. It is by no means indifferent to the pleasures of sight and hearing, but it sees something beyond them. Its worth must not be measured only by perfection of form, but also and chiefly, by the double power of expression which we have pointed out, and, as we must not omit to add, by the value of the sentiments and ideas expressed. This latter point is too often and wrongly ignored by artists.

Between two works which give evidence of equal talent—that is to say, of equal facility to grasp the true accents and characteristics of nature, and equal power to bring out both the inner meaning of things and the personality of the artist—we, for our part, would not hesitate to accord the preference to that of which the *Conception* showed the more vigorous intelligence and elevated feeling. The art critics seem to have made it one of their principles to take no account of choice of subject, but only to look at the technical result. Such a principle is plausible rather than true. The individuality of the author can never be excluded from a work, and choice of subject is frequently one of the points by which this individuality is most clearly indicated.

It is true, of course, that elevation of sentiment can never take the place of art talent. On this point we cannot too strongly condemn the practice of academic juries who, on the one hand, reward mere mechanical labour simply because it has been exercised upon what are called classic subjects; and, on the other, persecute more independent artists to punish their obstinacy in deserting the beaten track. Nothing, then, can be further from our thoughts than to require critics to substitute, in every case, consideration of the subject for that of the work itself; or to condemn *à priori* all artists who remain faithful to the traditions, ideas, and sentiments of the past. In these, indeed, some find their only inspiration. We only wish to affirm our conviction that choice of subject is not so indifferent a matter as some say it is, and that it must be taken into account as of considerable weight in determining an opinion of a work of art.

The necessity for this is one consequence of the distinction which we have established between decorative and expressive art. The former, solely devoted to the gratification of eye and ear, affords no measure of its success beyond the pleasure which it gives. The latter, whose chief object is to express the feelings and ideas, and, through them, to manifest the power of conception and expansion possessed by the artist, must obviously be estimated, partly at least, by the moral or other value of the ideas and sentiments in question. And, as the value of a work depends directly upon the capability of its author, and as many artists have been about equal in their technical ability, we must be ready to acknowledge that moral and intellectual superiority is a real superiority, and is naturally marked by the possession of an instinctive and spontaneous power of sympathy. . . .

STYLE

Style is the man, says Buffon; and he is right. Get some one who *can* read, to read a page of Demosthenes *and* of Cicero, of Bossuet and of Massillon, of Corneille and of Racine, of Lamartine and of Victor Hugo. However slight may be your literary perceptions, you will at once notice that no two of them sound the same. Apart altogether from the subjects or ideas, which may be identical, each one has an air, an accent, which can never either be confounded or replaced. In some of them we find elegance, finesse, grace, the most seductive and soothing harmony; in others, a force and *élan* like the sound of a trumpet, enough to awaken the Seven Sleepers.

Style only exists by virtue of what Bürger calls *the law of separation.* "A being only exists in consequence of his separation from other beings. . . . . . . [sic] This law of successive detachment—which alone renders progress possible—may be proved to influence the course of religion, of politics, of literature and of art. What was the renaissance but a break in the continuity of the middle ages?" It is by style, by the manner of comprehension, of feeling and interpretation, that epochs, races, schools and indi-

viduals are separated and distinguished one from the other. In all
the arts, analogous differences are to be found; plainly marked,
in proportion as a more or less extensive field is offered for the
development of artistic personality. Michael Angelo ·and Raph-
ael, Leonardo and Veronese, Titian and Correggio, Rubens and
Rembrandt, resembled each other no more and no less than
Beethoven resembled Rossini; Weber, Mozart; or Wagner resembles Verdi. Each has his own style, his peculiar mode of thinking
and feeling, and of expressing those feelings and thoughts.[2]

Why have mediocre artists no style? For the same reasons that
they are mediocrities. The particular characteristic of mediocrity
is commonness or vulgarity of thought and feeling. At each
moment in the evolution of a social system, there is a general
level which marks, for that moment, the average value of the
human soul and intellect. Such works as rise above this general
level, imply an amount of talent or genius in exact proportion to
the amount of superior elevation and spontaneity which they
display. Mediocrity comes up to the general level, but does not
pass it; thus the mediocre artist thinks and feels like the ordinary
run of mankind, and has nothing to "separate" him from the
crowd. He may have a manner, an ensemble of habits of working
peculiar to himself; but he can have no style in the accurate sense
of the word. Facility is not style; for the latter is really a product,

---

[2] "Painting is perhaps more tell-tale than any other art. It is an absolutely
truthful witness to the moral state of a painter when he has brush in hand.
What he wills to do, that he really does. What his will only feebly desired is
obvious from the undecided result. What he willed not at all is, of course,
absent from his work, though he may not think so. Any distraction or
forgetfulness; any languor in feeling or shallow insight; any little relaxation
of efforts, or falling off in interest in his subject; any weariness of work or
insatiable passion for it; all the shadows of his nature and intermissions of his
sensibility: find a record in the finished work of the painter, as clear as if he
had literally made the world his confidant. We can conjecture, with certainty,
from the pictures of a conscientious portrait painter what his behaviour was
in presence of his sitters."—Eugène Fromentin, *Les Maîtres d'Autrefois*, p.
120.

What Fromentin here says of painting may be applied, more or less, to all
the arts; we may even say to all the manifestations of the soul of man. We do
not need to study the works of great painters and poets to be convinced of the
fact.

a reverberation, if we may use the word, from the soul itself, and
can no more be artificially acquired than can the sonorousness of
bronze or silver be acquired by lead.

*   *   *   *

. . . Style, which is a simple reflection of the artist's personality, is naturally found in the work of every artist who possesses
any personality. The indescribable quality, the "je ne sais quoi"
of which Fromentin speaks, is precisely the assemblage of qualities, the condition of being and temperament which caused Rubens to see things differently to Rembrandt. The two extracted
from one and the same object or subject, emotions widely different though congenial to their respective natures; just as a tight-
ened string in a concert room will vibrate in response to the note
which it would itself produce if struck. The one thing needful is
the power to vibrate, which is too often wanting.

The question of style has considerable importance. We might
even say that it includes the whole of æsthetics, which is in fact
the question of personality in art.

*   *   *   *

Truth and personality: these are the alpha and omega of art
formulas; *truth* as to facts, and the *personality* of the artist. But,
if we look more closely, we shall see that these two terms are in
reality but one. Truth as to fact, so far as art is concerned, is
above all the truth of our own sensations, of our own sentiments.
It is truth as we see it, as it appears modified by our own
temperaments, preferences, and physical organs. It is, in fact, our
personality itself. Reality, as given by the photographer, reality
taken from a point of view without connection with us or our
impressions, is the very negation of art. When this kind of truth
predominates in a work of art, we cry, "There is realism for you!"
Now, realism partakes of the nature of art, only because the most
downright of realists must, whether he will or not, put something
of his own individuality into his work. When, on the other hand,
the dominant quality is what we call human or personal truth,
then we at once exclaim, "Here is an artist!"

And the latter is the right meaning of the word. Art consists essentially in the predominance of subjectivity over objectivity; it is the chief distinction between it and science. The man intended for science, is he whose imagination has no modifying influence over the results of his direct observation. The artist, on the other hand, is one whose imagination, impressionability—in a word, whose personality, is so lively and excitable, that it spontaneously transforms everything, dyeing them in its own colours, and unconsciously exaggerating them in accordance with its own preferences.

We think ourselves justified, then, in calling art the direct and spontaneous manifestation of human personality. But we must not omit also to remember the fact that such personality—individual and particular as it is from some points of view—is nevertheless exposed to many successive and temporary modifications caused by the various kinds of civilisation through which it has had to pass. . . .

Clive Bell

The Aesthetic Hypothesis

It is improbable that more nonsense has been written about aesthetics than about anything else: the literature of the subject is not large enough for that. It is certain, however, that about no subject with which I am acquainted has so little been said that is at all to the purpose. The explanation is discoverable. He who would elaborate a plausible theory of aesthetics must possess two qualities—artistic sensibility and a turn for clear thinking. Without sensibility a man can have no aesthetic experience, and, obviously, theories not based on broad and deep aesthetic experience are worthless. Only those for whom art is a constant source of passionate emotion can possess the data from which profitable theories may be deduced; but to deduce profitable theories even from accurate data involves a certain amount of brain-work, and, unfortunately, robust intellects and delicate sensibilities are not inseparable. As often as not, the hardest thinkers have had no aesthetic experience whatever. I have a friend blessed with an intellect as keen as a drill, who, though he takes an interest in aesthetics, has never during a life of almost forty years been guilty of an aesthetic emotion. So, having no faculty for distinguishing a work of art from a handsaw, he is apt to rear up a pyramid of irrefragable argument on the hypothesis that a handsaw is a work of art. This defect robs his perspicuous and subtle reasoning of much of its value; for it has ever been a maxim that faultless logic can win but little credit for conclusions that are based on premises notoriously false. Every cloud, however, has its silver lining, and this insensibility, though unlucky in that it makes my

[Reprinted from *Art*. New York: Frederick A. Stokes Co., n.d., fourth edition. Pp. 3–37. Footnotes have been renumbered.]

friend incapable of choosing a sound basis for his argument, mercifully blinds him to the absurdity of his conclusions while leaving him in full enjoyment of his masterly dialectic. People who set out from the hypothesis that Sir Edwin Landseer was the finest painter that ever lived will feel no uneasiness about an aesthetic which proves that Giotto was the worst. So, my friend, when he arrives very logically at the conclusion that a work of art should be small or round or smooth, or that to appreciate fully a picture you should pace smartly before it or set it spinning like a top, cannot guess why I ask him whether he has lately been to Cambridge, a place he sometimes visits.

On the other hand, people who respond immediately and surely to works of art, though, in my judgment, more enviable than men of massive intellect but slight sensibility, are often quite as incapable of talking sense about aesthetics. Their heads are not always very clear. They possess the data on which any system must be based; but, generally, they want the power that draws correct inferences from true data. Having received aesthetic emotions from works of art, they are in a position to seek out the quality common to all that have moved them, but, in fact, they do nothing of the sort. I do not blame them. Why should they bother to examine their feelings when for them to feel is enough? Why should they stop to think when they are not very good at thinking? Why should they hunt for a common quality in all objects that move them in a particular way when they can linger over the many delicious and peculiar charms of each as it comes? So, if they write criticism and call it aesthetics, if they imagine that they are talking about Art when they are talking about particular works of art or even about the technique of painting, if, loving particular works they find tedious the consideration of art in general, perhaps they have chosen the better part. If they are not curious about the nature of their emotion, nor about the quality common to all objects that provoke it, they have my sympathy, and, as what they say is often charming and suggestive, my admiration too. Only let no one suppose that what they write and talk is aesthetics; it is criticism, or just "shop."

The starting-point for all systems of aesthetics must be the personal experience of a peculiar emotion. The objects that provoke this emotion we call works of art. All sensitive people agree that there is a peculiar emotion provoked by works of art. I do not mean, of course, that all works provoke the same emotion. On the contrary, every work produces a different emotion. But all these emotions are recognisably the same in kind; so far, at any rate, the best opinion is on my side. That there is a particular kind of emotion provoked by works of visual art, and that this emotion is provoked by every kind of visual art, by pictures, sculptures, buildings, pots, carvings, textiles, &c., &c., is not disputed, I think, by anyone capable of feeling it. This emotion is called the aesthetic emotion; and if we can discover some quality common and peculiar to all the objects that provoke it, we shall have solved what I take to be the central problem of aesthetics. We shall have discovered the essential quality in a work of art, the quality that distinguishes works of art from all other classes of objects.

For either all works of visual art have some common quality, or when we speak of "works of art" we gibber. Everyone speaks of "art," making a mental classification by which he distinguishes the class "works of art" from all other classes. What is the justification of this classification? What is the quality common and peculiar to all members of this class? Whatever it be, no doubt it is often found in company with other qualities; but they are adventitious—it is essential. There must be some one quality without which a work of art cannot exist; possessing which, in the least degree, no work is altogether worthless. What is this quality? What quality is shared by all objects that provoke our aesthetic emotions? What quality is common to Sta. Sophia and the windows at Chartres, Mexican sculpture, a Persian bowl, Chinese carpets, Giotto's frescoes at Padua, and the masterpieces of Poussin, Piero della Francesca, and Cézanne? Only one answer seems possible—significant form. In each, lines and colours combined in a particular way, certain forms and relations of forms, stir our aesthetic emotions. These relations and combinations of lines and colours, these aesthetically moving forms, I call "Significant Form"; and "Significant Form" is the one quality common to all works of visual art.

At this point it may be objected that I am making aesthetics a purely subjective business, since my only data are personal experiences of a particular emotion. It will be said that the objects that provoke this emotion vary with each individual, and that therefore a system of aesthetics can have no objective validity. It must be replied that any system of aesthetics which pretends to be based on some objective truth is so palpably ridiculous as not to be worth discussing. We have no other means of recognising a work of art than our feeling for it. The objects that provoke aesthetic emotion vary with each individual. Aesthetic judgments are, as the saying goes, matters of taste; and about tastes, as everyone is proud to admit, there is no disputing. A good critic may be able to make me see in a picture that had left me cold things that I had overlooked, till at last, receiving the aesthetic emotion, I recognise it as a work of art. To be continually pointing out those parts, the sum, or rather the combination, of which unite to produce significant form, is the function of criticism. But it is useless for a critic to tell me that something is a work of art; he must make me feel it for myself. This he can do only by making me see; he must get at my emotions through my eyes. Unless he can make me see something that moves me, he cannot force my emotions. I have no right to consider anything a work of art to which I cannot react emotionally; and I have no right to look for the essential quality in anything that I have not *felt* to be a work of art. The critic can affect my aesthetic theories only by affecting my aesthetic experience. All systems of aesthetics must be based on personal experience—that is to say, they must be subjective.

Yet, though all aesthetic theories must be based on aesthetic judgments, and ultimately all aesthetic judgments must be matters of personal taste, it would be rash to assert that no theory of aesthetics can have general validity. For, though A, B, C, D are the works that move me, and A, D, E, F the works that move you, it may well be that x is the only quality believed by either of us to be common to all the works in his list. We may all agree about aesthetics, and yet differ about particular works of art. We may differ as to the presence or absence of the quality x. My immediate object will be to show that significant form is the only quality common and peculiar to all the works of visual art that move me;

and I will ask those whose aesthetic experience does not tally with mine to see whether this quality is not also, in their judgment, common to all works that move them, and whether they can discover any other quality of which the same can be said.

Also at this point a query arises, irrelevant indeed, but hardly to be suppressed: "Why are we so profoundly moved by forms related in a particular way?" The question is extremely interesting, but irrelevant to aesthetics. In pure aesthetics we have only to consider our emotion and its object: for the purposes of aesthetics we have no right, neither is there any necessity, to pry behind the object into the state of mind of him who made it. Later, I shall attempt to answer the question; for by so doing I may be able to develop my theory of the relation of art to life. I shall not, however, be under the delusion that I am rounding off my theory of aesthetics. For a discussion of aesthetics, it need be agreed only that forms arranged and combined according to certain unknown and mysterious laws do move us in a particular way, and that it is the business of an artist so to combine and arrange them that they shall move us. These moving combinations and arrangements I have called, for the sake of convenience and for a reason that will appear later, "Significant Form."

A third interruption has to be met. "Are you forgetting about colour?" someone inquires. Certainly not; my term "significant form" included combinations of lines and of colours. The distinc-between form and colour is an unreal one; you cannot conceive a colourless line or a colourless space; neither can you conceive a formless relation of colours. In a black and white drawing the spaces are all white and all are bounded by black lines; in most oil paintings the spaces are multi-coloured and so are the boundaries; you cannot imagine a boundary line without any content, or a content without a boundary line. Therefore, when I speak of significant form, I mean a combination of lines and colours (counting white and black as colours) that moves me aesthetically.

Some people may be surprised at my not having called this "beauty." Of course, to those who define beauty as "combinations of lines and colours that provoke aesthetic emotion," I willingly concede the right of substituting their word for mine. But most of us, however strict we may be, are apt to apply the epithet "beautiful" to objects that do not provoke that peculiar emotion produced by works of art. Everyone, I suspect, has called a butterfly or a flower beautiful. Does anyone feel the same kind of emotion for a butterfly or a flower that he feels for a cathedral or a picture? Surely, it is not what I call an aesthetic emotion that most of us feel, generally, for natural beauty. I shall suggest, later, that some people may, occasionally, see in nature what we see in art, and feel for her an aesthetic emotion; but I am satisfied that, as a rule, most people feel a very different kind of emotion for birds and flowers and the wings of butterflies from that which they feel for pictures, pots, temples and statues. Why these beautiful things do not move us as works of art move is another, and not an aesthetic, question. For our immediate purpose we have to discover only what quality is common to objects that do move us as works of art. In the last part of this chapter, when I try to answer the question—"Why are we so profoundly moved by some combinations of lines and colours?" I shall hope to offer an acceptable explanation of why we are less profoundly moved by others.

Since we call a quality that does not raise the characteristic aesthetic emotion "Beauty," it would be misleading to call by the same name the quality that does. To make "beauty" the object of the aesthetic emotion, we must give to the word an over-strict and unfamiliar definition. Everyone sometimes uses "beauty" in an unaesthetic sense; most people habitually do so. To everyone except perhaps here and there an occasional aesthete, the commonest sense of the word is unaesthetic. Of its grosser abuse, patent in our chatter about "beautiful huntin' " and "beautiful shootin'," I need not take account; it would be open to the precious to reply that they never do so abuse it. Besides, here there is no danger of confusion between the aesthetic and the non-aesthetic use; but when we speak of a beautiful woman there is. When an ordinary man speaks of a beautiful woman he certainly does not mean only that she moves him aesthetically; but when an artist calls a withered old hag beautiful he may sometimes mean what he means when he calls a battered torso beautiful. The ordinary man, if he be also a man of taste, will call the battered torso beautiful, but he will not call a withered hag beautiful because, in the matter of women, it is not to the aesthetic quality that the hag may possess, but to some other quality that he assigns the epithet. Indeed, most of us never dream of going for aesthetic emotions to human beings, from whom we ask something very different. This "something," when we find it in a young woman, we are apt to call "beauty." We live in a nice age. With the man-in-the-street "beautiful" is more often than not synonymous with "desirable"; the word does not necessarily connote any aesthetic reaction whatever, and I am tempted to believe that in the minds of many the sexual flavour of the word is stronger than the aesthetic. I have noticed a consistency in those to whom the most beautiful thing in the world is a beautiful woman, and the next most beautiful thing a picture of one. The confusion between aesthetic and sensual beauty is not in their case so great as might be supposed. Perhaps there is none; for perhaps they have never had an aesthetic emotion to confuse with their other emotions. The art that they call "beautiful" is generally closely related to the women. A beautiful picture is a photograph of a pretty girl; beautiful music, the music that provokes emotions similar to those provoked by young ladies in musical farces; and beautiful poetry, the poetry that recalls the same emotions felt, twenty years earlier, for the rector's daughter. Clearly the word "beauty" is used to connote the objects of quite distinguishable emotions, and that is a reason for not employing a term which would land me inevitably in confusions and misunderstandings with my readers.

On the other hand, with those who judge it more exact to call these combinations and arrangements of form that provoke our aesthetic emotions, not "significant form," but "significant relations of form," and then try to make the best of two worlds, the aesthetic and the metaphysical, by calling these relations "rhythm," I have no quarrel whatever. Having made it clear that by "significant form" I mean arrangements and combinations that move us in a particular way, I willingly join hands with those who prefer to give a different name to the same thing.

The hypothesis that significant form is the essential quality in a work of art has at least one merit denied to many more famous and more striking—it does help to explain things. We are all familiar with pictures that interest us and excite our admiration, but do not move us as works of art. To this class belongs what I call "Descriptive Painting"—that is, painting in which forms are used not as objects of emotion, but as means of suggesting emotion or conveying information. Portraits of psychological and historical value, topographical works, pictures that tell stories and suggest situations, illustrations of all sorts, belong to this class. That we all recognise the distinction is clear, for who has not said that such and such a drawing was excellent as illustration, but as a work of art worthless? Of course many descriptive pictures possess, amongst other qualities, formal significance, and are therefore works of art: but many more do not. They interest us; they may move us too in a hundred different ways, but they do not move us aesthetically. According to my hypothesis they are not works of art. They leave untouched our aesthetic emotions because it is not their forms but the ideas or information suggested or conveyed by their forms that affect us.

Few pictures are better known or liked than Frith's "Paddington Station"; certainly I should be the last to grudge it its popularity. Many a weary forty minutes have I whiled away disentangling its fascinating incidents and forging for each an imaginary past and an improbable future. But certain though it is that Frith's masterpiece, or engravings of it, have provided thousands with half-hours of curious and fanciful pleasure, it is not less certain that no one has experienced before it one half-second of aesthetic rapture—and this although the picture contains several pretty passages of colour, and is by no means badly painted. "Paddington Station" is not a work of art; it is an interesting and amusing document. In it line and colour are used to recount anecdotes, suggest ideas, and indicate the manners and customs of an age: they are not used to provoke aesthetic emotion. Forms and the relations of forms were for Frith not objects of emotion, but means of suggesting emotion and conveying ideas.

The ideas and information conveyed by "Paddington Station" are so amusing and so well presented that the picture has considerable value and is well worth preserving. But, with the perfection of photographic processes and of the cinematograph, pictures of this sort are becoming otiose. Who doubts that one of those *Daily Mirror* photographers in collaboration with a *Daily Mail* reporter can tell us far more about "London day by day" than any Royal Academician? For an account of manners and fashions we shall go, in future, to photographs, supported by a little bright journalism, rather than to descriptive painting. Had the imperial academicians of Nero, instead of manufacturing incredibly loathsome imitations of the antique, recorded in fresco and mosaic the manners and fashions of their day, their stuff, though artistic rubbish, would now be an historical gold-mine. If only they had been Friths instead of being Alma Tademas! But photography has made impossible any such transmutation of modern rubbish. Therefore it must be confessed that pictures in the Frith tradition are grown superfluous; they merely waste the hours of able men who might be more profitably employed in works of a wider beneficence. Still, they are not unpleasant, which is more than can be said for that kind of descriptive painting of which "The Doctor" is the most flagrant example. Of course "The Doctor" is not a work of art. In it form is not used as an object of emotion, but as a means of suggesting emotions. This alone suffices to make it nugatory; it is worse than nugatory because the emotion it suggests is false. What it suggests is not pity and admiration but a sense of complacency in our own pitifulness and generosity. It is sentimental. Art is above morals, or, rather, all art is moral because, as I hope to show presently, works of art are immediate means to good. Once we have judged a thing a work of art, we have judged it ethically of the first importance and put it beyond the reach of the moralist. But descriptive pictures which are not works of art, and, therefore, are not necessarily means to good states of mind, are proper objects of the ethical philosopher's attention. Not being a work of art, "The Doctor" has none of the immense ethical value possessed by all objects that provoke aesthetic ecstasy; and the state of mind to which it is a means, as illustration, appears to me undesirable.

The works of those enterprising young men, the Italian Futurists, are notable examples of descriptive painting. Like the Royal

Academicians, they use form, not to provoke aesthetic emotions, but to convey information and ideas. Indeed, the published theories of the Futurists prove that their pictures ought to have nothing whatever to do with art. Their social and political theories are respectable, but I would suggest to young Italian painters that it is possible to become a Futurist in thought and action and yet remain an artist, if one has the luck to be born one. To associate art with politics is always a mistake. Futurist pictures are descriptive because they aim at presenting in line and colour the chaos of the mind at a particular moment; their forms are not intended to promote aesthetic emotion but to convey information. These forms, by the way, whatever may be the nature of the ideas they suggest, are themselves anything but revolutionary. In such Futurist pictures as I have seen—perhaps I should except some by Severini—the drawing, whenever it becomes representative as it frequently does, is found to be in that soft and common convention brought into fashion by Besnard some thirty years ago, and much affected by Beaux-Art students ever since. As works of art, the Futurist pictures are negligible; but they are not to be judged as works of art. A good Futurist picture would succeed as a good piece of psychology succeeds; it would reveal, through line and colour, the complexities of an interesting state of mind. If Futurist pictures seem to fail, we must seek an explanation, not in a lack of artistic qualities that they never were intended to possess, but rather in the minds the states of which they are intended to reveal.

Most people who care much about art find that of the work that moves them most the greater part is what scholars call "Primitive." Of course there are bad primitives. For instance, I remember going, full of enthusiasm, to see one of the earliest Romanesque churches in Poitiers (Notre-Dame-la-Grande), and finding it as ill-proportioned, over-decorated, coarse, fat and heavy as any better class building by one of those highly civilised architects who flourished a thousand years earlier or eight hundred later. But such exceptions are rare. As a rule primitive art is good—and here again my hypothesis is helpful—for, as a rule, it is also free from descriptive qualities. In primitive art you will find no accurate representation; you will find only significant form. Yet no other art moves us so profoundly. Whether we consider Sumerian sculpture or pre-dynastic Egyptian art, or archaic Greek, or the Wei and T'ang masterpieces,[1] or those early Japanese works of which I had the luck to see a few superb examples (especially two wooden Bodhisattvas) at the Shepherd's Bush Exhibition in 1910, or whether, coming nearer home, we consider the primitive Byzantine art of the sixth century and its primitive developments amongst the Western barbarians, or, turning far afield, we consider that mysterious and majestic art that flourished in Central and South America before the coming of the white men, in every case we observe three common characteristics—absence of representation, absence of technical swagger, sublimely impressive form. Nor is it hard to discover the connection between these three. Formal significance loses itself in preoccupation with exact representation and ostentatious cunning.[2]

Naturally, it is said that if there is little representation and less saltimbancery in primitive art, that is because the primitives were unable to catch a likeness or cut intellectual capers. The contention is beside the point. There is truth in it, no doubt, though, were I a critic whose reputation depended on a power of impress-

[1] The existence of the Ku K'ai-chih makes it clear that the art of this period (fifth to eighth centuries), was a typical primitive movement. To call the great vital art of the Liang, Chen, Wei, and Tang dynasties a development out of the exquisitely refined and exhausted art of the Han decadence —from which Ku K'ai-chih is a delicate straggler—is to call Romanesque sculpture a development out of Praxiteles. Between the two something has happened to refill the stream of art. What had happened in China was the spiritual and emotional revolution that followed the onset of Buddhism.

[2] This is not to say that exact representation is bad in itself. It is indifferent. A perfectly represented form may be significant, only it is fatal to sacrifice significance to representation. The quarrel between significance and illusion seems to be as old as art itself, and I have little doubt that what makes most palaeolithic art so bad is a preoccupation with exact representation. Evidently palaeolithic draughtsmen had no sense of the significance of form. Their art resembles that of the more capable and sincere Royal Academicians: it is a little higher than that of Sir Edward Poynter and a little lower than that of the late Lord Leighton. That this is no paradox let the cave-drawings of Altamira, or such works as the sketches of horses found at Bruniquel and now in the British Museum, bear witness. If the ivory head of a girl from the Grotte du Pape, Brassempouy (*Musée St. Germain*) and the ivory torso found at the same place (*Collection St. Cric*), be, indeed, palaeolithic, then there were good palaeolithic artists who created and did not imitate form. Neolithic art is, of course, a very different matter.

ing the public with a semblance of knowledge, I should be more cautious about urging it than such people generally are. For to suppose that the Byzantine masters wanted skill, or could not have created an illusion had they wished to do so, seems to imply ignorance of the amazingly dexterous realism of the notoriously bad works of that age. Very often, I fear, the misrepresentation of the primitives must be attributed to what the critics call, "wilful distortion." Be that as it may, the point is that, either from want of skill or want of will, primitives neither create illusions, nor make display of extravagant accomplishment, but concentrate their energies on the one thing needful—the creation of form. Thus have they created the finest works of art that we possess.

Let no one imagine that representation is bad in itself; a realistic form may be as significant, in its place as part of the design, as an abstract. But if a representative form has value, it is as form, not as representation. The representative element in a work of art may or may not be harmful; always it is irrelevant. For, to appreciate a work of art we need bring with us nothing from life, no knowledge of its ideas and affairs, no familiarity with its emotions. Art transports us from the world of man's activity to a world of aesthetic exaltation. For a moment we are shut off from human interests; our anticipations and memories are arrested; we are lifted above the stream of life. The pure mathematician rapt in his studies knows a state of mind which I take to be similar, if not identical. He feels an emotion for his speculations which arises from no perceived relation between them and the lives of men, but springs, inhuman or super-human, from the heart of an abstract science. I wonder, sometimes, whether the appreciators of art and of mathematical solutions are not even more closely allied. Before we feel an aesthetic emotion for a combination of forms, do we not perceive intellectually the rightness and necessity of the combination? If we do, it would explain the fact that passing rapidly through a room we recognise a picture to be good, although we cannot say that it has provoked much emotion. We seem to have recognised intellectually the rightness of its forms without staying to fix our attention, and collect, as it were, their emotional significance. If this were so, it would be permissible to inquire whether it was the forms themselves or our perception of their rightness and necessity that caused aesthetic emotion. But I do not think I need linger to discuss the matter here. I have been inquiring why certain combinations of forms move us; I should not have travelled by other roads had I enquired, instead, why certain combinations are perceived to be right and necessary, and why our perception of their rightness and necessity is moving. What I have to say is this: the rapt philosopher, and he who contemplates a work of art, inhabit a world with an intense and peculiar significance of its own; that significance is unrelated to the significance of life. In this world the emotions of life find no place. It is a world with emotions of its own.

To appreciate a work of art we need bring with us nothing but a sense of form and colour and a knowledge of three-dimensional space. That bit of knowledge, I admit, is essential to the appreciation of many great works, since many of the most moving forms ever created are in three dimensions. To see a cube or a rhomboid as a flat pattern is to lower its significance, and a sense of three-dimensional space is essential to the full appreciation. of most architectural forms. Pictures which would be insignificant if we saw them as flat patterns are profoundly moving because, in fact, we see them as related planes. If the representation of three-dimensional space is to be called "representation," then I agree that there is one kind of representation which is not irrelevant. Also, I agree that along with our feeling for line and colour we must bring with us our knowledge of space if we are to make the most of every kind of form. Nevertheless, there are magnificent designs to an appreciation of which this knowledge is not necessary: so, though it is not irrelevant to the appreciation of some works of art it is not essential to the appreciation of all. What we must say is that the representation of three-dimensional space is neither irrelevant nor essential to all art, and that every other sort of representation is irrelevant.

That there is an irrelevant representative or descriptive element in many great works of art is not in the least surprising. Why it is not surprising I shall try to show elsewhere. Representation is not of necessity baneful, and highly realistic forms may be extremely significant. Very often, however, representation is a sign of weakness in an artist. A painter too feeble to create forms that provoke more than a little aesthetic emotion will try to eke that little out by suggesting the emotions of life. To evoke the emotions of life he must use representation. Thus a man will paint an execution, and, fearing to miss with his first barrel of significant form, will try to hit with his second by raising an emotion of fear or pity. But if in the artist an inclination to play upon the emotions of life is often the sign of a flickering inspiration, in the spectator a tendency to seek, behind form, the emotions of life is a sign of defective sensibility always. It means that his aesthetic emotions are weak or, at any rate, imperfect. Before a work of art people who feel little or no emotion for pure form find themselves at a loss. They are deaf men at a concert. They know that they are in the presence of something great, but they lack the power of apprehending it. They know that they ought to feel for it a tremendous emotion, but it happens that the particular kind of emotion it can raise is one that they can feel hardly or not at all. And so they read into the forms of the work those facts and ideas for which they are capable of feeling emotion, and feel for them the emotions that they can feel—the ordinary emotions of life. When confronted by a picture, instinctively they refer back its forms to the world from which they came. They treat created form as though it were imitated form, a picture as though it were a photograph. Instead of going out on the stream of art into a new world of aesthetic experience, they turn a sharp corner and come straight home to the world of human interests. For them the significance of a work of art depends on what they bring to it; no new thing is added to their lives, only the old material is stirred. A good work of visual art carries a person who is capable of appreciating it out of life into ecstasy: to use art as a means to the emotions of life is to use a telescope for reading the news. You will notice that people who cannot feel pure aesthetic emotions remember pictures by their subjects; whereas people who can, as often as not, have no idea what the subject of a picture is. They have never noticed the representative element, and so when they discuss pictures they talk about the shapes of forms and the relations and quantities of colours. Often they can tell by the quality of a single line whether or no a man is a good artist. They are concerned only with lines and colours, their relations and quantities and qualities; but from these they win an emotion more profound and far more sublime than any that can be given by the description of facts and ideas.

This last sentence has a very confident ring—over-confident, some may think. Perhaps I shall be able to justify it, and make my meaning clearer too, if I give an account of my own feelings about music. I am not really musical. I do not understand music well. I find musical form exceedingly difficult to apprehend, and I am sure that the profounder subtleties of harmony and rhythm more often than not escape me. The form of a musical composition must be simple indeed if I am to grasp it honestly. My opinion about music is not worth having. Yet, sometimes, at a concert, though my appreciation of the music is limited and humble, it is pure. Sometimes, though I have a poor understanding, I have a clean palate. Consequently, when I am feeling bright and clear and intent, at the beginning of a concert for instance, when something that I can grasp is being played, I get from music that pure aesthetic emotion that I get from visual art. It is less intense, and the rapture is evanescent; I understand music too ill for music to transport me far into the world of pure aesthetic ecstasy. But at moments I do appreciate music as pure musical form, as sounds combined according to the laws of a mysterious necessity, as pure art with a tremendous significance of its own and no relation whatever to the significance of life; and in those moments I lose myself in that infinitely sublime state of mind to which pure visual form transports me. How inferior is my normal state of mind at a concert. Tired or perplexed, I let slip my sense of form, my aesthetic emotion collapses, and I begin weaving into the harmonies, that I cannot grasp, the ideas of life. Incapable of feeling the austere emotions of art, I begin to read into the musical forms human emotions of terror and mystery, love and hate, and spend the minutes, pleasantly enough, in a world of turbid and inferior feeling. At such times, were the grossest pieces of onomatopoeic representation— the song of a bird, the galloping of horses, the cries of children, or the laughing of demons—to be introduced into the symphony, I should not be offended. Very likely I should be pleased; they would afford new points of departure for new trains of romantic feeling or heroic thought. I know very well what has happened. I have been using art as a means to the emotions of life and reading into it the ideas of life. I have been cutting blocks with a razor. I have tumbled from the superb peaks of aesthetic exaltation to the snug foothills of warm humanity. It is a jolly country. No one need be ashamed of enjoying himself there. Only no one who has ever been on the heights can help feeling a little crestfallen in the cosy valleys. And let no one imagine, because he has made merry in the warm tilth and quaint nooks of romance, that he can even guess at the austere and thrilling raptures of those who have climbed the cold, white peaks of art.

About music most people are as willing to be humble as I am. If they cannot grasp musical form and win from it a pure aesthetic emotion, they confess that they understand music imperfectly or not at all. They recognise quite clearly that there is a difference between the feeling of the musician for pure music and that of the cheerful concert-goer for what music suggests. The latter enjoys his own emotions, as he has every right to do, and recognises their inferiority. Unfortunately, people are apt to be less modest about their powers of appreciating visual art. Everyone is inclined to believe that out of pictures, at any rate, he can get all that there is to be got; everyone is ready to cry "humbug" and "impostor" at those who say that more can be had. The good faith of people who feel pure aesthetic emotions is called in question by those who have never felt anything of the sort. It is the prevalence of the representative element, I suppose, that makes the man in the street so sure that he knows a good picture when he sees one. For I have noticed that in matters of architecture, pottery, textiles, &c., ignorance and ineptitude are more willing to defer to the opinions of those who have been blest with peculiar sensibility. It is a pity that cultivated and intelligent men and women cannot be induced to believe that a great gift of aesthetic appreciation is at least as rare in visual as in musical art. A comparison of my own experience in both has enabled me to discriminate very clearly between pure and impure appreciation. Is it too much to ask that others should be as honest about their feelings for pictures as I have been about mine for music? For I

am certain that most of those who visit galleries do feel very
much what I feel at concerts. They have their moments of pure
ecstasy; but the moments are short and unsure. Soon they fall
back into the world of human interests and feel emotions, good
no doubt, but inferior. I do not dream of saying that what they
get from art is bad or nugatory; I say that they do not get the best
that art can give. I do not say that they cannot understand art;
rather I say that they cannot understand the state of mind of
those who understand it best. I do not say that art means nothing
or little to them; I say they miss its full significance. I do not
suggest for one moment that their appreciation of art is a thing
to be ashamed of; the majority of the charming and intelligent
people with whom I am acquainted appreciate visual art impurely; and, by the way, the appreciation of almost all great
writers has been impure. But provided that there be some frac-
tion of pure aesthetic emotion, even a mixed and minor appreciation of art is, I am sure, one of the most valuable things in the
world—so valuable, indeed, that in my giddier moments I have
been tempted to believe that art might prove the world's salva-
tion.

Yet, though the echoes and shadows of art enrich the life of the
plains, her spirit dwells on the mountains. To him who woos, but
woos impurely, she returns enriched what is brought. Like the
sun, she warms the good seed in good soil and causes it to bring
forth good fruit. But only to the perfect lover does she give a new
strange gift—a gift beyond all price. Imperfect lovers bring to art
and take away the ideas and emotions of their own age and
civilisation. In twelfth-century Europe a man might have been
greatly moved by a Romanesque church and found nothing in a
T'ang picture. To a man of a later age, Greek sculpture meant
much and Mexican nothing, for only to the former could he
bring a crowd of associated ideas to be the objects of familiar
emotions. But the perfect lover, he who can feel the profound
significance of form, is raised above the accidents of time and
place. To him the problems of archaeology, history, and hagiog-
raphy are impertinent. If the forms of a work are significant its
provenance is irrelevant. Before the grandeur of those Sumerian
figures in the Louvre he is carried on the same flood of emotion

to the same aesthetic ecstasy as, more than four thousand years ago, the Chaldean lover was carried. It is the mark of great art that its appeal is universal and eternal.[3] Significant form stands charged with the power to provoke aesthetic emotion in anyone capable of feeling it. The ideas of men go buzz and die like gnats; men change their institutions and their customs as they change their coats; the intellectual triumphs of one age are the follies of another; only great art remains stable and unobscure. Great art remains stable and unobscure because the feelings that it awakens are independent of time and place, because its kingdom is not of this world. To those who have and hold a sense of the significance of form what does it matter whether the forms that move them were created in Paris the day before yesterday or in Babylon fifty centuries ago? The forms of art are inexhaustible; but all lead by the same road of aesthetic emotion to the same world of aesthetic ecstasy.

[3] Mr. Roger Fry permits me to make use of an interesting story that will illustrate my view. When Mr. Okakura, the Government editor of *The Temple Treasures of Japan,* first came to Europe, he found no difficulty in appreciating the pictures of those who from want of will or want of skill did not create illusions but concentrated their energies on the creation of form. He understood immediately the Byzantine masters and the French and Italian Primitives. In the Renaissance painters, on the other hand, with their descriptive pre-occupations, their literary and anecdotic interests, he could see nothing but vulgarity and muddle. The universal and essential quality of art, significant form, was missing, or rather had dwindled to a shallow stream, overlaid and hidden beneath weeds, so the universal response, aesthetic emotion, was not evoked. It was not till he came on to Henri-Matisse that he again found himself in the familiar world of pure art. Similarly, sensitive Europeans who respond immediately to the significant forms of great Oriental art, are left cold by the trivial pieces of anecdote and social criticism so lovingly cherished by Chinese dilettanti. It would be easy to multiply instances did not decency forbid the labouring of so obvious a truth.

Henri Bergson

from *Laughter*

What is the object of art? Could reality come into direct
contact with sense and consciousness, could we enter into
immediate communion with things and with ourselves, probably
art would be useless, or rather we should all be artists, for then
our soul would continually vibrate in perfect accord with nature.
Our eyes, aided by memory, would carve out in space and fix in
time the most inimitable of pictures. Hewn in the living marble
of the human form, fragments of statues, beautiful as the relics of
antique statuary, would strike the passing glance. Deep in our
souls we should hear the strains of our inner life's unbroken
melody,—a music that is ofttimes gay, but more frequently plain-
tive and always original. All this is around and within us, and yet
no whit of it do we distinctly perceive. Between nature and
ourselves, nay, between ourselves and our own consciousness a
veil is interposed: a veil that is dense and opaque for the common
herd,—thin, almost transparent, for the artist and the poet. What
fairy wove that veil? Was it done in malice or in friendliness? We
had to live, and life demands that we grasp things in their
relations to our own needs. Life is action. Life implies the acceptance only of the *utilitarian* side of things in order to respond to
them by appropriate reactions: all other impressions must be
dimmed or else reach us vague and blurred. I look and I think I
see, I listen and I think I hear, I examine myself and I think I am
reading the very depths of my heart. But what I see and hear of
the outer world is purely and simply a selection made by my
senses to serve as a light to my conduct; what I know of myself is

[Reprinted from *Laughter,* trans. Cloudsley Brereton and Fred Roth-
well. London: Macmillan Co., Ltd., 1911. Pp. 150–171.]

what comes to the surface, what participates in my actions. My senses and my consciousness, therefore, give me no more than a practical simplification of reality. In the vision they furnish me of myself and of things, the differences that are useless to man are obliterated, the resemblances that are useful to him are emphasised; ways are traced out for me in advance, along which my activity is to travel. These ways are the ways which all mankind has trod before me. Things have been classified with a view to the use I can derive from them. And it is this classification I perceive, far more clearly than the colour and the shape of things. Doubtless man is vastly superior to the lower animals in this respect. It is not very likely that the eye of a wolf makes any distinction between a kid and a lamb; both appear to the wolf as the same identical quarry, alike easy to pounce upon, alike good to devour. We, for our part, make a distinction between a goat and a sheep; but can we tell one goat from another, one sheep from another? The *individuality* of things or of beings escapes us, unless it is materially to our advantage to perceive it. Even when we do take note of it—as when we distinguish one man from another—it is not the individuality itself that the eye grasps, *i.e.,* an entirely original harmony of forms and colours, but only one or two features that will make practical recognition easier.

In short, we do not see the actual things themselves; in most cases we confine ourselves to reading the labels affixed to them. This tendency, the result of need, has become even more pronounced under the influence of speech; for words—with the exception of proper nouns—all denote genera. The word, which only takes note of the most ordinary function and commonplace aspect of the thing, intervenes between it and ourselves, and would conceal its form from our eyes, were that form not already masked beneath the necessities that brought the word into existence. Not only external objects, but even our own mental states, are screened from us in their inmost, their personal aspect, in the original life they possess. When we feel love or hatred, when we are gay or sad, is it really the feeling itself that reaches our consciousness with those innumerable fleeting shades of meaning and deep resounding echoes that make it something altogether our own? We should all, were it so, be novelists or poets or

musicians. Mostly, however, we perceive nothing but the outward
display of our mental state. We catch only the impersonal aspect
of our feelings, that aspect which speech has set down once for all
because it is almost the same, in the same conditions, for all men.
Thus, even in our own individual, individuality escapes our ken.
We move amidst generalities and symbols, as within a tilt-yard in
which our force is effectively pitted against other forces; and
fascinated by action, tempted by it, for our own good, on to the
field it has selected, we live in a zone midway between things and
ourselves, externally to things, externally also to ourselves. From
time to time, however, in a fit of absentmindedness, nature raises
up souls that are more detached from life. Not with that intentional, logical, systematical detachment—the result of reflection
and philosophy—but rather with a natural detachment, one innate in the structure of sense or consciousness, which at once
reveals itself by a virginal manner, so to speak, of seeing, hearing
or thinking. Were this detachment complete, did the soul no
longer cleave to action by any of its perceptions, it would be the
soul of an artist such as the world has never yet seen. It would
excel alike in every art at the same time; or rather, it would fuse
them all into one. It would perceive all things in their native
purity: the forms, colours, sounds of the physical world as well as
the subtlest movements of the inner life. But this is asking too
much of nature. Even for such of us as she has made artists, it is
by accident, and on one side only, that she has lifted the veil. In
one direction only has she forgotten to rivet the perception to the
need. And since each direction corresponds to what we call a
sense—through one of his senses, and through that sense alone, is
the artist usually wedded to art. Hence, originally, the diversity
of arts. Hence also the speciality of predispositions. This one
applies himself to colours and forms, and since he loves colour for
colour and form for form, since he perceives them for their sake
and not for his own, it is the inner life of things that he sees
appearing through their forms and colours. Little by little he
insinuates it into our own perception, baffled though we may be
at the outset. For a few moments at least, he diverts us from the
prejudices of form and colour that come between ourselves and
reality. And thus he realises the loftiest ambition of art, which

here consists in revealing to us nature. Others, again, retire within themselves. Beneath the thousand rudimentary actions which are the outward and visible signs of an emotion, behind the commonplace, conventional expression that both reveals and conceals an individual mental state, it is the emotion, the original mood, to which they attain in its undefiled essence. And then, to induce us to make the same effort ourselves, they contrive to make us see something of what they have seen: by rhythmical arrangement of words, which thus become organised and animated with a life of their own, they tell us—or rather suggest—things that speech was not calculated to express. Others delve yet deeper still. Beneath these joys and sorrows which can, at a pinch, be translated into language, they grasp something that has nothing in common with language, certain rhythms of life and breath that are closer to man than his inmost feelings, being the living law—varying with each individual—of his enthusiasm and despair, his hopes and regrets. By setting free and emphasising this music, they force it upon our attention; they compel us, willy-nilly, to fall in with it, like passers-by who join in a dance. And thus they impel us to set in motion, in the depths of our being, some secret chord which was only waiting to thrill. So art, whether it be painting or sculpture, poetry or music, has no other object than to brush aside the utilitarian symbols, the conventional and socially accepted generalities, in short, everything that veils reality from us, in order to bring us face to face with reality itself. It is from a misunderstanding on this point that the dispute between realism and idealism in art has arisen. Art is certainly only a more direct vision of reality. But this purity of perception implies a break with utilitarian convention, an innate and specially localised disinterestedness of sense or consciousness, in short, a certain immateriality of life, which is what has always been called idealism. So that we might say, without in any way playing upon the meaning of the words, that realism is in the work when idealism is in the soul, and that it is only through ideality that we can resume contact with reality.

Dramatic art forms no exception to this law. What drama goes forth to discover and brings to light, is a deep-seated reality that is veiled from us, often in our own interests, by the necessities of life. What is this reality? What are these necessities? Poetry always expresses inward states. But amongst these states some arise mainly from contact with our fellow-men. They are the most intense as well as the most violent. As contrary electricities attract each other and accumulate between the two plates of the condenser from which the spark will presently flash, so, by simply bringing people together, strong attractions and repulsions take place, followed by an utter loss of balance, in a word, by that electrification of the soul known as passion. Were man to give way to the impulse of his natural feelings, were there neither social nor moral law, these outbursts of violent feeling would be the ordinary rule in life. But utility demands that these outbursts should be foreseen and averted. Man must live in society, and consequently submit to rules. And what interest advises, reason commands: duty calls, and we have to obey the summons. Under this dual influence has perforce been formed an outward layer of feelings and ideas which make for permanence, aim at becoming common to all men, and cover, when they are not strong enough to extinguish it, the inner fire of individual passions. The slow progress of mankind in the direction of an increasingly peaceful social life has gradually consolidated this layer, just as the life of our planet itself has been one long effort to cover over with a cool and solid crust the fiery mass of seething metals. But volcanic eruptions occur. And if the earth were a living being, as mythology has feigned, most likely when in repose it would take delight in dreaming of these sudden explosions, whereby it suddenly resumes possession of its innermost nature. Such is just the kind of pleasure that is provided for us by drama. Beneath the quiet humdrum life that reason and society have fashioned for us, it stirs something within us which luckily does not explode, but which it makes us feel in its inner tension. It offers nature her revenge upon society. Sometimes it makes straight for the goal, summoning up to the surface, from the depths below, passions that produce a general upheaval. Sometimes it effects a flank movement, as is often the case in contemporary drama; with a skill that is frequently sophistical, it shows up the inconsistencies of society; it exaggerates the shams and shibboleths of the social law; and so indirectly, by merely dissolving or corroding the outer crust, it again brings us back to the inner core. But, in both cases, whether it weakens society or strengthens nature, it has the same end in view: that of laying bare a secret portion of our-selves,—what might be called the tragic element in our character. This is indeed the impression we get after seeing a stirring drama. What has just interested us is not so much what we have been told about others as the glimpse we have caught of ourselves —a whole host of ghostly feelings, emotions and events that would fain have come into real existence, but, fortunately for us, did not. It also seems as if an appeal had been made within us to certain ancestral memories belonging to a far-away past—memo-ries so deep-seated and so foreign to our present life that this latter, for a moment, seems something unreal and conventional, for which we shall have to serve a fresh apprenticeship. So it is indeed a deeper reality that drama draws up from beneath our superficial and utilitarian attainments, and this art has the same end in view as all the others.

Hence it follows that art always aims at what is *individual*. What the artist fixes on his canvas is something he has seen at a certain spot, on a certain day, at a certain hour, with a colouring that will never be seen again. What the poet sings of is a certain mood which was his, and his alone, and which will never return. What the dramatist unfolds before us is the life-history of a soul, a living tissue of feelings and events—something, in short, which has once happened and can never be repeated. We may, indeed, give general names to these feelings, but they cannot be the same thing in another soul. They are *individualised*. Thereby, and thereby only, do they belong to art; for generalities, symbols or even types, form the current coin of our daily perception. How, then, does a misunderstanding on this point arise?

The reason lies in the fact that two very different things have been mistaken for each other: the generality of things and that of the opinions we come to regarding them. Because a feeling is generally recognised as true, it does not follow that it is a general feeling. Nothing could be more unique than the character of Hamlet. Though he may resemble other men in some respects, it is clearly not on that account that he interests us most. But he is universally accepted and regarded as a living character. In this sense only is he universally true. The same holds good of all the other products of art. Each of them is unique, and yet, if it bear the stamp of genius, it will come to be accepted by everybody. Why will it be accepted? And if it is unique of its kind, by what sign do we know it to be genuine? Evidently, by the very effort it forces us to make against our predispositions in order to see sincerely. Sincerity is contagious. What the artist has seen we shall probably never see again, or at least never see in exactly the same way; but if he has actually seen it, the attempt he has made to lift the veil compels our imitation. His work is an example which we take as a lesson. And the efficacy of the lesson is the exact standard of the genuineness of the work. Consequently, truth bears within itself a power of conviction, nay, of conversion, which is the sign that enables us to recognise it. The greater the work and the more profound the dimly apprehended truth, the longer may the effect be in coming, but, on the other hand, the more universal will that effect tend to become. So the universality here lies in the effect produced, and not in the cause.

Altogether different is the object of comedy. Here it is in the work itself that the generality lies. Comedy depicts characters we have already come across and shall meet with again. It takes note of similarities. It aims at placing types before our eyes. It even creates new types, if necessary. In this respect it forms a contrast to all the other arts.

The very titles of certain classical comedies are significant in themselves. Le Misanthrope, l'Avare, le Joueur, le Distrait, etc., are names of whole classes of people; and even when a character comedy has a proper noun as its title, this proper noun is speedily swept away, by the very weight of its contents, into the stream of common nouns. We say "a Tartuffe," but we should never say "a Phèdre" or "a Polyeucte."

Above all, a tragic poet will never think of grouping around the chief character in his play secondary characters to serve as simplified copies, so to speak, of the former. The hero of a tragedy represents an individuality unique of its kind. It may be possible to imitate him, but then we shall be passing, whether consciously or not, from the tragic to the comic. No one is like him, because he is like no one. But a remarkable instinct, on the

contrary, impels the comic poet, once he has elaborated his
central character, to cause other characters, displaying the same
general traits, to revolve as satellites round him. Many comedies
have either a plural noun or some collective term as their title.
"Les Femmes savantes," *"Les* Précieuses ridicules," *"Le Monde
où* l'on s'ennuie," etc., represent so many rallying points on the
stage adopted by different groups of characters, all belonging to
one identical type. It would be interesting to analyse this tendency in comedy. Maybe dramatists have caught a glimpse of a fact
recently brought forward by mental pathology, viz. that cranks of
the same kind are drawn, by a secret attraction, to seek each
other's company. Without precisely coming within the province
of medicine, the comic individual, as we have shown, is in some
way absentminded, and the transition from absentmindedness to
crankiness is continuous. But there is also another reason. If the
comic poet's object is to offer us types, that is to say, characters
capable of self-repetition, how can he set about it better than by
showing us, in each instance, several different copies of the same
model? That is just what the naturalist does in order to define a
species. He enumerates and describes its main varieties.

This essential difference between tragedy and comedy, the
former being concerned with individuals and the latter with
classes, is revealed in yet another way. It appears in the first draft
of the work. From the outset it is manifested by two radically
different methods of observation.

Though the assertion may seem paradoxical, a study of other
men is probably not necessary to the tragic poet. We find some of
the great poets have lived a retiring, homely sort of life, without
having a chance of witnessing around them an outburst of the
passions they have so faithfully depicted. But, supposing even
they had witnessed such a spectacle, it is doubtful whether they
would have found it of much use. For what interests us in the
work of the poet is the glimpse we get of certain profound moods
or inner struggles. Now, this glimpse cannot be obtained from
without. Our souls are impenetrable to one another. Certain
signs of passion are all that we ever apperceive externally. These
we interpret—though always, by the way, defectively—only by
analogy with what we have ourselves experienced. So what we

experience is the main point, and we cannot become thoroughly acquainted with anything but our own heart—supposing we ever get so far. Does this mean that the poet has experienced what he depicts, that he has gone through the various situations he makes his characters traverse, and lived the whole of their inner life? Here, too, the biographies of poets would contradict such a supposition. How, indeed, could the same man have been Macbeth, Hamlet, Othello, King Lear, and many others? But then a distinction should perhaps here be made between the personality *we have* and all those we might have had. Our character is the result of a choice that is continually being renewed. There are points—at all events there seem to be—all along the way, where we may branch off, and we perceive many possible directions though we are unable to take more than one. To retrace one's steps, and follow to the end the faintly distinguishable directions, appears to be the essential element in poetic imagination. Of course, Shakespeare was neither Macbeth, nor Hamlet, nor Othello; still, he *might have been* these several characters if the circumstances of the case on the one hand, and the consent of his will on the other, had caused to break out into explosive action what was nothing more than an inner prompting. We are strangely mistaken as to the part played by poetic imagination, if we think it pieces together its heroes out of fragments filched from right and left, as though it were patching together a harlequin's motley. Nothing living would result from that. Life cannot be recomposed; it can only be looked at and reproduced. Poetic imagination is but a fuller view of reality. If the characters created by a poet give us the impression of life, it is only because they are the poet himself,—a multiplication or division of the poet,—the poet plumbing the depths of his own nature in so powerful an effort of inner observation that he lays hold of the potential in the real, and takes up what nature has left as a mere outline or sketch in his soul in order to make of it a finished work of art.

Altogether different is the kind of observation from which comedy springs. It is directed outwards. However interested a dramatist may be in the comic features of human nature, he will hardly go, I imagine, to the extent of trying to discover his own.

Besides, he would not find them, for we are never ridiculous except in some point that remains hidden from our own consciousness. It is on others, then, that such observation must perforce be practised. But it will, for this very reason, assume a character of generality that it cannot have when we apply it to ourselves. Settling on the surface, it will not be more than skin-deep, dealing with persons at the point at which they come into contact and become capable of resembling one another. It will go no farther. Even if it could, it would not desire to do so, for it would have nothing to gain in the process. To penetrate too far into the personality, to couple the outer effect with causes that are too deep-seated, would mean to endanger and in the end to sacrifice all that was laughable in the effect. In order that we may be tempted to laugh at it, we must localise its cause in some intermediate region of the soul. Consequently, the effect must appear to us as an average effect, as expressing an average of mankind. And, like all averages, this one is obtained by bringing together scattered data, by comparing analogous cases and extracting their essence, in short by a process of abstraction and generalisation similar to that which the physicist brings to bear upon facts with the object of grouping them under laws. In a word, method and object are here of the same nature as in the inductive sciences, in that observation is always external and the result always general.

And so we come back, by a roundabout way, to the double conclusion we reached in the course of our investigations. On the one hand, a person is never ridiculous except through some mental attribute resembling absentmindedness, through something that lives upon him without forming part of his organism, after the fashion of a parasite; that is the reason this state of mind is observable from without and capable of being corrected. But, on the other hand, just because laughter aims at correcting, it is expedient that the correction should reach as great a number of persons as possible. This is the reason comic observation instinctively proceeds to what is general. It chooses such peculiarities as admit of being reproduced and consequently are not indissolubly bound up with the individuality of a single person, —a possibly common sort of uncommonness, so to say,—peculiar-

ities that are held in common. By transferring them to the stage,
it creates works which doubtless belong to art in that their only
visible aim is to please, but which will be found to contrast with
other works of art by reason of their generality and also of their
scarcely confessed or scarcely conscious intention to correct and
instruct. So we were probably right in saying that comedy lies
midway between art and life. It is not disinterested as genuine art
is. By organising laughter, comedy accepts social life as a natural
environment, it even obeys an impulse of social life. And in this
respect it turns its back upon art, which is a breaking away from
society and a return to pure nature.

A. C. Bradley

Poetry for Poetry's Sake

The words 'Poetry for poetry's sake' recall the famous phrase
'Art for Art.' It is far from my purpose to examine the possible
meanings of that phrase, or all the questions it involves. I propose to state briefly what I understand by 'Poetry for poetry's
sake,' and then, after guarding against one or two misapprehensions of the formula, to consider more fully a single problem
connected with it. And I must premise, without attempting to
justify them, certain explanations. We are to consider poetry in
its essence, and apart from the flaws which in most poems accompany their poetry. We are to include in the idea of poetry the
metrical form, and not to regard this as a mere accident or a mere
vehicle. And, finally, poetry being poems, we are to think of a
poem as it actually exists; and, without aiming here at accuracy,
we may say that an actual poem is the succession of experiences
—sounds, images, thoughts, emotions—through which we pass
when we are reading as poetically as we can.[1] Of course this
imaginative experience—if I may use the phrase for brevity—differs with every reader and every time of reading: a poem exists in
innumerable degrees. But that insurmountable fact lies in the
nature of things and does not concern us now.

What then does the formula 'Poetry for poetry's sake' tell us
about this experience? It says, as I understand it, these things.
First, this experience is an end in itself, is worth having on its
own account, has an intrinsic value. Next, its *poetic* value is this

[1] Note A [following this selection].

[Reprinted from *Oxford Lectures on Poetry*. London: Macmillan
and Co., Ltd., and St. Martin's Press, Inc., 1934. Pp. 4–34. Footnotes
have been renumbered.]

intrinsic worth alone. Poetry may have also an ulterior value as a
means to culture or religion; because it conveys instruction, or
softens the passions, or furthers a good cause; because it brings
the poet fame or money or a quiet conscience. So much the
better: let it be valued for these reasons too. But its ulterior
worth neither is nor can directly determine its poetic worth as a
satisfying imaginative experience; and this is to be judged entirely from within. And to these two positions the formula would
add, though not of necessity, a third. The consideration of ulterior ends, whether by the poet in the act of composing or by the
reader in the act of experiencing, tends to lower poetic value. It
does so because it tends to change the nature of poetry by taking
it out of its own atmosphere. For its nature is to be not a part,
nor yet a copy, of the real world (as we commonly understand
that phrase), but to be a world by itself, independent, complete,
autonomous; and to possess it fully you must enter that world,
conform to its laws, and ignore for the time the beliefs, aims, and
particular conditions which belong to you in the other world of
reality.

Of the more serious misapprehensions to which these statements may give rise I will glance only at one or two. The offensive
consequences often drawn from the formula 'Art for Art' will be
found to attach not to the doctrine that Art is an end in itself,
but to the doctrine that Art is the whole or supreme end of
human life. And as this latter doctrine, which seems to me
absurd, is in any case quite different from the former, its consequences fall outside my subject. The formula 'Poetry is an end in
itself' has nothing to say on the various questions of moral
judgment which arise from the fact that poetry has its place in a
many-sided life. For anything it says, the intrinsic value of poetry
might be so small, and its ulterior effects so mischievous, that it
had better not exist. The formula only tells us that we must not
place in antithesis poetry and human good, for poetry is one kind
of human good; and that we must not determine the intrinsic
value of this kind of good by direct reference to another. If we
do, we shall find ourselves maintaining what we did not expect.
If poetic value lies in the stimulation of religious feelings, *Lead,
kindly Light* is no better a poem than many a tasteless version of

a Psalm: if in the excitement of patriotism, why is *Scots, wha hae* superior to *We don't want to fight?* if in the mitigation of the passions, the Odes of Sappho will win but little praise: if in instruction, Armstrong's *Art of preserving Health* should win much.

Again, our formula may be accused of cutting poetry away from its connection with life. And this accusation raises so huge a problem that I must ask leave to be dogmatic as well as brief. There is plenty of connection between life and poetry, but it is, so to say, a connection underground. The two may be called different forms of the same thing: one of them having (in the usual sense) reality, but seldom fully satisfying imagination; while the other offers something which satisfies imagination but has not full 'reality.' They are parallel developments which nowhere meet, or, if I may use loosely a word which will be serviceable later, they are analogues. Hence we understand one by help of the other, and even, in a sense, care for one because of the other; but hence also, poetry neither is life, nor, strictly speaking, a copy of it. They differ not only because one has more mass and the other a more perfect shape, but because they have different *kinds* of existence. The one touches us as beings occupying a given position in space and time, and having feelings, desires, and purposes due to that position: it appeals to imagination, but appeals to much besides. What meets us in poetry has not a position in the same series of time and space, or, if it has or had such a position, it is taken apart from much that belonged to it there; [2] and therefore it makes no direct appeal to those feelings, desires, and purposes, but speaks only to contemplative imagination—imagination the reverse of empty or emotionless, imagination saturated with the results of 'real' experience, but still contemplative. Thus, no doubt, one main reason why poetry has poetic value for us is that it presents to us in its own way something which we meet in another form in nature or life; and yet the test of its poetic value for us lies simply in the question whether it satisfies our imagination; the rest of us, our knowledge or conscience, for example, judging it only so far as they appear

[2] Note B.

transmuted in our imagination. So also Shakespeare's knowledge or his moral insight, Milton's greatness of soul, Shelley's 'hate of hate' and 'love of love,' and that desire to help men or make them happier which may have influenced a poet in hours of meditation —all these have, as such, no poetical worth: they have that worth only when, passing through the unity of the poet's being, they reappear as qualities of imagination, and then are indeed mighty powers in the world of poetry.

I come to a third misapprehension, and so to my main subject. This formula, it is said, empties poetry of its meaning: it is really a doctrine of form for form's sake. 'It is of no consequence what a poet says, so long as he says the thing well. The *what* is poetically indifferent: it is the *how* that counts. Matter, subject, content, substance, determines nothing; there is no subject with which poetry may not deal: the form, the treatment, is everything. Nay, more: not only is the matter indifferent, but it is the secret of Art to "eradicate the matter by means of the form," '—phrases and statements like these meet us everywhere in current criticism of literature and the other arts. They are the stock-in-trade of writers who understand of them little more than the fact that somehow or other they are not 'bourgeois.' But we find them also seriously used by writers whom we must respect, whether they are anonymous or not; something like one or another of them might be quoted, for example, from Professor Saintsbury, the late R. A. M. Stevenson, Schiller, Goethe himself; and they are the watchwords of a school in the one country where Aesthetics has flourished. They come, as a rule, from men who either practise one of the arts, or, from study of it, are interested in its methods. The general reader—a being so general that I may say what I will of him—is outraged by them. He feels that he is being robbed of almost all that he cares for in a work of art. 'You are asking me,' he says, 'to look at the Dresden Madonna as if it were a Persian rug. You are telling me that the poetic value of *Hamlet* lies solely in its style and versification, and that my interest in the man and his fate is only an intellectual or moral interest. You allege that, if I want to enjoy the poetry of *Crossing the Bar,* I must not mind what Tennyson says there, but must consider solely his way of saying it. But in that case I can care no more for a poem than I do for a set of nonsense verses; and I do not believe that the authors of *Hamlet* and *Crossing the Bar* regarded their poems thus.'

These antitheses of subject, matter, substance on the one side, form, treatment, handling on the other, are the field through which I especially want, in this lecture, to indicate a way. It is a field of battle; and the battle is waged for no trivial cause; but the cries of the combatants are terribly ambiguous. Those phrases of the so-called formalist may each mean five or six different things. Taken in one sense they seem to me chiefly true; taken as the general reader not unnaturally takes them, they seem to me false and mischievous. It would be absurd to pretend that I can end in a few minutes a controversy which concerns the ultimate nature of Art, and leads perhaps to problems not yet soluble; but we can at least draw some plain distinctions which, in this controversy, are too often confused.

In the first place, then, let us take 'subject' in one particular sense; let us understand by it that which we have in view when, looking at the title of an un-read poem, we say that the poet has chosen this or that for his subject. The subject, in this sense, so far as I can discover, is generally something, real or imaginary, as it exists in the minds of fairly cultivated people. The subject of *Paradise Lost* would be the story of the Fall as that story exists in the general imagination of a Bible-reading people. The subject of Shelley's stanzas *To a Skylark* would be the ideas which arise in the mind of an educated person when, without knowing the poem, he hears the word 'skylark.' If the title of a poem conveys little or nothing to us, the 'subject' appears to be either what we should gather by investigating the title in a dictionary or other book of the kind, or else such a brief suggestion as might be offered by a person who had read the poem, and who said, for example, that the subject of *The Ancient Mariner* was a sailor who killed an albatross and suffered for his deed.

Now the subject, in this sense (and I intend to use the word in no other), is not, as such, inside the poem, but outside it. The contents of the stanzas *To a Skylark* are not the ideas suggested by the work 'skylark' to the average man; they belong to Shelley just as much as the language does. The subject, therefore, is not the matter *of* the poem at all; and its opposite is not the *form* of the poem, but the whole poem. The subject is one thing; the poem, matter and form alike, another thing. This being so, it is surely obvious that the poetic value cannot lie in the subject, but lies entirely in its opposite, the poem. How can the subject determine the value when on one and the same subject poems may be written of all degrees of merit and demerit; or when a perfect poem may be composed on a subject so slight as a pet sparrow, and, if Macaulay may be trusted, a nearly worthless poem on a subject so stupendous as the omnipresence of the Deity? The 'formalist' is here perfectly right. Nor is he insisting on something unimportant. He is fighting against our tendency to take the work of art as a mere copy or reminder of something already in our heads, or at the best as a suggestion of some idea as little removed as possible from the familiar. The sightseer who promenades a picture-gallery, remarking that this portrait is so like his cousin, or that landscape the very image of his birthplace, or who, after satisfying himself that one picture is about Elijah, passes on rejoicing to discover the subject, and nothing but the subject, of the next—what is he but an extreme example of this tendency? Well, but the very same tendency vitiates much of our criticism, much criticism of Shakespeare, for example, which, with all its cleverness and partial truth, still shows that the critic never passed from his own mind into Shakespeare's; and it may be traced even in so fine a critic as Coleridge, as when he dwarfs the sublime struggle of Hamlet into the image of his own un-happy weakness. Hazlitt by no means escaped its influence. Only the third of that great trio, Lamb, appears almost always to have rendered the conception of the composer.

Again, it is surely true that we cannot determine beforehand what subjects are fit for Art, or name any subject on which a good poem might not possibly be written. To divide subjects into two groups, the beautiful or elevating, and the ugly or vicious, and to judge poems according as their subjects belong to one of these groups or the other, is to fall into the same pit, to confuse with our pre-conceptions the meaning of the poet. What the thing is in the poem he is to be judged by, not by the thing as it was

before he touched it; and how can we venture to say beforehand
that he cannot make a true poem out of something which to us
was merely alluring or dull or revolting? The question whether,
having done so, he ought to publish his poem; whether the thing
in the poet's work will not be still confused by the incompetent
Puritan or the incompetent sensualist with the thing in *his* mind,
does not touch this point: it is a further question, one of ethics,
not of art. No doubt the upholders of 'Art for art's sake' will
generally be in favour of the courageous course, of refusing to
sacrifice the better or stronger part of the public to the weaker or
worse; but their maxim in no way binds them to this view.
Rossetti suppressed one of the best of his sonnets, a sonnet chosen
for admiration by Tennyson, himself extremely sensitive about
the moral effect of poetry; suppressed it, I believe, because it was
called fleshly. One may regret Rossetti's judgment and at the
same time respect his scrupulousness; but in any case he judged
in his capacity of citizen, not in his capacity of artist.

So far then the 'formalist' appears to be right. But he goes too
far, I think, if he maintains that the subject is indifferent and
that all subjects are the same to poetry. And he does not prove his
point by observing that a good poem might be written on a pin's
head, and a bad one on the Fall of Man. That truth shows that
the subject *settles* nothing, but not that it counts for nothing.
The Fall of Man is really a more favourable subject than a pin's
head. The Fall of Man, that is to say, offers opportunities of
poetic effects wider in range and more penetrating in appeal.
And the fact is that such a subject, as it exists in the general
imagination, has some aesthetic value before the poet touches it.
It is, as you may choose to call it, an inchoate poem or the débris
of a poem. It is not an abstract idea or a bare isolated fact, but an
assemblage of figures, scenes, actions, and events, which already
appeal to emotional imagination; and it is already in some degree
organized and formed. In spite of this a bad poet would make a
bad poem on it; but then we should say he was unworthy of the
subject. And we should not say this if he wrote a bad poem on a
pin's head. Conversely, a good poem on a pin's head would
almost certainly transform its subject far more than a good poem

on the Fall of Man. It might revolutionize its subject so completely that we should say, 'The subject may be a pin's head, but the substance of the poem has very little to do with it.'

This brings us to another and a different antithesis. Those figures, scenes, events, that form part of the subject called the Fall of Man, are not the substance of *Paradise Lost;* but in *Paradise Lost* there are figures, scenes, and events resembling them in some degree. These, with much more of the same kind, may be described as its substance, and may then be contrasted with the measured language of the poem, which will be called its form. Subject is the opposite not of form but of the whole poem. Substance is within the poem, and its opposite, form, is also within the poem. I am not criticizing this antithesis at present, but evidently it is quite different from the other. It is practically the distinction used in the old-fashioned criticism of epic and drama, and it flows down, not unsullied, from Aristotle. Addison, for example, in examining *Paradise Lost* considers in order the fable, the characters, and the sentiments; these will be the substance: then he considers the language, that is, the style and numbers; this will be the form. In like manner, the substance or meaning of a lyric may be distinguished from the form.

Now I believe it will be found that a large part of the controversy we are dealing with arises from a confusion between these two distinctions of substance and form, and of subject and poem. The extreme formalist lays his whole weight on the form because he thinks its opposite is the mere subject. The general reader is angry, but makes the same mistake, and gives to the subject praises that rightly belong to the substance.[3] I will read an example of what I mean. I can only explain the following words of a good critic by supposing that for the moment he has fallen into this confusion: 'The mere matter of all poetry—to wit, the appearances of nature and the thoughts and feelings of men— being unalterable, it follows that the difference between poet and

[3] What is here called 'substance' is what people generally mean when they use the word 'subject' and insist on the value of the subject. I am not arguing against this usage, or in favour of the usage which I have adopted for the sake of clearness. It does not matter which we employ, so long as we and others know what we mean. (I use 'substance' and 'content' indifferently.)

poet will depend upon the manner of each in applying language, metre, rhyme, cadence, and what not, to this invariable material.' What has become here of the substance of *Paradise Lost*—the story, scenery, characters, sentiments, as they are in the poem? They have vanished clean away. Nothing is left but the form on one side, and on the other not even the subject, but a supposed invariable material, the appearances of nature and the thoughts and feelings of men. Is it surprising that the whole value should then be found in the form?

So far we have assumed that this antithesis of substance and form is valid, and that it always has one meaning. In reality it has several, but we will leave it in its present shape, and pass to the question of its validity. And this question we are compelled to raise, because we have to deal with the two contentions that the poetic value lies wholly or mainly in the substance, and that it lies wholly or mainly in the form. Now these contentions, whether false or true, may seem at least to be clear; but we shall find, I think, that they are both of them false, or both of them, nonsense: false if they concern anything outside the poem, nonsense if they apply to something in it. For what do they evidently imply? They imply that there are in a poem two parts, factors, or components, a substance and a form; and that you can conceive them distinctly and separately, so that when you are speaking of the one you are not speaking of the other. Otherwise how can you ask the question, In which of them does the value lie? But really in a poem, apart from defects, there are no such factors or components; and therefore it is strictly nonsense to ask in which of them the value lies. And on the other hand, if the substance and the form referred to are not in the poem, then both the contentions are false, for its poetic value lies in itself.

What I mean is neither new nor mysterious; and it will be clear, I believe, to any one who reads poetry poetically and who closely examines his experience. When you are reading a poem, I would ask—not analysing it, and much less criticizing it, but allowing it, as it proceeds, to make its full impression on you through the exertion of your recreating imagination—do you then apprehend and enjoy as one thing a certain meaning or substance, and as another thing certain articulate sounds, and do you somehow compound these two? Surely you do not, any more than you apprehend apart, when you see some one smile, those lines in the face which express a feeling, and the feeling that the lines express. Just as there the lines and their meaning are to you one thing, not two, so in poetry the meaning and the sounds are one: there is, if I may put it so, a resonant meaning, or a meaning resonance. If you read the line, 'The sun is warm, the sky is clear,' you do not experience separately the image of a warm sun and clear sky, on the one side, and certain unintelligible rhythmical sounds on the other; nor yet do you experience them together, side by side; but you experience the one *in* the other. And in like manner, when you are really reading *Hamlet,* the action and the characters are not something which you conceive apart from the words; you apprehend them from point to point *in* the words, and the words as expressions of them. Afterwards, no doubt, when you are out of the poetic experience but remember it, you may by analysis decompose this unity, and attend to a substance more or less isolated, and a form more or less isolated. But these are things in your analytic head, not in the poem, which is *poetic* experience. And if you want to have the poem again, you cannot find it by adding together these two products of decomposition; you can only find it by passing back into poetic experience. And then what you recover is no aggregate of factors, it is a unity in which you can no more separate a substance and a form than you can separate living blood and the life in the blood. This unity has, if you like, various 'aspects' or 'sides,' but they are not factors or parts; if you try to examine one, you find it is also the other. Call them substance and form if you please, but these are not the reciprocally exclusive substance and form to which the two contentions *must* refer. They do not 'agree,' for they are not apart: they are one thing from different points of view, and in that sense identical. And this identity of content and form, you will say, is no accident; it is of the essence of poetry in so far as it is poetry, and of all art in so far as it is art. Just as there is in music not sound on one side and a meaning on the other, but expressive sound, and if you ask what is the meaning you can only answer by pointing to the sounds; just as in painting there is not a meaning *plus* paint, but a meaning *in* paint, or significant paint, and no man can really express the meaning in any other way than in paint and in *this* paint; so in a poem the true content and the true form neither exist nor can be imagined apart. When then you are asked whether the value of a poem lies in a substance got by decomposing the poem, and present, as such, only in reflective analysis, or whether the value lies in a form arrived at and existing in the same way, you will answer, 'It lies neither in one, nor in the other, nor in any addition of them, but in the poem, where they are not.'

We have then, first, an antithesis of subject and poem. This is clear and valid; and the question in which of them does the value lie is intelligible; and its answer is, In the poem. We have next a distinction of substance and form. If the substance means ideas, images, and the like taken alone, and the form means the measured language taken by itself, this is a possible distinction, but it is a distinction of things not in the poem, and the value lies in neither of them. If substance and form mean anything *in* the poem, then each is involved in the other, and the question in which of them the value lies has no sense. No doubt you may say, speaking loosely, that in this poet or poem the aspect of substance is the more noticeable, and in that the aspect of form; and you may pursue interesting discussions on this basis, though no principle or ultimate question of value is touched by them. And apart from that question, of course, I am not denying the usefulness and necessity of the distinction. We cannot dispense with it. To consider separately the action or the characters of a play, and separately its style or versification, is both legitimate and valuable, so long as we remember what we are doing. But the true critic in speaking of these apart does not really think of them apart; the whole, the poetic experience, of which they are but aspects, is always in his mind; and he is always aiming at a richer, truer, more intense repetition of that experience. On the other hand, when the question of principle, of poetic value, is raised, these aspects *must* fall apart into components, separately conceivable; and then there arise two heresies, equally false, that the value lies in one of two things, both of which are outside the poem, and therefore where its value cannot lie.

On the heresy of the separable substance a few additional words will suffice. This heresy is seldom formulated, but perhaps some unconscious holder of it may object: 'Surely the action and the characters of *Hamlet* are in the play; and surely I can retain these, though I have forgotten all the words. I admit that I do not possess the whole poem, but I possess a part, and the most important part.' And I would answer: 'If we are not concerned with any question of principle, I accept all that you say except the last words, which do raise such a question. Speaking loosely, I agree that the action and characters, as you perhaps conceive them, together with a great deal more, are in the poem. Even then, however, you must not claim to possess all of this kind that is in the poem; for in forgetting the words you must have lost innumerable details of the action and the characters. And, when the question of value is raised, I must insist that the action and characters, as you conceive them, are not in *Hamlet* at all. If they are, point them out. You cannot do it. What you find at any moment of that succession of experiences called *Hamlet* is words. In these words, to speak loosely again, the action and characters (more of them than you can conceive apart) are focussed; but your experience is not a combination of them, as ideas, on the one side, with certain sounds on the other; it is an experience of something in which the two are indissolubly fused. If you deny this, to be sure I can make no answer, or can only answer that I have reason to believe that you cannot read poetically, or else are misinterpreting your experience. But if you do not deny this, then you will admit that the action and characters of the poem, as you separately imagine them, are no part of it, but a product of it in your reflective imagination, a faint analogue of one aspect of it taken in detachment from the whole. Well, I do not dispute, I would even insist, that, in the case of so long a poem as *Hamlet,* it may be necessary from time to time to interrupt the poetic experience, in order to enrich it by forming such a product and dwelling on it. Nor, in a wide sense of "poetic," do I question the poetic value of this product, as you think of it apart from the poem. It resembles our recollections of the heroes of history or legend, who move about in our imaginations, "forms more real than living man," and are worth much to us though we do not remember anything they said. Our ideas and images of the "substance" of a poem have this poetic value, and more, if they are at all adequate. But they cannot determine the poetic value of the poem, for (not to speak of the competing claims of the "form") nothing that is outside the poem can do that, and they, as such, are outside it.' [4]

Let us turn to the so-called form—style and versification. There is no such thing as mere form in poetry. All form is expression. Style may have indeed a certain aesthetic worth in partial abstraction from the particular matter it conveys, as in a well-built sentence you may take pleasure in the build almost apart from the meaning. Even so, style is expressive—presents to sense, for example, the order, ease, and rapidity with which ideas move in the writer's mind—but it is not expressive of the meaning of that particular sentence. And it is possible, interrupting poetic experience, to decompose it and abstract for comparatively separate consideration this nearly formal element of style. But the aesthetic value of style so taken is not considerable; [5] you could not read with pleasure for an hour a composition which had no other merit. And in poetic experience you never apprehend this value by itself; the style is here expressive also of a particular meaning, or rather is one aspect of that unity whose other aspect is meaning. So that what you apprehend may be called indifferently an expressed meaning or a significant form. Perhaps on this point I may in Oxford appeal to authority, that of Matthew Arnold and Walter Pater, the latter at any rate an authority whom the formalist will not despise. What is the gist of Pater's teaching about style, if it is not that in the end the one virtue of style is truth or adequacy; that the word, phrase, sentence, should express perfectly the writer's perception, feeling, image, or thought; so that, as we read a descriptive phrase of Keats's, we exclaim, 'That is the thing itself'; so that, to quote Arnold, the words are 'symbols equivalent with the thing symbol-

---

[4] These remarks will hold good, *mutatis mutandis,* if by 'substance' is understood the 'moral' or the 'idea' of a poem, although perhaps in one instance out of five thousand this may be found in so many words in the poem.

[5] On the other hand, the absence, or worse than absence, of style, in this sense, is a serious matter.

ized,' or, in our technical language, a form identical with its content? Hence in true poetry it is, in strictness, impossible to express the meaning in any but its own words, or to change the words without changing the meaning. A translation of such poetry is not really the old meaning in a fresh dress; it is a new product, something like the poem, though, if one chooses to say so, more like it in the aspect of meaning than in the aspect of form.

No one who understands poetry, it seems to me, would dispute this, were it not that, falling away from his experience, or misled by theory, he takes the word 'meaning' in a sense almost ludicrously inapplicable to poetry. People say, for instance, 'steed' and 'horse' have the same meaning; and in bad poetry they have, but not in poetry that *is* poetry.

> 'Bring forth the horse!' The horse was brought:
> In truth he was a noble steed!

says Byron in *Mazeppa*. If the two words mean the same here, transpose them:

> 'Bring forth the steed!' The steed was brought:
> In truth he was a noble horse!

and ask again if they mean the same. Or let me take a line certainly very free from 'poetic diction':

> To be or not to be, that is the question.

You may say that this means the same as 'What is just now occupying my attention is the comparative disadvantages of continuing to live or putting an end to myself.' And for practical purposes—the purpose, for example, of a coroner—it does. But as the second version altogether misrepresents the speaker at that moment of his existence, while the first does represent him, how can they for any but a practical or logical purpose be said to have the same sense? Hamlet was well able to 'unpack his heart with words,' but he will not unpack it with our paraphrases.

These considerations apply equally to versification. If I take the famous line which describes how the souls of the dead stood waiting by the river, imploring a passage from Charon:

Tendebantque manus ripae ulterioris amore;

and if I translate it, 'and were stretching forth their hands in longing for the further bank,' the charm of the original has fled. Why has it fled? Partly (but we have dealt with that) because I have substituted for five words, and those the words of Virgil, twelve words, and those my own. In some measure because I have turned into rhythmless prose a line of verse which, as mere sound, has unusual beauty. But much more because in doing so I have also changed the *meaning* of Virgil's line. What that meaning is *I* cannot say: Virgil has said it. But I can see this much, that the translation conveys a far less vivid picture of the outstretched hands and of their remaining outstretched, and a far less poignant sense of the distance of the shore and the longing of the souls. And it does so partly because this picture and this sense are conveyed not only by the obvious meaning of the words, but through the long-drawn sound of 'tendebantque,' through the time occupied by the five syllables and therefore by the idea of 'ulterioris,' and through the identity of the long sound 'or' in the penultimate syllables of 'ulterioris amore'—all this, and much more, apprehended not in this analytical fashion, nor as *added* to the beauty of mere sound and to the obvious meaning, but in unity with them and so as expressive of the poetic meaning of the whole.

It is always so in fine poetry. The value of versification, when it is indissolubly fused with meaning, can hardly be exaggerated. The gift for feeling it, even more perhaps than the gift for feeling the value of style, is the *specific* gift for poetry, as distinguished from other arts. But versification, taken, as far as possible, all by itself, has a very different worth. Some aesthetic worth it has; how much, you may experience by reading poetry in a language of which you do not understand a syllable.[6] The pleasure is quite appreciable, but it is not great; nor in actual poetic experience

6 Note C.

do you meet with it, as such, at all. For, I repeat, it is not *added* to the pleasure of the meaning when you read poetry that you do understand: by some mystery the music is then the music *of* the meaning, and the two are one. However fond of versification you might be, you would tire very soon of reading verses in Chinese; and before long of reading Virgil and Dante if you were ignorant of their languages. But take the music as it is *in* the poem, and there is a marvellous change. Now

> It gives a very echo to the seat
> Where love is throned;

or 'carries far into your heart,' almost like music itself, the sound

> Of old, unhappy, far-off things
> And battles long ago.

What then is to be said of the following sentence of the critic quoted before: 'But when any one who knows what poetry is reads—

> Our noisy years seem moments in the being
> Of the eternal silence,

he sees that, quite independently of the meaning, . . . there is one note added to the articulate music of the world—a note that never will leave off resounding till the eternal silence itself gulfs it'? I must think that the writer is deceiving himself. For I could quite understand his enthusiasm, if it were an enthusiasm for the music of the meaning; but as for the music, 'quite independently of the meaning,' so far as I can hear it thus (and I doubt if any one who knows English can quite do so), I find it gives some pleasure, but only a trifling pleasure. And indeed I venture to doubt whether, considered as mere sound, the words are at all exceptionally beautiful, as Virgil's line certainly is.

When poetry answers to its idea and is purely or almost purely poetic, we find the identity of form and content; and the degree of purity attained may be tested by the degree in which we feel it hopeless to convey the effect of a poem or passage in any form but its own. Where the notion of doing so is simply ludicrous, you have quintessential poetry. But a great part even of good poetry, especially in long works, is of a mixed nature; and so we find in it no more than a partial agreement of a form and substance which remain to some extent distinct. This is so in many passages of Shakespeare (the greatest of poets when he chose, but not always a conscientious poet) ; passages where something was wanted for the sake of the plot, but he did not care about it or was hurried. The conception of the passage is then distinct from the execution, and neither is inspired. This is so also, I think, wherever we can truly speak of merely decorative effect. We seem to perceive that the poet had a truth or fact—philosophical, agricultural, social—distinctly before him, and then, as we say, clothed it in metrical and coloured language. Most argumentative, didactic, or satiric poems are partly of this kind; and in imaginative poems anything which is really a mere 'conceit' is mere decoration. We often deceive ourselves in this matter, for what we call decoration has often a new and genuinely poetic content of its own; but wherever there is mere decoration, we judge the poetry to be not wholly poetic. And so when Wordsworth inveighed against poetic diction, though he hurled his darts rather wildly, what he was rightly aiming at was a phraseology, not the living body of a new content, but the mere worn-out body of an old one.[7]

In pure poetry it is otherwise. Pure poetry is not the decoration of a preconceived and clearly defined matter: it springs from the creative impulse of a vague imaginative mass pressing for development and definition. If the poet already knew exactly what he meant to say, why should he write the poem? The poem would in fact already be written. For only its completion can reveal, even to him, exactly what he wanted. When he began and while he was at work, he did not possess his meaning; it possessed him. It was not a fully formed soul asking for a body: it was an inchoate soul in the inchoate body of perhaps two or three vague ideas and a few scattered phrases. The growing of this body into its full stature and perfect shape was the same thing as the gradual self-definition of the meaning.[8] And this is the reason why such poems strike us as creations, not manufactures, and have the

[7] This paragraph is criticized in Note D.
[8] Note E.

magical effect which mere decoration cannot produce. This is
also the reason why, if we insist on asking for the meaning of
such a poem, we can only be answered 'It means itself.'

And so at last I may explain why I have troubled myself and
you with what may seem an arid controversy about mere words.
It is not so. These heresies which would make poetry a compound
of two factors—a matter common to it with the merest prose, *plus*
a poetic form, as the one heresy says: a poetical substance *plus* a
negligible form, as the other says—are not only untrue, they are
injurious to the dignity of poetry. In an age already inclined to
shrink from those higher realms where poetry touches religion
and philosophy, the formalist heresy encourages men to taste
poetry as they would a fine wine, which has indeed an aesthetic
value, but a small one. And then the natural man, finding an
empty form, hurls into it the matter of cheap pathos, rancid
sentiment, vulgar humour, bare lust, ravenous vanity—everything which, in Schiller's phrase [9] the form should extirpate, but
which no mere form can extirpate. And the other heresy—which
is indeed rather a practice than a creed—encourages us in the
habit so dear to us of putting our own thoughts or fancies into
the place of the poet's creation. What he meant by *Hamlet,* or the
Ode to a Nightingale, or *Abt Vogler,* we say, is this or that which
we knew already; and so we lose what he had to tell us. But he
meant what he said, and said what he meant.

Poetry in this matter is not, as good critics of painting and
music often affirm, different from the other arts; in all of them
the content is one thing with the form. What Beethoven meant
by his symphony, or Turner by his picture, was not something
which you can name, but the picture and the symphony. Meaning they have, but *what* meaning can be said in no language but
their own: and we know this, though some strange delusion
makes us think the meaning has less worth because we cannot put
it into words. Well, it is just the same with poetry. But because
poetry is words, we vainly fancy that some other words than its
own will express its meaning. And they will do so no more—or, if

[9] Not that to Schiller 'form' meant mere style and versification.

you like to speak loosely, only a trifle more—than words will express the meaning of the Dresden Madonna.[10] Something a little like it they may indeed express. And we may find analogues of the meaning of poetry outside it, which may help us to appropriate it. The other arts, the best ideas of philosophy or religion, much that nature and life offer us or force upon us, are akin to it. But they are only akin. Nor is it the expression of them. Poetry does not present to imagination our highest knowledge or belief, and much less our dreams and opinions; but it, content and form in unity, embodies in its own irreplaceable way something which embodies itself also in other irreplaceable ways, such as philosophy or religion. And just as each of these gives a satisfaction which the other cannot possibly give, so we find in poetry, which cannot satisfy the needs they meet, that which by their natures they cannot afford us. But we shall not find it fully if we look for something else.

And now, when all is said, the question will still recur, though now in quite another sense, What does poetry mean?[11] This unique expression, which cannot be replaced by any other, still seems to be trying to express something beyond itself. And this, we feel, is also what the other arts, and religion, and philosophy are trying to express: and that is what impels us to seek in vain to translate the one into the other. About the best poetry, and not only the best, there floats an atmosphere of infinite suggestion. The poet speaks to us of one thing, but in this one thing there seems to lurk the secret of all. He said what he meant, but his meaning seems to beckon away beyond itself, or rather to expand into something boundless which is only focussed in it; something also which, we feel, would satisfy not only the imagination, but the whole of us; that something within us, and without, which everywhere

> makes us seem
> To patch up fragments of a dream,
> Part of which comes true, and part
> Beats and trembles in the heart.

[10] Note F.
[11] Note G.

Those who are susceptible to this effect of poetry find it not only, perhaps not most, in the ideals which she has sometimes described, but in a child's song by Christina Rossetti about a mere crown of wind-flowers, and in tragedies like *Lear,* where the sun seems to have set for ever. They hear this spirit murmuring its undertone through the *Aeneid,* and catch its voice in the song of Keats's nightingale, and its light upon the figures on the Urn, and it pierces them no less in Shelley's hopeless lament, *O world, O life, O time,* than in the rapturous ecstasy of his *Life of Life.* This all-embracing perfection cannot be expressed in poetic words or words of any kind, nor yet in music or in colour, but the suggestion of it is in much poetry, if not all, and poetry has in this suggestion, this 'meaning,' a great part of its value. We do it wrong, and we defeat our own purposes, when we try to bend it to them:

> We do it wrong, being so majestical,
> To offer it the show of violence;
> For it is as the air invulnerable,
> And our vain blows malicious mockery.

It is a spirit. It comes we know not whence. It will not speak at our bidding, nor answer in our language. It is not our servant; it is our master.

NOTE A

The purpose of this sentence was not, as has been supposed, to give a definition of poetry. To define poetry as something that goes on in us when we read poetically would be absurd indeed. My object was to suggest to my hearers in passing that it is futile to ask questions about the end, or substance, or form of poetry, if we forget that a poem is neither a mere number of black marks on a white page, nor such experience as is evoked in us when we read these marks as we read, let us say, a newspaper article; and I suppose my hearers to know, sufficiently for the purpose of the lecture, how that sort of reading differs from poetical reading.

The truths thus suggested are so obvious, when stated, that I thought a bare reminder of them would be enough. But in fact the mistakes we make about 'subject,' 'substance,' 'form,' and the like, are due not solely to misapprehension of our poetic experience, but to our examining what is not this experience. The whole lecture may be called an expansion of this statement.

The passage to which the present note refers raises difficult questions which any attempt at a 'Poetics' ought to discuss. I will mention three. (1) If the experience called a poem varies 'with every reader and every time of reading' and 'exists in innumerable degrees,' what is the poem itself, if there is such a thing? (2) How does a series of successive experiences form *one* poem? (3) If the object in the case of poetry and music ('arts of hearing') is a succession somehow and to some extent unified, how does it differ in this respect from the object in 'arts of sight'—a building, a statue, a picture?

NOTE B

A lyric, for example, may arise from 'real' emotions due to transitory conditions peculiar to the poet. But these emotions and conditions, however interesting biographically, are poetically irrelevant. The poem, what the poet *says*, is universal, and is appropriated by people who live centuries after him and perhaps know nothing of him and his life; and if it arose from mere imagination it is none the worse (or the better) for that. So far as it cannot be appropriated without a knowledge of the circumstances in which it arose, it is probably, so far, faulty (probably, because the difficulty *may* come from our distance from the whole mental world of the poet's time and country) .

What is said in the text applies equally to all the arts. It applies also to such aesthetic apprehension as does not issue in a work of art. And it applies to this apprehension whether the object belongs to 'Nature' or to 'Man.' A beautiful landscape is not a 'real' landscape. Much that belongs to the 'real' landscape is ignored when it is apprehended aesthetically; and the painter only carries this unconscious idealisation further when he deliberately alters the 'real' landscape in further ways.

All this does not in the least imply that the 'real' thing, where there is one (personal emotion, landscape, historical event, etc.) , is of small importance to the aesthetic apprehension or the work of art. But it is relevant only as it appears *in* that apprehension or work.

If an artist alters a reality (*e.g.* a well-known scene or historical character) so much that his product clashes violently with our familiar ideas, he may be making a mistake: not because his product is untrue to the reality (this by itself is perfectly irrelevant) , but because the 'untruth' may make it difficult or impossible for others to appropriate his product, or because this product may be aesthetically inferior to the reality even as it exists in the general imagination.

NOTE C

For the purpose of the experiment you must, of course, know the sounds denoted by the letters, and you must be able to make out the rhythmical scheme. But the experiment will be vitiated if you get some one who understands the language to read or recite to you poems written in it, for he will certainly so read or recite as to convey to you something of the meaning through the sound (I do not refer of course to the logical meaning) .

Hence it is clear that, if by 'versification taken by itself' one means the versification of a *poem,* it is impossible under the requisite conditions to get at this versification by itself. The versification of a poem is always, to speak loosely, influenced by the sense. The bare metrical scheme, to go no further, is practically never followed by the poet. Suppose yourself to know no English, and to perceive merely that in its general scheme

It gives a very echo to the seat

is an iambic line of five feet; and then read the line as you would have to read it; and then ask if *that* noise is the sound of the line *in the poem*.

In the text, therefore, more is admitted than in strictness should be admitted. For I have assumed for the moment that you can hear the sound of poetry if you read poetry which you do not in the least understand, whereas in fact that sound cannot be produced at all except by a person who knows something of the meaning.

NOTE D

This paragraph has not, to my knowledge, been adversely criticised, but it now appears to me seriously misleading. It refers to certain kinds of poetry, and again to certain passages in poems, which we feel to be less poetical than some other kinds or passages. But this difference of degree in poeticalness (if I may use the word) is put as a difference between 'mixed' and 'pure' poetry; and that distinction is, I think, unreal and mischievous. Further, it is implied that in less poetical poetry there necessarily is only a partial unity of content and form. This (unless I am now mistaken) is a mistake, and a mistake due to failure to hold fast the main idea of the lecture. Naturally it would be most agreeable to me to re-write the paragraph, but if I reprint it and expose my errors the reader will perhaps be helped to a firmer grasp of that idea.

It is true that where poetry is most poetic we feel most decidedly how impossible it is to separate content and form. But where poetry is less poetic and does not make us feel this unity so decidedly, it does not follow that the unity is imperfect. Failure or partial failure in this unity is always (as in the case of Shakespeare referred to) a failure on the part of the *poet* (though it is not always due to the same causes). It does not lie of necessity in the nature of a particular kind of poetry (*e.g.* satire) or in the nature of a particular passage. All poetry cannot be equally poetic, but *all* poetry ought to maintain the unity of content and form, and, in that sense, to be 'pure.' Only in certain kinds, and in certain passages, it is more difficult for the poet to maintain it than in others.

Let us take first the 'passages' and suppose them to occur in one of the more poetic kinds of poetry. In certain parts of any epic or tragedy matter has to be treated which, though necessary to the whole, is not in itself favourable to poetry, or would not in itself be a good 'subject.' But it is the business of the poet to do his best to make this matter poetry, and pure poetry. And, if he succeeds, the passage, though it will probably be less poetic than the bulk of the poem, will exhibit the complete unity of content and form. It will not strike us as a mere bridge between other passages; it will be enjoyable for itself; and it will not occur to us to think that the poet was dealing with an un-poetic 'matter' and found his task difficult or irksome. Shakespeare frequently does not trouble himself to face this problem and leaves an imperfect unity. The conscientious artists, like Virgil, Milton, Tennyson, habitually face it and frequently solve it.[12] And when they wholly or partially fail, the fault is still *theirs*. It is, in one sense, due to the 'matter,' which set a hard problem; but they would be the first to declare that *nothing* in the poem ought to be only mixedly poetic.

In the same way, satire is not in its nature a highly poetic kind of poetry, but it ought, in its own kind, to be poetry throughout, and therefore ought not to show a merely partial unity of content and form. If the satirist makes us exclaim 'This is sheer prose wonderfully well disguised,' that is a fault, and *his* fault (unless it happens to be ours). The idea that a tragedy or lyric could really be reproduced in a form not its own strikes us as ridiculous; the idea that a satire could so be reproduced seems much less ridiculous; but if it were true the satire would not be poetry at all.

---

[12] In Schiller's phrase, they have extirpated the mere 'matter.' We often say that they do this by dint of style. This is roughly true, but in strictness it means, as we have seen, not that they decorate the mere 'matter' with a mere 'form,' but that they produce a new content-form.

The reader will now see where, in my judgment, the paragraph is wrong. Elsewhere it is, I think, right, though it deals with a subject far too large for a paragraph. This is also true of the next paragraph, which uses the false distinction of 'pure' and 'mixed,' and which will hold in various degrees of poetry in various degrees poetical.

It is of course possible to use a distinction of 'pure' and 'mixed' in another sense. Poetry, whatever its kind, would be pure as far as it preserved the unity of content and form; mixed, so far as it failed to do so—in other words, failed to be poetry and was partly prosaic.

NOTE E

It is possible therefore that the poem, as it existed at certain stages in its growth, may correspond roughly with the poem as it exists in the memories of various readers. A reader who is fond of the poem and often thinks of it, but remembers only half the words and perhaps fills up the gaps with his own words, may possess something like the poem as it was when half-made. There are readers again who retain only what they would call the 'idea' of the poem; and the poem *may* have begun from such an idea. Others will forget all the words, and will not profess to remember even the 'meaning,' but believe that they possess the 'spirit' of the poem. And what they possess may have, I think, an immense value. The poem, of course, it is not; but it may answer to the state of imaginative feeling or emotional imagination which was the germ of the poem. This is, in one sense, quite definite: it would not be the germ of a decidedly different poem: but in another sense it is indefinite, comparatively structureless, more a 'stimmung' than an idea.

Such correspondences, naturally, must be very rough, if only because the readers have been at one time in contact with the fully grown poem.

NOTE F

I should be sorry if what is said here and elsewhere were taken to imply depreciation of all attempts at the interpretation of works of art. As regards poetry, such attempts, though they cannot possibly express the whole meaning of a poem, may do much to facilitate the poetic apprehension of that meaning. And, although the attempt is still more hazardous in the case of music and painting, I believe it may have a similar value. That its results *may* be absurd or disgusting goes without saying, and whether they are ever of use to musicians or the musically educated I do not know. But I see no reason why an exceedingly competent person should not try to indicate the emotional tone of a composition, movement, or passage, or the changes of feeling within it, or even, very roughly, the 'idea' he may suppose it to embody (though he need not imply that the composer had any of this before his mind). And I believe that such indications, however inadequate they must be, may greatly help the uneducated lover of music to hear more truly the music itself.

NOTE G

This new question has 'quite another sense' than that of the question, What is the meaning or content expressed by the form of a poem? The new question asks, What is it that the *poem,* the unity of this content and form, is trying to express? This 'beyond' is beyond the content as well as the form.

Of course, I should add, it is not *merely* beyond them or outside of them. If it were, they (the poem) could not 'suggest' it. They are a partial manifestation of it, and point beyond themselves to it, both because they *are* a manifestation and because this is partial.

The same thing is true, not only (as is remarked in the text) of the other arts and of religion and philosophy, but also of what is commonly called reality. This reality is a manifestation of a different order from poetry, and in certain important respects a much more imperfect manifestation. Hence, as was pointed out (p. 55, note B), poetry is not a copy of it, but in dealing with it idealises it, and in doing so produces in certain respects a fuller manifestation. On the other hand, that imperfect 'reality' has for us a character in which poetry is deficient,—the character in virtue of which we call it 'reality.' It is, we feel, thrust upon us, not made by us or by any other man. And in this respect it seems more akin than poetry to that 'beyond,' or absolute, or perfection, which we want, which partially expresses itself in both, and which could not be perfection and could not satisfy us if it were not real (though it cannot be real in the same sense as that imperfect 'reality'). This seems the ultimate ground of the requirement that poetry, though no copy of 'reality,' should not be mere 'fancy,' but should refer to, and interpret, that 'reality.' For that reality, however imperfectly it reveals perfection, is at least no mere fancy. (Not that the merest fancy can fail to reveal something of perfection.)

The lines quoted on p. 71 are from a fragment of Shelley's, beginning 'Is it that in some brighter sphere.'

Two

The Nature and Identity
of a Work of Art

Part Two. Selected Readings

Beardsley, Monroe C. *Aesthetics*. New York, 1958, Ch. 1.

Henze, Donald. "Is the Work of Art a Construct?" *Journal of Philosophy*, 52: 433–439 (1955).

Jenkins, Iredell. "The Aesthetic Object," *Review of Metaphysics*, 11: 3–11 (1957).

Margolis, Joseph. "The Identity of a Work of Art," *Mind*, 68: 34–51 (1959).

———. "The Mode of Existence of a Work of Art," *Review of Metaphysics*, 12: 26–34 (1958).

Meager, R. "The Uniqueness of a Work of Art," *Proceedings of the Aristotelian Society*, 53: 205–226 (1952–1953).

Pepper, Stephen. "Further Considerations on the Aesthetic Work of Art," *Journal of Philosophy*, 49: 274–279 (1952).

Sartre, Jean-Paul. "Conclusion," *The Psychology of Imagination*. New York, 1948.

Stevenson, Charles S. "On 'What Is a Poem?'," *Philosophical Review*, 66: 329–362 (1957).

Wacker, Jeanne. "Particular Works of Art," *Mind*, 69: 223–234 (1960).

Introduction

After having studied the material in Part One on the nature of art, the reader is now confronted with discussions about what one might call the product of the artistic process—the work of art—the novel, painting, sculpture, or other form.

How does one know that what he is seeing or reading, for example, is a work of art? He might be reading what is called a novel, but is it a work of art? Is a lemon pie a work of art? If so, why? Furthermore, where is the work of art located? Does it exist objectively? Is a sculpture a mere representation of the work of art that exists in the artist's mind, or is it itself the work of art with no prior or other existence? Are the many performances of *Hamlet* all works of art, or are they merely variations and interpretations of the essentially unrepeatable *Hamlet*? Are imitations and reprints of paintings works of art?

All such questions and many more inevitably enter into any thorough discussion of the nature and identity of works of art. The essays that follow not only discuss some of the problems involved in talking about works of art, but some of them also offer answers to such problems.

Manuel Bilsky

The Significance of Locating the Art Object

Many recent writers on esthetic theory have worried about the exact location of the work of art.[1] Few of them, however, have questioned the importance of talking about this problem. Does such a discussion have any genuine significance, or are considerations of this sort largely gratuitous? Does it make any difference whether the work of art is here, there, or the other place; whether it is *really* the artist's experience, the physical stimulus, or the spectator's experience? In this paper it will be no part of my purpose to argue that it is in one rather than another of the possible places, that its mode of existence is of one sort rather than another; I shall be concerned only with the significance of raising the issue. I shall in effect be asking Peirce's question: Is there a difference which makes a difference?

Before we try to answer this question, however, there is a job of analysis to be done. What precise meaning can be attached to the assertion that the work of art is the artist's experience, the physical stimulus, or the spectator's experience? One way to approximate such precision is to look for the various meanings, or senses, which are relevant to each of these. In other words what I want to do in this preliminary stage is to take each of these three possibilities and show some of the senses in which it may be, or

---

[1] See R. Wellek and A. Warren, *Theory of Literature,* chap. xii. Also I. A. Richards, *Principles of Literary Criticism,* chap. xxx; and C. I. Lewis, *An Analysis of Knowledge and Valuation,* chap. xv.

[Reprinted from *Philosophy and Phenomenological Research,* 13: 531–536 (1953).]

has been, used.[2] This procedure will enable us to move on to the question of significance, with which we are primarily concerned. For the moment I hold the explanation as to how the one will enable us to do the other. Let us for simplicity symbolize the three possibilities as, respectively, AE, PS, and SE.

The first alternative is to say the work of art is AE, the artist's experience. As it stands this is rather ambiguous. As has been suggested, one way to remove the ambiguity, at least partially, is to subject the expression "the artist's experience" to analysis: we can ask about its different senses. Some of the possibilities are:

AE_1: It might refer to the experience the artist had which gave rise to the work. Proust's actual commerce with a family like the Verdurins could, in this sense, have been the basis of *Swann's Way*. Van Gogh's rejection by a hostile society resulted, possibly, in his suffusing many of his paintings with a golden glow.

AE_2: Another sense of the expression could be the imaginative recollection of AE_1. The basic experience and its attendant emotions might then be "recollected in tranquility," and this recollection could be responsible for the actual poem, painting, or musical composition. (It is doubtful whether this can be clearly distinguished from AE_1; that it, could we ever get a pure example of AE_1, one that does not contain some recall?)

AE_3: Croce has devoted nearly a whole book to the explication of our third sense. Here the artist's experience is expression, something which, if I read Croce correctly, qualifies in varying degrees all experience. This sense, however, is perhaps identical with AE_1.[3]

---

[2] Although I have suggested only three, I do not mean to imply that these exhaust the possibilities. There may be more, but, as will be seen presently, that there are will not affect the outcome of this investigation.

[3] I do not pretend to have listed all the possible senses of "the artist's experience." It might also be plausibly argued here that I have given only one of the senses: a careful examination of the above would probably show that the distinctions I have suggested can be collapsed. All three senses are merely variations or elaborations of the idealist thesis. Neither of these considerations, however, has any significant bearing on what follows.

What does this kind of analysis disclose now if we say the work of art is *PS,* the physical stimulus? This in turn can be construed in several different ways. But it is slightly more complicated than *AE,* since the media of the three standard art objects—a musical composition, a painting, and a literary work—are so different. But since getting involved in the intricacies of distinguishing among these three will not help much here, let us avoid this by concentrating on one of them, a painting. What are some of the senses, then, in which we may be speaking about the work of art as the physical stimulus?

PS_1: Formalists like Clive Bell and Roger Fry have given us one sense of *PS.* The formal properties of the painting consti-tute the esthetic object. The yellow of the sunflower, rather than the sunflower itself, contributes to the work of art, properly speaking. The lines of the painting, not what the lines designate, are significant: the "significant form" elicits the unique esthetic emotion of the formalists.

PS_2: Some estheticians reject the form-content distinction in the physical stimulus although they agree as to locus. While agreeing that the form of the painting is properly the work of art, they hold that the form consists of everything that can be found on the canvas. There is danger here, if we try to push the distinction between PS_1 and PS_2, of becoming embroiled in the formalist controversy. This, however, may best be side-stepped for the purposes of this discussion.

PS_3: The dispositional view gives us the ground for our third sense. Here the esthetic object is the physical stimulus, but we do not talk about colors and lines, just as we do not worry about whether the painting is sad or the sadness is in us. We talk instead of a set of dispositions, powers, or tendencies; and it is these that properly constitute the work of art.

With the somewhat abashed realization of having given a rather cavalier treatment to a number of tremendously difficult and complicated problems, I move on to the third way of talking about the work of art: it is the spectator's experience. When we scrutinize the expression "the spectator's experience," we find that it also bears many senses.

SE_1: Any one person's experience as he reads the poem, looks at the painting, or listens to the musical composition, is the work of art in this first sense. If I read "Dover Beach" today and again tomorrow, two works of art are involved. The same is true if I read the poem and you also read it.

SE_2: This and the following two are classes of experiences. SE_2 consists of the majority of the experiences of all those who have ever read the poem. If someone had read it twice, both experiences would be members of this class. The class, or type, following Peirce, is the esthetic object.

SE_3: This class is more restricted. The poem, we might say, consists of the experiences which all *qualified* readers have. The restriction might be even more specific: the class is made up of the experiences which the English teachers at Harvard University have.

SE_4: This is the class which I. A. Richards ends up with in his *Principles of Literary Criticism*. It consists of the experience of the artist as he contemplates his completed product plus all those experiences which are similar in certain important respects to it.

So much for the preparatory stage. We may now return to our primary problem: Is it important to talk about the locus of the art object? One way of defending the affirmative answer is to say that in criticism and in esthetics generally the locus will determine the nature of many statements. The difference will really make a difference. If we take such a statement, therefore, and shift the locus around, we should be able to see whether the shift influences the nature of the statement. Now, what kinds of statements shall we select as the bases for this examination? What statements in esthetics and criticism will best serve as vehicles for our test cases? We want a variety which will give us a cross section of all possible statements. I propose the following: (1) an interpretive judgment, e.g., "X is symbolic," (2) an evaluative judgment, e.g., "*X* is excellent." These two are the kinds most frequently found in practical criticism; they are statements about particular works of art. The next two are statements found in esthetic theory rather than practical criticism: (3) "Clarity is a criterion of esthetic value," (4) "Beauty is a tertiary property." These, it will be noticed, exemplify the two cardinal problems in esthetics: the standard and the definition of esthetic value.

The next step is to take each of the above four statements and show its relation to the locus of the art object. We could take one of the four and go through the whole list of possible locations, seeing what effect each locus has on the nature of the statement, and similarly for the other three. But such an exhaustive study is not really necessary for our purposes. If we correlate each statement with a pair of the possible locations, e.g., ask whether it makes any difference to the nature of the statement if we start with *PS* or *SE*, we should get a fairly good indication as to how our question is to be answered. Let us start, then, with the first, an interpretive judgment.

An interpretive judgment would be one of the following form: "Maria symbolizes the artist in society." (The reference is to the main character in James Joyce's short story, *Clay.*) Now suppose we start with AE_2 and SE_3. Let us assume further that Joyce, in recollecting his original experience, did *not* conceive Maria symbolically. Let us also assume that SE_3 is symbolic; that is, the members of the English faculty of Harvard all have experiences which indicate that Maria is a symbolic figure in the way suggested.

Now consider another person: he wants to find out whether the story is symbolic. He is faced by two possibilities: if he listens to Joyce, he learns that the story is not symbolic; if he listens to the professors, it is symbolic. Hence, it is obviously true that the kind of answer he gets depends on where he locates the work of art. If it is AE_2, it is not symbolic; if it is SE_3, it is. But suppose now he asks whether the story is *really* symbolic. Would it then make any difference where he starts? He would certainly get two candidates for the answer to his question. But in order to get the definitive answer, it does not seem as though it would make any difference where he starts. Further inquiry along these lines would probably yield little more than a clarification of "interpretive," i.e., how its meaning differs from "factual" or "evaluative."

An example of an evaluative judgment would be: *"Clay* is an excellent short story." Will this type of judgment be affected by the starting point? In this instance let us assume as our points of origin SE_2 and SE_3. Suppose now the judgment of SE_2 is that *Clay* is a poor specimen of short-story writing, while SE_3 indicates that the story is superior. Is it a good story? If we are satisfied with the implied relativism, our choice of starting points does determine what the answer will be. If the work of art is identified with the experiences of the majority of the readers, the answer is no; if with the professors, the answer is yes. This situation parallels the one involving interpretive judgments. And again it is possible to ask whether the story is *really* a good one. But to do so takes us, in the way indicated before, far beyond the immediate question.

"Clarity is a criterion of esthetic value." How is a statement of this sort affected by the locus of the work of art? Here let us use as our starting points AE_3 and PS_2. In the former, since the work of art is equated with expression, the question of clarity does not arise (Croce does raise it, but illegitimately, it seems to me) — whether or not the expression is externalized, that is, put into a communicable form, is irrelevant to its status as a work of art. Equating the esthetic object with AE_3, therefore, precludes the use of any such standard. Actually, this can be extended to include any standard. Thus, on one interpretation of Croce, something is either beautiful or not beautiful; there can be no degrees of beauty. A thing can not be more or less beautiful than something else.

What follows if we regard the work of art as PS_2? Can we talk about standards if the art object is the physical stimulus?[4] Obviously we can. I look at the great Dutch paintings of the seventeenth century, and I say, "Everyone of them exhibits unity in variety." I am, of course, dodging the problem of making the transition from the empirical to the normative, but that need not

---

[4] We must be careful here not to confuse this question with one regarding a statement like "X is clear." Such a statement is in most respects just like interpretive judgments.

concern us. In a perfectly good sense it is possible to talk about standards when the work of art is regarded as PS_2.

Finally, we look at a statement like, "Beauty is a tertiary property." We need go no further than the pair used in the preceding paragraph to see that here too the choice of starting points makes a significant difference in the nature of statements of this sort. If we assume that the work of art is PS_2, we can at least postulate a "tertiary property," as C. E. M. Joad, for example, does. But if the work of art is AE_3, the question of tertiary properties, in this sense, does not arise. Since the primary-secondary distinction collapses, the possibility of a tertiary property falls with it.

But let us examine this situation a little more closely. We can do this by varying both the test statement and the starting points. "Art," let us say, "is the communication of an experience, predominantly emotional, from one mind to another." Equating the work of art with SE_4 would render such a statement impossible. If we talk about communication, there must be a medium, or vehicle. If we then say the communication is effected by the vehicle; for SE_4, what would it be? Ordinarily, we would say it is the work of art; but since this, for SE_4, is a set of experiences similar to that of the artist as he contemplates his completed product, obviously it will not do. A way to get around this difficulty would be to say that the vehicle is the physical stimulus, and this generates the work of art, but this seems an unnecessary circumlocution, besides flying in the face of ordinary usage; i.e., people do not ordinarily speak of a work of art as a set of experiences, etc. Another difficulty would arise if the artist were dead. Since his experience is the touchstone by which other candidates are either excluded or included in SE_4, we could never specify what the work of art is—the standard, or touchstone, would obviously not be available.[5]

If we equate the work of art with PS_3, however, these difficulties

---

[5] This objection to Richards's proposed definition is so obvious that one wonders how he could ever seriously have entertained it; and yet, paradoxically, it is just this definition, forcing the attention of the critic on the experience of the reader, that played such a large part in influencing the so-called "new criticism."

vanish. We could speak of PS_3 as arising from the artist's experience—this would accord with ordinary usage—and being the vehicle which communicates it to the spectator. Now if we ask, "What is communicated?" we could answer that the artist's experience is communicated to the spectator by means of the work of art, PS_3. In addition, starting with PS_3 as the locus, we could talk intelligibly about the artist's recreating his own experience for himself by contemplating the work of art. This would be impossible with SE_4, since the work of art *is* his own experience, among others.

The results of this discussion should be obvious. In both practical criticism and esthetic theory, where we start, where we locate the work of art affects significantly the kinds of statements that can be made about it. Examination of four models, or test statements—one interpretive, one evaluative, one concerning standards, and one definitional—has shown that in each case the nature of the statement was definitely governed by the locus of the art object. Hence, the problem is important, perhaps even the most crucial one in esthetics, and deserves careful discussion and analysis.

Richard Rudner

The Ontological Status of the Esthetic Object

In this discussion I shall be concerned with a certain puzzle which C. I. Lewis brings to light in *An Analysis of Knowledge and Valuation* regarding the ontological status of the esthetic object, and with the solution he proposes.

The "science of esthetics," Lewis feels, is quite undeveloped. And this he believes may be ascribed, in part at least, to the fact that a "marked diversity . . . obtains amongst objects of esthetic interest and to the fact that some classes of them [the objects] . . . are phenomena of extreme complexity" (p. 469).

To demonstrate this complexity, Lewis chooses as an example a musical composition.

> Consider what entity it is which is termed "Beethoven's Fifth Symphony." A musical composition is not a physical object: any particular rendition of it is a physical entity of its own complex sort; but between the rendition and the thing itself, there is an obvious difference. The rendition may not and presumably will not, realize exactly the musical intention of the composer or the esthetic possibilities represented by the composition (pp. 469–470).

It is important, if one is to understand Lewis, to be clear about what is being suggested here. Or, if this is not accomplishable, to be clear about some of the things which are not being suggested. First then, the esthetic object in music is no particular rendition of a score. It is not the actual physical sound waves which constitute any rendition; it is not the printed score from which

[Reprinted from *Philosophy and Phenomenological Research*, 10: 380–388 (1950).]

the orchestra is playing; and, curiously enough, it is not what we might normally call the phenomenal content of the mind—that is to say, it is *never* any particular *heard* music. Moreover, the passage suggests that it may be one or the other of two things. It may be, we gather, either "the musical intention of the composer," or, it may be the full, presumably unrealizable, "esthetic possibilities of the composition." There is, I should say, although Lewis fails to point this out, an evident difference between the two last named; for there is a perfectly good sense in which we might say of a particular composer that his own musical intention does not coincide with the composition's esthetic possibilities.

But these are only initial considerations; when we come to products of literary art, we find "an even wider gap between the thing itself and the apprehension of it" (p. 470). Consider a poem for example. "Here," Lewis tells us, "we must ordinarily provide our own rendition; and in so doing we may not only miss a part of the intended meaning but inadvertently introduce certain grace-notes and variations of our own" (p. 470). As for the drama, this he feels is the most complex of all esthetic entities. In some of the above respects, he finds it like music, in others, like poetry. But this much he decides is clear: that "a drama cannot be identified with any physical object" (p. 470).

It will, perhaps, be best to give the remainder of Mr. Lewis's thoughts on the gap between physical work and actual esthetic object in his own words. He is here as succinct as an adequate paraphrase would be. He tells us, then, that

> On these points, a painting, a cathedral, or a piece of sculpture seems to differ from a musical composition or a literary product. A picture, edifice or statue may likewise fail to incorporate fully the intention of the creator. But at least esthetic objects of these classes are embodied once for all in physical individuals; and the distinction of any entity so incorporated from the physical embodiment of it seems uncalled for. On second thought, however, this difference can be viewed as one of degree rather than of kind. For example, when we stand before a masterpiece of painting or of sculpture, we may be reminded of something which is common to this physical object and various more or less adequate reproductions of it, some of which we may have

observed before. Is it this canvas or this marble which is the object of esthetic contemplation, or is this only the "original" and most adequate incorporation of it; the thing itself being an abstract entity here embodied or approximated to, in these fading pigments or this stone which already shows the marks of time? Even in the case of objects found in nature, the esthetic orientation may be directed upon an ideality not physically present: if the landscape should be intriguing, still the sketcher will at once begin moving this a little in his mind's eye and eliminating that; and in any case the eye of the beholder performs something of the same office. Do such considerations allow the simple identification of any kind of esthetic object with a physical thing; or must we rather say that even the artist's original is an instance and an "imitation" only of an entity which itself is abstract and ideal? And between those physical conditions which qualify presentation of it and those further and psychological conditions which likewise qualify its appearance to any subject, is there any fundamental difference of kind or only one of manner or degree; the true object being separated from our apprehension by a whole series of accidents of phenomenal appearance, some outward and physical, some inward and psychological? (pp. 470–471).

From all of these considerations, Lewis finds that there emerge three possible candidates for the office of "the basic category of esthetics—*the* esthetic object" (p. 471). These are "first, the intention of the artist or the ideal which that intention projects" (p. 471). It should be pointed out that this is actually a double candidate—although Lewis nowhere explicitly recognizes that this is the case. The second candidate is "the kind of abstract entity which may be instanced in two printings of a poem or two renditions of a piece of music" (p. 471). Finally, the third is "the physical individual which incorporates this abstraction or approximates to this ideal, and serves on some occasions as the vehicle of its presentation" (p. 471).

Each of these prospects is now considered in turn. With respect to the intention of the artist (which Lewis seems to be taking as identical with the "ideal that intention projects"), two factors seem to favor its selection: a) it seems to be important in attempting to bring about "truer renditions" to look beyond the physical art work to what the artist intends; and, b) it is "obvious" that if we found the adequate and accurate "laws of esthetics" they would "project as their exemplars, idealities rather than actualities, whether art-produced or natural" (p. 471).

On the other hand, neither of these two factors gives us a "compelling" reason for taking esthetic objects to be transcendental entities—a position to which Lewis feels acceptance of this first candidate commits us and to which, at this particular point, he seems reluctant to be committed. To accept candidate 1, would, with respect to natural esthetic objects at least, make us guilty of the pathetic fallacy.

Also ruled out is the third candidate. The physical individual, in the light of what has already been said, cannot be the esthetic object. Also presumably ruled out, I might add, although Lewis seems to have forgotten this dark horse, is the phenomenal individual. In the case of music, for example, neither the physical sound waves nor the *phenomenally* heard music could be regarded as the esthetic object.

This leaves Lewis with the second candidate, i.e., the "abstract entity which may be instanced in two printings of a poem or two renditions of a piece of music."

The task which now confronts the expositor of Lewis in this connection, namely that of making clear what is meant by "abstract entity" here—or of telling what kind of a thing it is, is one which seems singularly difficult to accomplish. First of all, it is something which is "literally actualized and exemplified by physical occasions—and not merely approximated to or 'imitated' by physical things" (p. 472). This, Lewis feels, is sufficient to differentiate it from the artist's intention or projected ideal which, one gathers, is never actualized but is only approximated or merely imitated by the creation. Similarly, it is also different from the physical art work—as has been already indicated above—but it does depend on the physical art work insofar as it cannot be presented as the esthetic object without the physical art work. Nevertheless, it is not "literally embodied in the physical thing which serves on any occasion as the medium of its presentation" (p. 473).

Where is it to be located? Well, "this abstraction, or its instance is to be located in a context of the physical object." In the case of a poem, its locus will be something he calls "a mentally associated context."

Let us, taking poetry as our example (as does Lewis), call this abstract esthetic object The Poem with a capital "T" and capital "P." The Poem then, is not located in the poem which presents it. However, The Poem does have properties in common with the poem—for example, its language pattern, or the temporal sequence of sounds. But, *The* Poem itself being "constituted by meanings . . . physically symbolized, lies in the *context associated with* this physical entity which presents it" (p. 474).

What now is an associated context? Lewis, I'm afraid, is not very kind to us on this point. All that he tells us is that a correct associated context is what an individual *must* bring to the presentation in order correctly to understand The Poem presented—and moreover, that which is so brought, belongs to The Poem—presumably this means, is a part of it.

Let me use his own words to sum up thus far:

> The poem is an abstraction which is actualized in the instances of its presentation, through the medium of some physical vehicle. It is an entity essentially repeatable in, or common to, different physical events or things which instance it. But it must be observed that this abstractness of it is *not* the kind by which universals like triangularity or honesty or incompatibility stand in contrast to anything which is sensuously qualitative and imaginal. It has the literal character of esthesis: we shall call it an esthetic essence (pp. 474–5).

For Lewis, then, the esthetic object is not, to use his words in a wide sense, any particular rendition of an art work. It is rather an abstract entity. Particular renditions are concrete "instances" of the esthetic object but are not identical with it. It must be admitted that Lewis gives us very little specific information about what kind of a thing an abstract esthetic object could be, or about how it can be "embodied" in an "instance." How is it that we experience the abstract esthetic object when what seems present is merely a concrete instance? Lewis says we bring with us to the experience an "associated context." But this is scarcely illuminating. Finally, why should Lewis feel it incumbent to thus multiply the types of entities permissible in his esthetic ontology?

All of these things seem at the outset quite puzzling. We can, however, without too much difficulty gain some inkling of the kind of eventuality which motivates Lewis in the direction he takes. It is a fact that we do call two (frequently obviously different) renditions of *Beethoven's Fifth Symphony* by the same name. We feel that the art work, *Fifth Symphony,* which Beethoven created is one thing, one art work. We feel, also, that there is an overwhelming likelihood that no particular rendition of the symphony does more than approximate the "primal" symphony which was actually Beethoven's creation. One way of solving the difficulty thus presented, it would seem, would be to regard the "primal" symphony as an abstract entity of which particular renditions are instances.

Now, it seems clear, that any complete esthetic theory must account for this difficulty whether it be apparent or real. With respect to Lewis's account, I propose to show, negatively, that Lewis's solution has counter-intuitive consequences and is hence untenable as an analysis; and positively, I shall indicate a direction in which a solution might lie that may not have counter-intuitive consequences.

Lewis's analysis has as a consequence that the symphony which Beethoven composed was not something having the same "ontological status" with any heard symphony or with the physical score which Beethoven wrote out. Moreover, since Lewis is surely not proposing that anything which is imagined (in the sense of the content of someone's imaginings) is *thereby* abstract, on Lewis's view what Beethoven was imagining when he was writing the score (or preparing to write the score) was not insofar abstract and hence not the esthetic object either. But what activities *vis a vis* creation other than writing out the score, "imagining out" the music, or "working out" phrases on the piano, was Beethoven undertaking when he composed the *Fifth Symphony?* One does not see how the product of these actions as such need be an abstract entity; this is true as well of the imagining of music. Think of a tune. Let any simple melody run through the mind. This "tune" may be different from a heard tune just because it isn't *heard,* i.e., just because it isn't directly causally connected with an event consisting of the impingement of sound waves on the ear. But wherein are we justified in maintaining disparate status in level for the imagined tune and the heard tune? The fact that frequently the hearing of tunes is mistaken for the mere imagining of them, the fact that frequently the imagining of tunes is mistaken for the hearing of them, and the fact that we are sometimes at a loss to know whether we have just imagined or actually heard some familiar melody, seems to be decisive against any theory which holds that heard music is concrete but imagined music abstract. If Lewis's position commits him to hypostatizing as the esthetic object, an abstract entity which cannot be the product of the artist's activities, then a counter-intuitive consequence of the position is that Beethoven did not compose the *Fifth Symphony*. I am not, however, here attempting to demonstrate that a creator's activities could not issue in an abstract entity. Rather, my point is that Lewis does not show us how they could so issue, an obvious desideratum for any such theory. More importantly, I shall show that the difficulties, i.e., the problematic locutions, which lead Lewis to posit an abstract entity, can be accounted for without taking such a step.

There is some evidence that Lewis is thinking of the relationship between the abstract art work and a particular rendition of it as being analogous to or identical with the type-token or symbol-token relationship which is frequently described in linguistic studies. In a given book, carbonic configurations similar to

man

may make a number of appearances. Each occurrence, however, is not thought of as the occurrence of a different word, but rather as a different token or instance of *the* word or symbol "man." On different pages where a configuration similar to

man

appears, we are said to have the same word, "man," but different tokens or instances of it. Lewis's thesis may be that this is also the case for the *Fifth Symphony* and particular renditions of it. But such a position would also have counter-intuitive consequences in esthetics. In linguistic studies the symbol is defined as the class of similar tokens.[1] But if the *Fifth Symphony* were defined as a class of similar renditions, we would again have as a counter-intuitive consequence a denial that Beethoven created the *Fifth Symphony*.

But the difficulty which seems to have set Lewis off does not in any event require the hypostatization of an abstract entity to take the place of the esthetic object. We do indeed say of two different musical renditions that they are both renditions of the *Fifth Symphony*. This, however, does not demonstrate that we have experienced two instances of the esthetic object—as is attested on a common sense level by the circumstance that we may react in an esthetically favorable way to the one and not the other. "Two renditions of the *Fifth Symphony*" can be interpreted as an ellipsis for "two musical renditions which are similar in a group of important respects." There is here no necessity for multiplying the types of ontological entity which shall be admitted to an Esthetic. Again, the sentence "Beethoven's *Fifth Symphony* is good but this is a bad rendition of it," could be taken as an ellipsis for "there is a musical rendition *called* Beethoven's *Fifth Symphony* which is pleasing esthetically but this musical rendition, while similar to it in important respects, is esthetically displeasing."[2] Here, too, there is no necessity for the manufacture of abstract entities. The problematic locutions are simply recognized as convenient shorthand.

In effect, what has been pointed out is that Lewis's question, "what is the esthetic object," is actually ambiguous; and that the source of his difficulties may lie in the confusion of at least two related but distinct problems. The question "what is the esthetic object" may, with some propriety, be taken as posing the problem: to what is our esthetic response directed; or it may be taken as posing the quite different problem: what, if anything, do names like *The Fifth Symphony* designate. That the problems are at least logically distinct can be seen in the possibility of

---

[1] *Cf.,* H. Reichenbach, *Elements of Symbolic Logic,* pp. 4–5. I am not, of course, here subscribing to the view which is expounded by Reichenbach.

[2] More rarely, perhaps, such a sentence is an ellipsis for: *"Beethoven's* composition [a particular thing] is esthetically pleasing, but this rendition, which is similar to it in important respects, is esthetically displeasing."

attributing the names of art works to non-experienceable abstract or ideal entities, a procedure which would leave the first of the problems mentioned above yet unsolved and would indeed dictate for it a differing answer. That they are in fact distinct problems has been evidenced (if the above considerations are cogent) by the solution, to the difficulties Lewis presents, which has been proposed. What we have been maintaining is that in typical pronouncements of esthetics, such as "that was a poor rendition *of* Beethoven's *Fifth*," the occurrence of the name of the art work is a syncategorematic one.[3] At the same time, we have maintained that there is an entity toward which we are esthetically responding. Lewis is forced to look for an "abstract entity with instances" because he assumes implicitly that what we have a given response to and that which the name of an art work designates, in typically esthetic locutions, must be the same thing. The way in which we use the names of art works confers a certain plausibility on the decision that their designata are abstract entities. But our ordinary experience of responses to concrete renditions renders the *same* answer to the other of the questions quite implausible. Other considerations aside, Lewis's difficulties, particularly the discomfort he manifests in the last pages of his treatment of esthetics, arise out of his attempts to make the one answer do for the two problems. Beyond this, our criticism has been that Lewis's solution to the question of the designata of names like *The Fifth Symphony* has only an apparent plausibility and should be rejected because it multiplies the types of ontological entity required beyond necessity.

Before continuing our discussion of Lewis's efforts in particular, it will be advisable to determine whether either one or both of the two problems we have delineated are uniquely esthetic problems; that is to say, whether there is a cogent sense in which the problem of the esthetic object may be interpreted as being of a different kind from the "problem of the object" in science and ordinary affairs. This latter problem presents a puzzle because of at least two unresolved difficulties which become apparent in Carnap's formulation in the *Logische Aufbau*. Suppose we want

[3] *Cf.* Quine, "Designation and Existence," *Journal of Philosophy*, Vol. XXXVI (1939).

to clarify the meaning of an expression like "x is objectively red." The notion derived from Carnap is that being objectively red can be explained as some function of looking red, and we get in effect the analysis

x is objectively red if and only if x would look red to a normal individual under normal conditions.

Two, so far as I know, unresolved problems which this formulation presents are the problem of counterfactuals,[4] and the apparent involvement of vicious circularity indicated by the usages of "normal." [5]

Now, this is a problem in ordinary affairs—in science and practical activity—because in ordinary affairs our primary concern lies with the orientation of suitable responses toward the "objective" object. But in esthetics, on the contrary (this may be just what distinguishes esthetics from ordinary affairs) the pertinent responses are those toward particular phenomenal contents in a sense independent of "objectivity" or to the clues to "objectivity" which such contents might afford. The distinction I think is complex and subtle, but there is a distinction. Perhaps it can be better elucidated by an example. The question in esthetics that I pose when I ask what is it to which we esthetically respond in an experience of, e.g., *The Magic Mountain,* is different in kind from the scientific question, what is observed when we examine a certain area of the sky. One kind of answer which might satisfy the first of these questions but not the second would be: the phenomenal words. The difference may perhaps even more clearly be exhibited when we contrast the typically esthetic question, to what do we respond in an esthetic experience of *The Magic Mountain,* with the question, what objectively, is *The Magic Mountain.* The phenomenal content to which I esthetically responded (and which might be, for example, causally related to the "objective" *Magic Mountain*) could not be the answer to the second of these questions. Moreover, the second of

---

[4] *Vide,* Nelson Goodman, "The Problem of Counterfactual Conditionals," *The Journal of Philosophy,* Vol. XLIV, No. 5 (1947), pp. 113–128.

[5] This formulation and its difficulties were brought to my attention by Morton G. White.

these questions would be a scientific rather than typically esthetic one.

The relevance of the foregoing to our consideration of Lewis is no doubt already obvious. The problem, what does an expression like *The Fifth Symphony* designate, which we took to be Lewis's primary concern, is not an esthetic problem, in the sense specified above, at all. Indeed, it is in all likelihood equivalent to the "scientific" problem, what is the objective *Fifth Symphony*.

For these reasons we have held that the occurrence of the names of art works in typically esthetic statements like "That was a poor rendition of *The Fifth Symphony*" is a non-designative one. It was this kind of locution in esthetics, it will be remembered, which led Lewis to hypostatize an abstract entity when he was confronted with the question of what we esthetically respond to. But no such entity is required when we realize that these locutions are a convenient shorthand of the type already described.

Nothing which has been said up to this point should, of course, be construed as questioning the propriety of referring to a particular rendition, i.e., some particular heard music, as Beethoven's *Fifth Symphony*. It is appropriate to call a rendition, Beethoven's *Fifth Symphony* rather than Beethoven's *Fourth Symphony* or *Sacre Du Printemps,* because the heard music is connected (at least causally) with a certain set of Beethoven's creative activities in a way in which it is not at all connected with another set or with Stravinsky.[6]

---

[6] The brief mention of the "connection" which is relevant in this essay is not meant to suggest that the establishment of the precise nature of the connection would not be a task of some difficulty.

Paul Ziff

The Task of Defining a Work of Art

One of the foremost problems of aesthetics has been to provide
a definition (or an analysis, or an explication, or an elucidation)
of the notion of a work of art. The solutions given by aestheticians to this problem have often been violently opposed to one
another; e.g., contrast Tolstoi's answer with that of his predeces-
sors. There is no doubt that the problem is a difficult one. But
what I should like to consider here is just why it is so difficult. In
this way I hope to make clear what is involved in such a definition and what an aesthetician must do, whether he knows it or
not, to justify his definition of a work of art.

I

Suppose a child does not understand what a book is, is merely
puzzled by people speaking about books. One of the many means
at hand to help him grasp the use of that word "book" would be
simply to show him a book. But one would not help or try to help
him by picking out a pocket book, or a diary with blank pages, or
a loose-leaf note book. What is wanted here is a perhaps fat book,
but not too fat, with a hard cover, perhaps a gold-lettered leather-bound book. If someone doesn't know but wants to know what
a table is, to learn the use of the word "table," it would not do to
begin by showing him an esoteric table with ninety-six legs, only
six inches high. Again one would take a good solid oak table with
a modest number of legs, an ordinary, everyday sort of table, not
a cabinet maker's nightmare. If we begin with a clear-cut case,
one no one would ordinarily be tempted to dispute, we can then

[Reprinted from *Philosophical Review*, 62: 58–78 (1953).]

shift to the less clear-cut, the disputed, cases. A clear-cut case is a
place to start from.

What would a clear-cut case of a work of art be? One is
inclined to say a painting like Poussin's "The Rape of the Sabine
Women," or Da Vinci's "Mona Lisa," or Rembrandt's "Night
Watch," would do here, that no one would want to object. But
suppose someone were to say, "No, none of these are works of
art." If, when we pointed to an ordinary everyday sort of table,
someone were to object, "No, that's not a table," we could and
should say he was clearly confused, in one way or another. Maybe
he imagined we had not pointed at the table, that we had
pointed at a chair; or we might suppose that he supposed the
word "table" was only and always applied to multiplication
tables; and so forth. Perhaps cultivated confusion at a sophisticated level, but nothing else but confusion, could be the root of a
dispute over our clear-cut example of a table; but a refusal to call
the Poussin, or the Da Vinci, or even the Rembrandt a work of
art, need not be the blossom of a merely blooming confusion. For
it is in fact possible to dispute whether any particular painting is
a work of art or not, and people do dispute such questions, in a
way that it is not in fact possible to dispute whether any particular object is a table or not.

And this is to say simply that there are and can be no clear-cut
cases of works of art in quite the same sense as there can be such
clear-cut cases of tables, chairs, and so forth. That this is so stems
partly from the fact that there are many uses of the phrase "work
of art" in a way in which there are very few uses of the word
"table." (For even though the word "table" does have many
diverse uses, e.g., one can speak of multiplication tables, dinner
tables, table lands, etc., there are very few uses of the word
"table" in connection with those ordinary everyday objects that
one customarily sits at and eats off of, i.e., tables. But in this
sense, there are many distinct and different and even "competing" uses of the phrase "work of art.") And it also stems partly
from the fact that among these many uses of the phrase "work of
art," some are aptly described as laudatory or eulogistic. The
many reasons why this is so will, I trust, become clear in the

course of this discussion. For the time being, even though the examples of works of art which I have cited might not or need not be accepted by everyone, they are the clearest cases available, and as such they provide a useful base for our explorations.

In selecting a clear-cut example of a carpenter's hammer, one could choose a hammer with a handle exactly twelve and three-quarters inches long. Perhaps the title of the book we pointed to, the leather-bound book with gold lettering, was *Anna Karenina*. But in describing or talking about the example of a hammer to a child who did not grasp the use of the word, one would not say, "The handle of the hammer is exactly twelve and three-quarters inches long." Instead, one would be much more apt to say, "The handle of the hammer is about a foot long," or something of that sort. In the kind of case we have envisaged, the former statement would, at best, be altogether misleading. Whether a description is liable to mislead depends roughly on why it is wanted. In describing the clear-cut case of a hammer, when we want to help someone understand how the word "hammer" is used, we mention those facts about the object that make it, in fact, such a clear-cut case. That is why we would not say, "The handle of the hammer is exactly twelve and three quarters inches long." This really does not matter; it does not affect and is entirely irrelevant to the status of the example as a clear-cut case. But the fact that the handle is about a foot long is really relevant here. Similarly, we would not mention the particular title of the book, which we were using as a clear-cut case; but the fact that it had a title would be relevant.

Suppose we point to Poussin's "The Rape of the Sabine Women" as our clearest available case of a work of art. We could describe it by saying, first, that it is a painting. Secondly, it was made, and what is more, made deliberately and self-consciously with obvious skill and care, by Nicolas Poussin. Thirdly, the painter intended it to be displayed in a place where it could be looked at and appreciated, where it could be contemplated and admired. In short, he intended it to be treated in a way very much like the way that works of art are customarily treated. In saying this I do not wish to suggest that Poussin intended his work to be exhibited in a museum gallery. I do not know, but I would suppose the painting was intended to be hung in some chateau, or something of that sort. So perhaps in this respect the painting is not treated in the way intended by the painter. But there is good reason to believe that the painter did intend the painting to be displayed in an appropriate manner, to be treated with care, and to be preserved for as long as possible. And there is good reason to believe that Poussin did intend the painting to be contemplated, studied, observed, admired, criticized, and discussed by some people, if not by just any people. Fourthly, the painting is or was exhibited in a museum gallery where people do contemplate, study, observe, admire, criticize, and discuss it. What I wish to refer to here by speaking of contemplating, studying, and observing a painting, is simply what we may do when we are concerned with a painting like this. For example, when we look at this painting by Poussin, we may attend to its sensuous features, to its "look and feel." Thus we attend to the play of light and color, to dissonances, contrasts, and harmonies of hues, values, and intensities. We notice patterns and pigmentation, textures, decorations, and embellishments. We may also attend to the structure, design, composition, and organization of the work. Thus we look for unity, and we also look for variety, for balance and movement. We attend to the formal interrelations and cross connections in the work, to its underlying structure. We are concerned with both two-dimensional and three-dimensional movements, the balance and opposition, thrust and recoil, of spaces and volumes. We attend to the sequences, overlaps, and rhythms of line, form, and color. We may also attend to the expressive, significant, and symbolic aspects of the work. Thus we attend to the subject matter, to the scene depicted, and to the interrelations between the formal structure and the scene portrayed. We attend to the emotional character of the presented forms, and so forth. This is, very roughly, what I have in mind when I speak of contemplating, studying, and observing this Poussin painting. (Lest there be any misunderstanding, let me say explicitly that I am not saying that when ordinary people either contemplate or study or observe or attend to or look at or in any way concern themselves with this Poussin painting, they do in fact always attend to or concern themselves with all of the aspects of the painting that I have here mentioned. This is plainly untrue. But it is true that some people, when they look at this painting, are concerned with some of its many aspects that I have mentioned, while other people concern themselves with other of its aspects. And it is true, certainly, that all of these aspects of the painting are attended to at one time or another, and occasionally even all by one very unordinary person at one time.) Fifthly, this work is a representational painting with a definite subject matter; it depicts a certain mythological scene. Sixthly, the painting has an elaborate and certainly complex formal structure. Finally, the painting is a good painting. And this is to say simply that the Poussin painting is worth contemplating, studying, and observing in the way I have ever so roughly described.

It must be clear that whether the Poussin painting does or does not in fact fit the description that I have given is totally irrelevant to what I am saying. For example, it is at least within the nebulous realm of possibility that I am much mistaken in saying it is a good painting. It is even more than merely possible that I have been misinformed about Poussin's intentions. And maybe I have made other mistakes as well. But whether this is so or not does not in the least matter, for I am not trying to show that the Poussin painting is in fact a work of art. Rather I am trying to clarify what may be meant by saying that the Poussin painting is a work of art. What is important here is this: Because I believe the Poussin painting does fit the description I have given, I believe that it is, and I have chosen it as, one of the clearest available cases of a work of art. Our concern here is only with the description and not with whether the description fits the particular case. Each of the various facts mentioned in the foregoing description are characteristic of a work of art; it is these characteristics that concern us.

In order to make clear what the difficulties are in formulating and justifying a definition of a work of art, in the following section I shall present what I take to be an adequate definition based on the preceding account of the Poussin painting. However, I shall not here attempt to show that the definition is in fact adequate.

II

All of the characteristics mentioned in the preceding description of the Poussin painting together constitute a set of characteristics. Several characteristics taken together constitute a set of characteristics if and only if all of the characteristics mentioned are relevant in determining whether something is or is not a work of art and if they are the only characteristics that are so relevant. Anything possessing all of these characteristics can then be said to be a characteristic case. Consequently, if the Poussin painting does in fact fit the description given above, it is such a characteristic case.

The set of characteristics given provides us with a set of sufficient conditions for something's being a work of art. Anything clearly satisfying these conditions can be said to be a work of art in exactly the same sense of the phrase "work of art" in which the Poussin painting can be said to be a work of art. It is important to notice that I said "clearly satisfying these conditions." The word "clearly" is crucial here. There is a temptation to say that the preceding description of the Poussin painting provides nothing more than a rough schema of what could be said about the work. This is not quite true, but it is a way of emphasizing the truth that there is a great deal of latitude in the various details of the description given. For example, one of the facts mentioned about the Poussin painting was that it is a representational work. Suppose we now consider a statue of Praxiteles: are we to say that it is representational? Someone might say that a statue cannot be representational in quite the same sense in which a painting can be. On the other hand, it could be claimed that both a statue and a painting can be said to be representational, in the very same sense of the word, but that they are merely different species of representative works. Again, someone might say that a sculptor does not make a statue in quite the same sense in which a painter makes his painting. And again it could be said that there is no difference in sense but only a difference in species. And this kind of question can be raised in connection with each of the characteristics mentioned.

I take it that we are inclined to speak of a difference in sense when we are impressed by, or wish to stress, dissimilarities. But when we are impressed by, or wish to stress, similarities, we are then inclined to speak of a mere difference in species. Now by speaking of a case that "clearly" satisfies the conditions given above, I mean to refer to a case in which there is no inclination to speak of a shift in sense with respect to any of the characteristics listed. Unless this point is attended to, it might mistakenly seem that we do not have a set of sufficient conditions, for one can conjure up some curious cases.

Suppose an object were found, satisfying the conditions given above, but with this one eccentricity: the scene depicted, and consequently the formal structure as well, changed periodically, without being changed. Imagine an object fitting the description, but having the peculiarity that, without being moved, it moved occasionally about the room. Thus in a way these odd objects behave somewhat like living organisms. One could be somewhat reluctant to call these things works of art. It would indeed be difficult to know what to say. Shall we say that our set of characteristics does not, therefore, provide a set of sufficient conditions? For we have not mentioned the fact that the object is a stable object, that it does not change or move about periodically of its own accord. This would be a mistake. We should be uncertain whether these odd objects were works of art solely because we should be uncertain whether they did in fact fit the description which we have given. It would be queer to say of an object that it was a painting and that it periodically moved about the room of its own accord. It would be equally queer to say of an object that it was a painting depicting a certain scene and that the scene periodically changed of its own accord. For facts like these cast doubt on whether the object is a painting in the sense of the word "painting" originally intended, and on whether the painting depicts a scene in the sense of the phrase "depicts a scene" originally intended. But if an object does clearly satisfy the conditions stated, there can be no doubt but that it can be said to be a work of art in the very same sense of the phrase "work of art" in which the Poussin painting can be said to be a work of art.

Although the above set of characteristics provides a set of

sufficient conditions, it does not provide a set of necessary and sufficient conditions. No one of the characteristics listed is necessarily a characteristic of a work of art. But a definition in terms of necessary and sufficient conditions is merely one kind of definition, one way of describing the use of a word or phrase. Another kind of definition, and the kind we are here concerned with, is one in terms of various subsets of a set of characteristics, or, in less exotic language, in terms of similarities to what I have called a characteristic case, a case in which an entire set of characteristics is exemplified.[1] The following examples should serve to clarify what is meant by speaking of similarities to a characteristic case.

Suppose we have a naturally formed stone object that has the shape of a woman reclining. Indeed, it looks as though some sculptor has fashioned it, though we know that this is not the case. What is more, it is worth contemplating, studying, and observing in a way analogous to the way described in connection with the Poussin painting. Further suppose that people do in fact contemplate, study, and observe it, that it is displayed in a museum, and so forth. In virtue of its similarities to the characteristic case, this object can be said to be a work of art. The points of similarity between this object and the Poussin painting constitute a particular subset of the set of characteristics listed above. Imagine this sort of case: we have a nonrepresentational painting, deliberately made by an artist, who intended it to be exhibited and displayed, and who wanted people to contemplate, study, and observe it. But in fact the painting is not worth contemplating, studying, and observing. What is more, no one does bother with it at all. It is not exhibited, displayed, and so forth; rather it is buried away in some cellar. This too, in virtue of its similarities to the characteristic case, can be said to be a work of art. Again, the points of similarity between this work and

---

[1] Let me note that I am deeply indebted to Professor Max Black, both through his published papers and from discussions with him, for many of the ideas in this paper. In particular, I have, I trust, here profited from his account of a definition in terms of overlapping and interacting criteria; cf. "The Definition of Scientific Method," *Science and Civilization,* ed. by R. C. Stauffer (Madison, University of Wisconsin Press, 1949).

the characteristic case constitute another subset of the set of characteristics given above.

In each of the preceding examples, when it was said that the object was a work of art in virtue of its similarities to the characteristic case, it was implicitly assumed that the similarities noted were sufficient to warrant the claim that the objects were works of art. No rule can be given to determine what is or is not a sufficient degree of similarity to warrant such a claim. If for one reason or another the dissimilarities become impressive (and what impresses one need not impress another), one is then reluctant to call the object a work of art. For example, a Greek vase is, in many ways, similar to a New England bean pot. Both are artifacts; both were made to serve domestic purposes; neither was intended to stand in a museum; and so forth. Nonetheless, a Greek vase is a work of art while a New England bean pot is not. To see that this is so, consider those points of similarity between a Greek vase and the Poussin painting that are also points of dissimilarity between a Greek vase and a New England bean pot. We do not, in fact, treat a New England bean pot in a way similar to the way we treat the Poussin painting; whereas we do, in fact, treat a Greek vase in a way quite similar to the way we treat the Poussin painting. We set up Greek vases on pedestals; we do display and exhibit them in museums and galleries, and what is more, it is worth while to do so. We do not in fact contemplate, study, observe, admire, criticize, and discuss bean pots in a way that we do Greek vases or in the way that we do the Poussin painting; furthermore, it seems most unlikely that it would be worth while to do so. Unlike bean pots, and like the Poussin painting, many Greek vases are representational. One is inclined to speak, and one does speak, of the formal structure of a Greek vase in a way similar to the way one speaks of the formal structure of the Poussin painting. We do not, in fact, speak of the formal structure of a bean pot, nor is there usually any inclination to do so. Now if one starts, as it were, from the Poussin painting and then shifts to the Greek vase, one begins to feel the strain. For a Greek vase was not (or so we are supposing) intended to be treated in a way similar to the way the Poussin painting is treated. It was designed to fulfill a specific utilitarian

function. Many Greek vases are not representational. They were
not, in the time of the Greeks (or so we are supposing), set up on
pedestals. They were not displayed and exhibited in museums
and galleries. They were not contemplated, studied, observed,
admired, criticized, and discussed in a way similar to the way in
which the Poussin painting is. One begins to feel the strain in
speaking of a Greek vase as a work of art. Now if one tries to
speak of a bean pot as a work of art, the strain becomes too great.
We have reached a breaking point, and one is inclined to say
things like, "A bean pot *cannot* be classed as a work of art." It is
only a matter of degree.

Finally, neither a poem, nor a novel, nor a musical composition can be said to be a work of art in the same sense of the
phrase in which a painting or a statue or a vase can be said to be
a work of art. For such things as poems, novels, musical compositions, possess none of the characteristics listed in our set of
characteristics. E.g., a poem is not exhibited or displayed; one
does not contemplate, study, and observe a poem; a poem is not
representational; and so forth. And even though a poem may
seem to possess some of the characteristics listed, for one can and
does speak of a good poem, the dissimilarities between what is
meant in speaking of a good poem and what is meant in speaking
of a good painting are sufficiently impressive to warrant our
saying it is a different sense of the word "good." All of this,
however, does not show that one cannot reasonably use the
phrase "work of art" to refer to poems, novels, musical compositions, as well as to paintings. If one wished to describe a use of
the phrase "work of art" in which there is such a systematic shift
in sense, one could do so in terms of several sets of characteristics.
One would take a clear-cut case of a poem and obtain a set of
characteristics, then a clear-cut case of a novel and obtain another
set, and so forth. Then something would be a work of art, in this
use of the phrase, if it possessed some subset of the set of characteristics pertaining to paintings, or some subset of the set of
characteristics pertaining to poems, and so forth. This may seem
an extremely complex way of using the phrase "work of art," but
it is actually often used in somewhat this way by critics who speak
of the "art of painting," the "art of poetry," and so forth. Such a

"blanket" use of the phrase may be warranted by the fact, if it is a fact, that each set of characteristics is analogous in composition to every other set; e.g., the analogue of contemplating a painting is reading a poem, the analogue of a good painting is a good poem, the analogue of display is publish, and so forth.

There is no need to elaborate this definition any further for the purposes of this discussion. The preceding account is sufficiently explicit to stir up and bring to the surface all the important difficulties that must be noted here.

III

The definition just given provides a rough description of only one use of the phrase "work of art." But this phrase is and has been used in many ways. So long as art remains what it has always been, something changing and varied, so long as there are artistic revolutions, the phrase "work of art," or some equivalent locution, will continue to be used in many ways. For when such revolutions occur, there is inevitably a shift in some uses of the phrase "work of art." Some understanding of the nature of the disputes that occur over what is and what is not a work of art during such periods of artistic revolution is essential to an understanding of what an aesthetician is doing in offering some one, and only one, definition of a work of art.

When nonrepresentational and abstract painting first attracted attention in the early part of this century, many people complained bitterly that the nonrepresentational and abstract works were not works of art. Thus one critic wrote: "The farce will end when people look at Post-Impressionist pictures as Mr. Sargent looked at those shown in London, 'absolutely skeptical as to their having any claim whatever to being works of art.' " [2] Other critics insisted, with equal vehemence, that the Post-Impressionist paintings most certainly were works of art. If one looks with an impartial eye at these disputes between the traditional and the modern critics, one thing is quite clear. In many cases the parties

[2] Royal Cortissoz, "The Post-Impressionist Illusion," *Three Papers on "Modernist Art,"* (New York, Amer. Acad. of Arts and Letters, 1924), p. 42. Reprinted from *Century Magazine*, April, 1913.

to the disputes were using the phrase "work of art" in more or less different ways. Indeed, the modern critics, the defenders of the new works, were introducing a more or less novel use of the phrase. To see that this is so, it is necessary to attend to some of the typical complaints that were voiced against modern art by the traditional critics.

In a review of the first exhibition of modern art in America, Mr. Kenyon Cox claimed that

> the real meaning of this Cubist movement is nothing else than the total destruction of the art of painting—that art of which the dictionary definition is "the art of representing, by means of figures and colors applied on a surface, objects presented to the eye or to the imagination." . . . Now the total destruction of painting as a representative art is a thing which a lover of painting could hardly envisage with entire equanimity, yet one may admit that such a thing might take place and yet an art remain that should have its own value. A Turkish rug or a tile from the Alhambra is nearly without representative purpose, but it has intrinsic beauty and some conceivable use. The important question is what it is proposed to substitute for this art of painting which the world has cherished since there were men definitely differentiated from beasts. Having abolished the representation of nature and all forms of recognized and traditional decoration; what will the "modernists" give us instead? [3]

It is often erroneously supposed that traditional critics held representation to be a necessary characteristic of a work of art. This is not true. Such critics did maintain that it was a relevant characteristic, but few insisted it was necessary in that without representation there could be no work of art. What is true is that traditional critics weighted this characteristic enormously, so that it was of paramount importance in determining whether a given work was or was not a work of art. In their reaction against this view, some of the modern critics have apparently gone to the extreme of suggesting that representation is wholly irrelevant to art. [4] In this respect, our definition would be apt to satisfy neither

[3] "The 'Modern' Spirit in Art," *op. cit.*, pp. 6–8. Reprinted from *Harper's Weekly*, March 15, 1913.
[4] Cf. Clive Bell, *Art*, pp. 28–30, where such a view is, or seems to be, suggested.

a conservative traditional critic nor an extreme modern critic. The shift in the notion of a work of art that was brought about through the modern developments was, with respect to the question of representation, primarily a shift in emphasis, and only secondarily a shift with respect to necessary conditions. The point is that representation was of paramount importance in virtue of the fact that "accurate" representation played the role of a necessary condition in determining what was and was not a good painting. This leads us to another point of difference between the traditional and modern critics.

I am inclined to suppose both traditional and modern critics would accept the seventh characteristic listed in our definition, viz., that the work be a good one, as a relevant characteristic of a work of art. (Whether they considered it to be a necessary characteristic is a difficult question that need not concern us here.) But it is fairly obvious that what the traditional critics meant in speaking of a good painting or a good drawing was somewhat different from what the modern critics meant. For example, Mr. Royal Cortissoz, in reviewing the first exhibition of modern art in America, severely criticized Van Gogh's drawing.

> The laws of perspective are strained. Landscape and other natural forms are set awry. So simple an object as a jug containing some flowers is drawn with the uncouthness of the immature, even childish, executant. From the point of view of the Post-Impressionist prophet, all this may be referred to inventive genius beating out a new artistic language. I submit that it is explained rather by incompetence suffused with egotism.[5]

Somewhat later in his review, while discussing Matisse's drawing, Mr. Cortissoz stated that

> whatever his ability may be, it is swamped in the contortions of his misshapen figures. The fact is that real genius in these matters will out. Degas, who has been all his life a disciple of Ingres, uses a magic of draftmanship akin to that of his idol, though the style and spirit of his work are wholly his own.[6]

[5] *Op. cit.*, p. 31.
[6] *Ibid.*, pp. 36–37.

It is, I take it, fairly clear that Mr. Cortissoz' notion of a good drawing, of a good painting, would today be objected to. For he, together with most traditional critics, apparently held that a necessary condition (though not, of course, a sufficient condition as is sometimes naïvely supposed) for a drawing to be considered a good drawing is that the perspective be "true," the form "realistic," and so forth. Few if any critics today would subscribe to this view.

Perhaps the clearest indication of the fact that the modern critics were using the phrase "work of art" in a more or less novel way is to be found in the oft-repeated charge that the new works had broken with tradition. For in claiming that there had been such a break, the traditional critics can be taken as claiming that the degree of similarity between the new works and those accepted in the tradition as works of art was insufficient to warrant the claim that the new works were works of art. The dissimilarities were felt to be overwhelming; the gap was held to be too great to bridge. The modern critics, of course, denied that there had been any such rupture, at least not with the tradition as they saw it; rather they insisted that tradition had been reasonably extended and developed. They repudiated the charge of a complete break by exhuming and pointing to the works of such people as El Greco to justify the modern use of distortion, just as somewhat later the Surrealists were to exhume the works of Acrimboldo and Bosch in an effort to make their own fantasies more palatable to the public. It is for this reason, among others, that the works of Matisse have so often been compared with Egyptian portraits, Japanese prints, and so forth, while the similarities between Picasso's work and practically everything in any tradition have been set forth exhaustively. Whether modern art did in fact break with European tradition is not a point that need concern us. But the fact that the tradition was at least extended cannot be denied and is here relevant. For this is merely another way of saying that there was some shift in the notion of a work of art. Let it be quite clear that I am not claiming to have here *shown* that the modern critics were introducing a somewhat novel use of the phrase "work of art." To show that such was the case, it would be necessary to present a great deal more evidence than I have done. But everything about the disputes between the traditional and the modern critics certainly suggests that the modern critics were in fact using the phrase "work of art" in a somewhat novel way. And if the likelihood of this is granted, that is sufficient for the purposes of this discussion.

Once it is realized that the modern critics were most likely using the phrase "work of art" in a somewhat novel way, there is, or is apt to be, a temptation to say that the disputes between the traditional and the modern critics were merely verbal. For one may be inclined to say that in a modern critic's use of the phrase, the new works were in fact works of art, while in a traditional critic's use, they were not. But this is a temptation which we must certainly resist. Even though it may be true that the new works were works of art in a modern critic's use of the phrase, and were not works of art in a traditional critic's use, it would be quite absurd to think that, therefore, the disputes were merely verbal. The disputes, in part, arose from conflicting decisions over the way to use the phrase "work of art," but such decisions were not and certainly need not be thought arbitrary. Decisions may not be true or false, but they can be reasonable or unreasonable, wise or unwise. In effect, the traditional critics maintained that their decision to use the phrase "work of art" in a traditional way was the most reasonable one, and consequently their use of the phrase was the most reasonable use; the modern critics made exactly the same claim in favor of their own somewhat radical use of the phrase. Sometimes these claims were made explicitly; at other times, such a claim is implicit in the criticism, favorable or unfavorable, given to the new works. To understand what is involved in such a claim and what is meant by speaking of a "reasonable use" of a word or phrase, it is necessary to see why it may be important to use a word or phrase in one way rather than another, and what there is that may be worth arguing about.

IV

There is no sense in speaking of a "reasonable use" of a word or phrase *in vacuo*. What is or is not a reasonable use depends on the particular context in which the question is raised, on the kind of considerations involved, and so forth. For example, if you want to be understood, you are well advised to use your words in some ordinary and familiar way; but if being understood is not at issue, this advice is not to the point. Not being understood may be one consequence of using a word or phrase in a particular way, but there may be other consequences, and consequences of a different kind. For example, it is, I suppose, no part of the meaning or the use of the phrase "excessive speed" that if a driver of a vehicle involved in an accident is held to have been driving at an excessive speed, he is likely to suffer certain penalties under the law. But even though this may be said to be no part of the use of the phrase, it is nevertheless an important fact which a jurist must keep in mind when attempting to specify the use of the phrase in a court of law. It would be unwise, for example, to lay down a ruling that would constitute a precedent for taking excessive speed to be any speed over posted limits. For a man may drive at a speed greater than the posted limit in an attempt to avoid an impending accident. It would be unreasonable to penalize him for making the attempt if it happened that even so he was unable to avoid the accident.

What I am saying is that once the legal consequences and implications of declaring a person to have been driving at an excessive speed are relatively fixed, we can then, in the light of these consequences and on the basis of certain moral and legal notions concerning the purposes to be accomplished by means of these consequences, say what is or is not a reasonable definition and a reasonable use of the phrase "excessive speed" in a court of law. (One can, of course, reverse this process and argue that once the notion of excessive speed is fairly well fixed in the sense indicated above, it is unreasonable to penalize a man merely for driving at an excessive speed. Thus someone could argue that his use of the phrase in the sense indicated above was reasonable, the consequences that are likely to occur in the course of using the phrase unreasonable. In a sense, the use of the phrase and the significant legal consequences likely to occur in the course of using the phrase each provide a standpoint for criticism. We can criticize either the use of the phrase in terms of the fairly fixed legal consequences or the legal consequences in terms of the fairly fixed use.)

To ask "What are the consequences and implications of something's being considered a work of art?" is to ask an equivocal question to which there can be no unequivocal answer. We must first know in what context we are to suppose the phrase "work of art" is being used. (Just so one can speak of the consequences of using the phrase "excessive speed" in one way or another only when the context is specified. In a court of law the use of such a phrase may have significant consequences which, in some other context, simply are not forthcoming.) In the context where critical disputes are carried on, there are in fact many significant consequences arising from the fact that a certain type of work is considered a work of art. For disputes between critics are not private affairs. They are carried on in a social context, and they are significant only when set in the framework provided by such a context.

It is, I suppose, no part of the meaning or the use of the phrase "work of art" that if a certain type of work is considered a work of art, works of this type will eventually find their way into a public museum. Nonetheless, public funds will, in fact, be spent on these works. The public will be advised to see and study such works. Books will be written and read about them, and so on. These are in fact some of the present characteristic social consequences of something's being considered a work of art in Western society. The social consequences and implications of something's being considered a work of art have varied in time, and no doubt they will continue to do so. For they are merely an aspect of the particular role art plays in a particular society, and as the character of the society changes, the role of art in the society may also change, together with the characteristic social consequences and implications of something's being considered a work of art in that society. Now although the traditional and the modern critics almost certainly disagreed about the specific characteristics of a work of art, they agreed both in their desires and in their expectations with regard to the characteristic social consequences and implications of something's being considered a work of art. Their agreement in this respect lent substance to their disputes over the use of the phrase "work of art." Indeed, the traditional critics explicitly and with great vehemence maintained that the Post-Impressionist works ought not to be placed in museums; that the public funds ought not to be spent on them; that the public would be ill-advised to spend its time looking at them or reading books about them; and so forth. All of this the modern critics explicitly and emphatically denied. (And this is one obvious reason why it would be quite absurd to call such disputes merely verbal.) Now to determine whether a certain type of work ought or ought not to be placed in a museum, purchased with public funds, and so on, it is necessary to consider what purposes it is to serve when once it has been purchased, when public funds have been spent on it, and so on. And this is to say that in order to determine what is or is not a reasonable use of the phrase "work of art," it is necessary to consider not only the characteristic social consequences and implications of something's being considered a work of art, but also the purposes to be accomplished by means of these consequences—i.e., the various functions of a work of art in society. The role that the functions of a work of art play in determining whether a particular use of the phrase "work of art" is reasonable or not, may be clarified by the following example.

Consider the second characteristic mentioned in our definition of a work of art, viz., that the work be made, deliberately and self-consciously with obvious skill and care, by some person. The traditional view would be that this is a necessary characteristic of a work of art. E.g., in *Art as Experience*, Dewey writes:

> Suppose, for the sake of illustration, that a finely wrought object, one whose texture and proportions are highly pleasing in perception, has been believed to be a product of some primitive people. Then there is discovered evidence that proves it to be an accidental natural product. As an external thing, it is now precisely what it was before. Yet at once it ceases to be a work of art and becomes a natural "curiosity." It now belongs in a museum of natural history, not in a museum of art.[7]

I am very much inclined to object to Dewey's use of the phrase "work of art," but it is most unlikely that such an objection can

[7] Page 48.

be made directly on the grounds that his use of the phrase is unreasonable. To see why this is so, it is necessary to see precisely what is at issue here. This may appear to be a relatively trivial point, one hardly worth disputing over; for there may in fact be fairly few natural objects that one is inclined to exhibit and display. What is and what is not excluded from a museum is in this case, however, of only secondary importance. The exclusion of a natural object from a museum of art is primarily of interest when viewed as symptomatic of a particular orientation toward the works that are in fact displayed in a museum. If one adopts a view similar to that of Dewey, there is a tendency to treat the work of art primarily as a "manifestation" of the artistic activity engaged in by the person who produced the object. One is then tempted to look through the work of art to the artist's "experiences," "feelings," and so forth. Furthermore, one is tempted to say that this "revealing" aspect of the work is essential to its functions as a work of art. Now the relevance of the artist's "experiences" to an appreciation of his work is an extremely complex problem which I shall not even attempt to consider here. But I mention these points in order to stress the fact that such considerations as these are relevant in attempting to determine whether the fact that the object was made by a person is or is not a necessary condition for its being a work of art. To claim that Dewey's traditional use of the phrase "work of art" is unreasonable would, in effect, be to claim that the mere fact that an object is an artifact does not suffice to show that it is thereby incapable of satisfactorily fulfilling the various functions of a work of art. But since such a claim would be made on the basis of a particular view of these functions, Dewey's use of the phrase ought properly to be considered in relation to his own view of what these functions are or ought to be.

There is no doubt but that the explicit disagreements between the traditional and the modern critics stemmed from more or less divergent conceptions of what the functions of a work of art are or ought to be in our society. In writing of the first exhibition of Post-Impressionist works in England, Roger Fry pointed out that the new movement in art "implied a reconsideration of the very

purpose and aim as well as methods of pictorial and plastic art." [8]
He characterized the purpose of the new art by saying it was
devoted to "the direct expression of feeling" and to the making
of "images which by the clearness of their logical structure, and
by their closely knit unity of texture, shall appeal to our disinterested and contemplative imagination with something of the same
vividness as the things of actual life appeal to our practical
activities." [9]

What Mr. Fry says here is, of course, quite vague, but he was
dealing with an extraordinarily difficult topic. Vague or not, he is
quite right in suggesting that modern works serve somewhat
different purposes from the accepted works that had preceded
them, no matter how difficult it may be to say precisely wherein
the difference lies. To consider but one aspect of this enormously
complicated question, a traditional view of a function of a work
of art was that it was to constitute an object of Beauty, which
would inspire, profit, and delight the beholder. Now "Beauty" is
not a term likely to be applied to a host of modern works, e.g., to
one like Picasso's "Guernica." "Guernica" is no doubt a magnificent, powerful, superbly conceived and executed work, but it is
not a thing of "Beauty." It is true that there are many paintings
in European tradition to which one would be equally reluctant
to apply the term "Beauty," e.g., Grünewald's "Crucifixion" in
the Isenheim altarpiece, but it is also true that the obvious
religious purpose of the Isenheim altarpiece is something more or
less alien to modern art. That modern works do in fact serve
somewhat different purposes from the accepted works that had
preceded them is perhaps best signalized by the technical innovations introduced and employed by the modern artists. The extent
of these innovations must not be underestimated.

It is true that the modern use of distortion has its analogue in
El Greco's work among others, but it is also true that El Greco's
work was practically ignored until the twentieth century. And of
course even his work appears naturalistic in contrast with a work
like "Les Demoiselles d'Avignon." To feel the full impact of the

[8] *Vision and Design* (Pelican Books, 1937) , p. 194.
[9] *Ibid.*, p. 195.

modern innovations in the use of color, it is merely necessary to see a work by Miro hung in a gallery alongside works done before 1850. Again one may admit that e.g., Poussin employed intense hues, and Giotto's work must have been quite brilliant at one time; but it is impossible to ignore the fact that many modern painters such as Miro and Matisse employ huge flat masses of color in an altogether new way, a way that is simply incompatible with and wholly alien to the spatial character of a Poussin painting. These and many other such technical innovations all herald the fact that modern paintings are devoted to somewhat different purposes and aims from those of the works that had preceded them. For the widespread adoption of new methods of working in art has, in fact, always been correlative to a more or less radical variation in the purposes and aims of art. (Just so the technical innovations of the monodic revolution in music at the beginning of the seventeenth century, the development of the so-called *stile moderno* or *seconda prattica* with its use of the thorough bass, the introduction of the recitative, and so forth, were the technical correlates of the development of secular music. Indeed, in the eyes of the modern critics of the period, the *stile antico* was seen as the sacred style appropriate to church music.)

Whether the traditional critics' disapproval of the purposes and aims of the new works stemmed from a failure to understand fully what these purposes and aims were, or whether this disapproval was based on a full understanding, is a purely historical question that need not concern us here. That they did disapprove is beyond question, for they voiced this disapproval in no uncertain terms; e.g., in concluding his review of the first exhibition of modern art in America, Mr. Cox adjured his readers to remember that

> it is for you that art is created, and judge honestly for yourselves whether this which calls itself art is useful to you or to the world. You are not infallible, but, in the main, your instincts are right, and, after all, you are the final judges. If your stomach revolts against this rubbish it is because it is not fit for human food.[10]

[10] *Op. cit.*, p. 18.

Most aestheticians today, I believe, would say the modern critics were right in contending that the Post-Impressionist paintings were works of art. Indeed, few people now dare to question the status of modern art as art, and those who do are at once labeled "Philistines" and "reactionaries." But if we say the modern critics were right—and I do not presume to question the matter here—if we say their decision to use the phrase "work of art" in a somewhat new way was a wise one and their use of the phrase was the most reasonable, we must not rashly assume that the traditional critics' use of the phrase "work of art" could be held to be unreasonable when examined on the basis of the traditional critics' own view of what the functions, purposes, and aims of a work of art are or ought to be. On the contrary, it is most likely that when so considered, their use of the phrase would prove to be quite reasonable. Thus an objection to their use of the phrase would most likely have to be made, and no doubt could be made, in terms of a prior objection to their view of what the functions of a work of art are or ought to be. (For one can reasonably dispute over the question of what the functions of a work of art are or ought to be just as one can reasonably dispute over what is or is not a reasonable use of the phrase "work of art.") In accepting the modern critics' decision, we are, in effect, accepting something of their view of what the present functions, purposes, and aims of a work of art are or ought to be in our society.

What then is an aesthetician doing when he offers some one and only one definition of a work of art? It should be clear that he is not describing the actual use of the phrase. As I have tried to indicate above, this phrase is and has been used in many ways. No one definition can mirror this manifold and varying usage. Instead, an aesthetician is describing one, perhaps new, use of the phrase "work of art," which he either implicitly or explicitly claims to be the most reasonable use of the phrase in the light of the characteristic social consequences and implications of something's being considered a work of art, and on the basis of what the functions, purposes, and aims of a work of art are or ought to be in our society. What these purposes and aims are or ought to be is a matter of here and now. For as the character of society changes, as new methods of working are developed, these purposes and aims will also change. With the development of new means there will be new ends that can be served, and with the appearance of new ends, new means will have to be developed to serve them. Art neither repeats itself nor stands still; it cannot if it is to remain art. An attempt to provide a definition and a justification of a definition of a work of art is, as Collingwood has stated, not "an attempt to investigate and expound eternal verities concerning the nature of an eternal object called Art"; rather it is an attempt to provide "the solution of certain problems arising out of the situation in which artists find themselves here and now." [11] An aesthetician is not and certainly ought not to be expected to be a seer foreseeing the future of art. He is not an oracle, though he may choose to speak like one. As new and different kinds of works are created, as the character of society changes and the role of art in society varies, as it has so often done throughout history, it may and most likely will be necessary to revise our definition of a work of art.

[11] *The Principles of Art,* p. vi.

Ruth Saw

What Is a "Work of Art"?

This examination of the concept "work of art" has been prompted by the desire to find a starting point for aesthetic inquiry which, to begin with at any rate, will arouse no dispute. A claim for general agreement such as Clive Bell's: "The starting point for all systems of aesthetics must be the personal experience of a peculiar emotion", is countered by I. A. Richards's "the phantom aesthetic state", and any attempt to claim "beauty" as the central concept is straightway confused by the varied contexts in which "beauty" and "beautiful" may function. We hear much more often of a beautiful stroke in cricket than in painting, and many of our moral judgments have an aesthetic flavour. An action may be bold, dashing, mean, underhanded, unimaginative, cringing, fine, as well as right or wrong. Aesthetic adjectives and adverbs may occur in any context, and part of our job is to separate out the various uses and establish their inter-relationships.

Even if we confine our attention to discourse about art, we find a bewildering variety in the application of aesthetic terms. A critical judgment may be upon the properties of a work of art considered as a sensible object, upon the artist's handling of his material, upon the ideas he is "expressing" in his work or upon the degree of success with which he communicates these ideas. Some critical judgments resemble moral judgments upon the artist and the importance of his ideas. A work may be described as slipshod, insincere, trivial, meretricious, or as a shirking of the artist's problem. A critic may distinguish between aspects and praise a work under one aspect: "good theatre, but negligible as

[Reprinted from *Philosophy*, 36: 18–29 (1961).]

drama". Judgment may be upon the performers, judged in as
many ways as was the composer or playwright, with the added
complication that the performer is an intermediary between artist and audience, and must be judged in this capacity too.
("What possessed this fine and subtle interpreter of German song
to present the most aristocratic of Mozart's characters as a Prus-
sian officer in a bad temper?") Our material is not only critical
talk about works of art but artists' opinions upon their own work
and that of their fellows, and both artists and critics mix their
critical opinions with aesthetic theory more or less well worked
out. Much aesthetic theory is misleading, because artists in words
are generally able to give a more complete account of their
problems and intentions than are painters, sculptors and
composers.

Discourse about works of art is further complicated by the
relationship of natural objects to paintings, sculptures and literary works of art. Much critical and aesthetic argument has been
engaged with the question of "representation" in art and of the
suitability of aesthetic experience which has a flavour of "natural" feeling towards "natural" objects. Some aesthetic theories
neglect the artist and take the object as given, treating it as if it
might have come into existence without human agency. Others
are based upon the relation of artist to spectator, still others
upon the relation of the artist to his world, but it is rare to find
any attempt at justification for concentrating upon one aspect
only of the complex situation, artist-making-object-for-human-
enjoyment.

In this confusion of discourse at different levels, we have no
generally accepted aesthetic principles to help us order our material. Critical pronouncements sometimes seem to assume principles, but they are of limited application and by no means generally accepted. It is as if in moral philosophy we could not assume
that truth speaking was right and lying wrong, not because of
variety of circumstance, but because the rightness or wrongness
itself was still in question. If we take aesthetic experiences or
situations as our starting point, we have to ask the person having
the experience or involved in the situation why he is or is not
enjoying the object, natural or man-made. If he is unskilled in

finding reasons for his enjoyment, he may mislead us by his answer, and if he is more or less sophisticated, he will probably give us an answer in which aesthetic theory is already involved, thus begging our question. If we begin with works of art, we can at least be sure that we have some undisputed facts; without any doubt whatever, there are pictures hanging on the walls of galleries, statues standing on pedestals, dramatic performances, ballets and operas in theatres and instrumentalists and singers performing in concert halls. These objects and performances have been made and prepared at great expense of time and money and audience and spectators are equally ready to expend great effort to look at and hear them. If we are troubled by the question of entertainment versus aesthetic enjoyment, we can at least say that some of our "objects" have been made and performed for aesthetic contemplation, some of our gallery-gazing, theatre and concert-going population do so contemplate these objects, and we may even go farther and say that aesthetic contemplation is the suitable reaction to these objects. I want to go farther still and say that aesthetic contemplation is the "normal" reaction, in the sense that it will count as a failure if a spectator looks at the object and is not moved to contemplation. I want to use the word "failure" because I think that to perceive a work of art is an achievement, and to track down the causes of the failure would throw light on aesthetic experience. (We all of us know the experience of being unable to look properly at a picture or a play because of some personal idiosyncrasy. "I know Lear is a great play, but I can't sit through it; I am squeamish about physical cruelty.")

We now have a factual starting point in the sense that there undoubtedly are objects described as works of art, and if there are aesthetic experiences, some of them undoubtedly occur when a man of sensibility submits himself actively and receptively to one of these objects. We must notice, however, that "work of art" is neither an entirely descriptive nor an entirely appraisive phrase—it represents a preliminary appraisal. This can be shown by noticing that in some contexts it is an insult to say of a picture that it is a work of art and in others, a compliment. A friend of mine visiting a very house-proud old lady, admired the little front parlour with these unfortunate words: "It is quite a little drawing room!" The old lady replied with extreme stateliness: "This *is* the drawing room." She was assuming the preliminary appraisal, "drawing room", but would not have rejected further admiration, such as, it has a pleasant outlook, it gets the evening sun and so on. Similarly, we might praise the painting of an amateur as "quite a work of art", meaning by that, that he ought to send it to an exhibition. We should not, visiting the studio of an academy artist, use these words; he assumes the preliminary appraisal, and like the old lady, will not reject further words of admiration. This is not, however, the end of the matter. On inspection of the picture, we might come to the opinion that the academician's assumption was unjustified. We have the expectation that established writers and painters will go on producing works of art, but there might come a moment when critics begin to say: "Mr. X is merely repeating himself." "Miss Y has written a typical Y-ish novel." How then, do pictures, plays, poems, novels, musical compositions and so on, become "works of art"?

In his *Aspects of the Novel,* Mr. E. M. Forster defines the novel, quoting M. Abel Chevalley, as "a fiction in prose of a certain extent". Mr. Forster specifies the extent. A novel, he says, is "any fictitious prose work over 50,000 words". What other definition, he asks, will fit *The Pilgrim's Progress, Marius the Epicurean, The Adventures of a Younger Son, The Magic Flute, The Journal of the Plague, Zuleika Dobson, Rasselas, Ulysses,* and *Green Mansions?* I am not concerned with this definition of the novel, but with what Mr. Forster is obviously wishing to contrast with the novel. From our point of view, he is beginning in *mediis rebus;* he is distinguishing the *established* novel from established short stories, scientific treatises, histories and travel books, not from *True under Trial, Gone with the Wind* and *The Sorrows of Satan,* which are "fictions in prose of a certain extent". He goes on to point out specific excellences of his examples, but he assumes, before he begins, that they are all works of art in the preliminary sense, that is, that they are worthy of serious critical attention. They are over all the hurdles, publisher, reviewers, critics, public: they now figure in courses in English Literature and are reprinted in *The World's Classics,* i.e. they have now become part of the tradition. "Novel" expresses this preliminary appraisal and "work of art" is an expression of exactly the same kind. It is the phrase for established works of all kinds, pictures, plays, novels, poems and so on. In applying the concept, we are not actually engaged in critical appraisal, but noting that the object is worth critical appraisal. We are marking off objects beneath serious critical attention from objects properly noticed by critics. "Work of art" distinguishes paintings in galleries from paintings used by manufacturers of chocolate boxes and birthday cards. It distinguishes films noticed by Miss Lejeune and Miss Powell, and short stories in "collections" from films and short stories that are noticed by nobody at all, but seen and read by hundreds.

One important question arises from this account of "work of art" considered as a preliminary appraisal: there are pictures in the basement of the Tate Gallery as well as on the walls, and books collecting dust on library shelves. Are these to be considered as "demoted" from their status as works of art? Here I must confess to being on uncertain ground; I do not know enough about the history of criticism to attempt an answer, but this is the way it seems to me. It seems to me that once a work of art has become established in the way described above, it may go in and out of fashion, but not cease to be a work of art. I cannot think that critics interested in the art of painting could be so completely blind to the painterly qualities of the works they praised as their own account of their reasons leads us to believe. Victorian critics who were fascinated by the vividness, incident and detail and by the story-telling power of pictures, must have accepted these pictures as worthy of serious consideration as pictures, even though they then went on to talk about them as if it were other qualities that mattered. I can more easily believe that they gave a misleading account of their reasons for liking pictures than that they never had an aesthetic experience when they looked at them. This is borne out by the way works of art go in and out of fashion. What changes is not the painterly qualities of pictures and our regard for them, but the way in which these qualities are obscured or underlined by liking or disliking for the qualities of the "vehicle". Victorian critics were delighted and we are revolted by the long lines of Burne-Jones damsels streaming down staircases with lilies in their hands. The damsels positively helped the Victorians to see and enjoy the long lines of robes and lily stalks, but prevented critics of later times. Frith is just now coming back into fashion, but critics do not say: "Now we see that the Victorians were right; the thing that matters is the life-like qualities of the incident and crowd scenes" but point out the painterly virtues of *Derby Day* and *Paddington Station*. The pictures always had these qualities and critics of the time would not have bothered with them if those qualities were lacking, but they took them for granted and then talked about qualities which, from our point of view, are irrelevant. Critics vary from one period to another in the kinds of reasons they give for their appreciation. When they concentrate, as they tend to do nowadays, upon the virtues proper to each art, what they say is much nearer to what aesthetic philosophers say, and so it seems to us "truer" criticism.

To sum up; the qualities that interest aestheticians *vis-à-vis* critics constitute a *sine qua non* for works of art; objects lacking these qualities are not worth critical attention. We might take as a parallel reasons given for their selections by judges at a flower show. It goes without saying that the plants exhibited must be healthy—they would not be put in if they were not. The judges take this for granted and then go on to talk about shape and size of bloom, truth of colour and so on. The most important quality, health of plant, is just not mentioned. Nobody would show a plant that had not this essential, nobody would show a picture, or get it shown, that lacked the essential qualities of painting. Its extra qualities *qua* novel, picture, play take it in and out of fashion, its basic quality puts it into a position to go in and out of fashion. Sometimes its "extra" qualities are estimated so highly that we overlook its lack of basic quality. This is more likely to happen in the literary arts. I do not think we should say that a picture was "great but not a work of art", though we might say that a novel was great, but not a work of art. Percy Lubbock goes so far as to say of *War and Peace,* that Tolstoy has "wasted" his subject, from the point of view of producing a work of art; I must hasten to point out that this occurs in many pages of praise for the vividness of the scenes and characters of the book. "Before the profusion of *War and Peace* the question of its general form is scarcely raised. It is enough that such a world should have been pictured; it is idle to look for the proportion and design in a book that contains a world." Nevertheless, the criticism has been raised, and we have an example of a great novel which is not a work of art. This will be anathema to the lovers of Tolstoy, but only because they think "work of art" such a high term of appraisal, and like *War and Peace* so much that they will withhold no term of praise from it. We can give all the other terms of praise to it, but just not this one. Some critics do not agree with Percy Lubbock's pronouncement and discover form in a more subtle and complex sense of the word in *War and Peace* and other works hitherto described as formless. There is also a tendency in contemporary literary criticism to emphasize the importance of the moral qualities of the work under discussion. "This is a good book, and by 'good' I mean good not in the aesthetic but in the moral sense, which is far more important." This critic, however, would not be concerned with the book at all if it were not good in the aesthetic sense. The author would not succeed in conveying moral quality if he were not a good writer.

At this point, I wish to consider some objections which have been raised to my account so far. It is said, rightly, that the appraisive character of "work of art" belongs also to ordinary words such as "rose" and "cabbage". A gardener, looking round your garden in which every rose bush was a mass of bloom, might say: "You haven't got a rose here." There is a difference though; the gardener is withholding the name "rose" from your "roses" because they are not good specimens of their kind and he could specify the respects in which they fell short. "That is a rose" is informative as well as appraisive, but there is no "kind" in an important sense of which a work of art is a specimen, and "That is a work of art" is almost entirely uninformative.

It is also objected that "work of art" is confined to paintings and sculptures, and that no one refers to novels, plays, poems, musical compositions as works of art. It is true that the *phrase* is not used in this context, but the concept is. We use "works" of writings and compositions in the same appraisive way. If we say "the works of X", we feel that X ought to be the name of a considerable author or composer. The difference between pictures and sculptures on the one hand, and literary and musical works on the other, is that artists and sculptors literally make the object with their own hands and place it before the public, while writers and composers give instructions for placing the object before the public. A man making a collection of "valuable literary and musical objects" would be using the concept "work of art", though he might never use the phrase.

We are now able to propose a tentative definition of "work of art". It is a picture, a play, a poem, etc., which has reached the public, been pronounced favourably upon by competent critics and is now considered to be a part of the tradition of English literature, French painting, and so on. We have proposed further, that it has reached this position by the excellence peculiar to it in its medium, though it may be valued highly for its human interest. This is more likely to be true of literature and painting. Many apparent differences of opinion may be traced to this double evaluation. Some critics and philosophers of art wish to use "work of art" to refer exclusively to works as displaying formal excellence, and confine "aesthetic experience" to the thrill of the recognition of form. These people look on the total work with its insight into human nature, its richness and variety, as the vehicle of form, and ask only that our attention shall not be distracted from form. Roger Fry, speaking of Rembrandt, praises his "sublime psychological imagination" and the supreme quality of his plastic constructions. He then goes on to say: "I do not know whether the world would not have gained had Rembrandt frankly divided his immoderate genius into a writer's and a painter's portion and kept them separate." We should thus be spared the clash of interest which leads our attention from one aspect to the other. Vernon Lee speaks of the representational element in painting as a useful relaxation from the effort of contemplating form. Its only criterion of usefulness is that it should confine our attention within the frame and bring it back to the formal aspect, refreshed. It is, of course, more usually held that the tension of competing interests and their mutual reinforcement is just what makes a Rembrandt picture satisfying. This leads me to my second proposal.

This is, that we should define "work of art" as a disjunction of named particulars, i.e. it is the *Odyssey, Œdipus Rex,* the *Virgin of the Rocks,* the Brandenburg Concerto or—through an indefinite list. We should then be able to satisfy both kinds of critics. Each work is in the list through its own merit, not by being a good specimen, for it need conform to no rules. All that we need ask is that it should continue to win delighted contemplation and lend itself to growing knowledge. "This is a work of art" says: "Look, listen, attend carefully, you will find it worth while." The intermediate concepts between "this" and "work of art" are useful only as directing attention to certain features of the individual object, and "setting" our attention in a certain way. Sometimes, indeed, the concepts may be a hindrance; we are prevented from receiving the full impact by looking with conceptually aroused expectations.

I want to emphasize the individuality of each work of art because I want to make room for both kinds of enjoyment. I sympathize with the austere delight of the formalists; it is difficult to achieve, but once experienced, it sets a standard which can never be forgotten. It might happen three or four times in a lifetime, and then not always in more than one art form. Those who have experienced it in one art form, tend to think that it belongs especially to that art, not realizing that for others the situation may be reversed. It seems to me most easily achieved in music, with the most difficulty, in literature. On the other hand, I sympathize, too, with the delight in the richness and variety of the human interest in many great plays, poems, novels and paintings. When people say that every detail matters, every quality is essential, we know what they mean. There is a close parallel here between the individuality of a work of art and of a human being. One of Wodehouse's young men, trying to persuade his mean and curmudgeonly uncle to invite his friend to stay, says: "You'll like Ronnie Fish—he's got an aunt in the looney bin." The uncle says: "Is that supposed to be a reason for liking him?" Of course the nephew is not doing anything so silly as offering a reason for liking his friend. Any one of the qualities of his friend reinstates for him the delightful whole upon which he loves to dwell. This is the way in which we dwell upon the delightful whole of a play or novel, thinking of each feature in turn and willing to let go of none, though not allowing the detail to obscure the whole. Neither the person nor the play is *an* anything at all, and we are continually discovering new features which belong to the individual but not in accordance with any concept.

We may now attempt a classification of works of art, not into kinds, but into groups which will help us in our analysis of critical discourse. Works of art are either:—

1. Things made by the artist's own hand and placed before the public, e.g. pictures and statues. These are works of art in the ordinary use of the term.

2. Instructions for placing the object before the public, e.g. musical scores, scripts of plays, novels, poems, etc. These fall into two categories. Musical scores and scripts give instructions for making an ephemeral object, a performance which must be repeated every time we wish to "have" the object. A relatively permanent object may be made, in accordance with the instructions, a recording which needs only mechanical skill to produce the performance. This, of course, will be one interpretation of the score or script, by a given cast or set of instrumentalists.[1] Blue prints give instructions for making a permanent object which may fall under the first heading.

3. (*a*) Performances of plays, ballets, musical compositions.

(*b*) Performances in which the performers are not carrying out the instructions of another artist, e.g. clowns, acrobats, some dancers.

4. (*a*) Things made for some useful end or some end other than contemplation, but which nevertheless arouse delighted contemplation.

---

[1] A definition by Justice Oliver Wendell Holmes is of interest here. Giving judgment in connection with a claim by composers for royalties from gramophone record makers he defined a composition as ". . . a rational collocation of sounds apart from concepts, reduced to a tangible expression from which the collocation can be reproduced either with or without continuous human intervention".

(*b*) Performances carried on for some end other than contemplation, but which nevertheless arouse it, e.g. sports, military tattoos, ritualistic ceremonies.

Several problems arise here in connection with one or other of our categories. Our first heading is relatively straightforward, the only problem arising in connection with prints and copies of paintings and copies and casts of statues. A copyist may be regarded as taking the picture or statue as a model for the making of another object, and he might be a draughtsman, or an artist appreciating the work of another so completely that he re-creates it. The copies and prints may be regarded as tokens of the same type among themselves, but it is difficult not to give the original a different status. It has a privileged position in that it sets the standard by which the others are judged as more or less adequate reproductions.

A connected but more difficult problem arises in connection with performances. There is no difficulty in regarding Shakespeare's MS. of *Hamlet* and all other copies as tokens of the same type. As contrasted with paintings, the original has only historical interest, copyists needing nothing but the ability to read and write. When it comes to performances, we have a problem of quite a different type. Performances are judged as better or worse than one another even though we have no standard against which to measure them. Critics sometimes appear to assume that the performance which comes closest to the playwright's intention is the best, and when he is still living, or has approved a performance within living memory, then we might be able to claim a certain performance as standard. Nicolas Nabokov, writing on the Moscow Art Theatre says: "Fortunately or unfortunately, I belong to a generation which saw Chekhov's plays at the Moscow Art Theatre in what was largely the original cast, and these performances became for me a kind of Platonic model." On the other hand, not all playwrights and composers are the best interpreters of their own work, not all poets the best readers of their own poems. The various performances might each better be regarded as a work of art in its own right, Oliver's *Hamlet*, Pavlova's *Swan Lake*, Beecham's *Sinfonia* appearing in our list of named particulars. The "copyists" make their appearances as lesser performers modelling themselves on the artists of stage and orchestra.

Playwrights differ in their view of the function of actors and producers. There is the dramatist who, by every means in his power, tries to ensure that nothing shall be left to the actor's own initiative. For him, the business of the producer is simply to place the play before the audience with no interposition of personality. Bernard Shaw with his minute stage directions is a dramatist of this kind. Others look on the actors as collaborators and the script as incomplete—the work of art coming into existence with each performance. Composers are similarly divided: some tend to think of instrumentalists as a mere means of giving the music to the audience, some going so far as to claim that the sound produced by instrumentalists, while charming and delightful, is essential to the appreciation of music, except for the musically illiterate. Some architects claim that the blue print is the work of art, and the building the work of craftsmen.

No matter what view architects may take of the function of master builders, there is no doubt that buildings as well as furniture, pottery and carpets are pleasing objects and are sometimes described as beautiful. They are works of art if our criterion is that we should delight in their "look". But there is an important difference between the work of artists and that of craftsmen. Objects made for use are judged by a double standard, one connected with their adaptation to their use and one connected with their look. This may not be decisive. The tension between competing criteria of look and use may give aesthetic satisfaction; the teapot must look as if it will pour out well and pour out well. For me, however, the decisive difference is that craft objects are not importantly individual. It would be sensible to ask a craftsman making a chair to make us another just like it, but not a painter painting a picture. We could ask him to paint another picture, but we should have to wait and see what it was like. It is no accident that craft objects cannot figure in our list of named objects. Any chair of Chippendale's best period will do; there is a tradition of English furniture making, but it is bound up with a way of living, and part of our enjoyment derives from the realization that there were fortunate people who sat upon Chippendale chairs every day. If they had never been used, but made especially for a museum, they would be different objects.

Our discussion of craft objects is complicated by some cases which fall between and which seem to come from both sides. There are artists whose work leads to such critical comment as "this is the efficient orchestration of a triviality", "as near perfect theatre work as it is possible to imagine", "technical perfection, but the artist has nothing to say". From the side of craft, some objects fulfill their end with such mastery that they take their place among the classics of literature. Newton's *Principia* is so well written that it might appear in our list, and some detective stories come out of their category of wit-exercising writings and rank as novels.

Processes as objects of aesthetic appraisal may be of several kinds. If someone is cutting out a frock with barely enough material, but by twisting and turning the pattern gets it with hardly a snippet over, we might say: "That was quite a work of art." We should not say it if the cutter out was simply economizing. In praising the performance, we are not concerned with the movements of the performer, nor with the product, but simply with the neat and ingenious adaptation of means to end. On the other hand, what we usually describe as an artist in dressmaking, is one who, with great slashings of the scissors and with no regard for waste, makes an object which is pleasing in itself and in relation to a particular person and a particular occasion. There are performances in which the performers are simply placing the work of another artist before us, but we may also value their work as good in its own right. There are finished performances of bad plays as well as productions which faithfully render the work of the playwright.

There is another important class of aesthetically pleasing performances in which the performers are not carrying out the instructions of another artist, but are acting spontaneously. The star performers in ice hockey, cricket, football and sports generally, are valued as much for their elegance in action as their run-making and goal-getting ability. Sports commentators use the terms of aesthetic appraisal as freely as do art critics: footballers are described as "intuitive artist", "inspired clowns", and there is the general run of good solid craftsmen.

We may notice in conclusion, that critics make their names in connection with the work of particular artists, even with particular works, and not with poetry, painting or the drama in general. If we want to follow the advice of a dramatic critic, it is more important to know which particular plays he appreciates than what his views on drama are. We might allow him one or two blind spots, but he must be sound on most of the great plays.

In this paper I have not been concerned with the requirements which people in general assume for giving the title "work of art", "artist" to things, processes and people. These requirements appear to relate almost entirely to the ways in which the artist works and the ways in which the work was produced. Asked whether Congo's pictures are works of art, almost every unsophisticated person answers that they could not be, since a chimpanzee is not capable of expressing his experiences. Some add a further reason, that Congo cheated, or rather someone cheated on his behalf, by giving him the brushes already filled with paint and taking away his canvas when it was judged he had done enough to it. Rocks and stones worn by wind and rain so that they look like a piece by Henry Moore are similarly refused the title "work of art". In both these cases, sophisticated people tend to say that it entirely depends on the look—if Congo's paintings look well, they may be works of art, and so may weather-worn rocks. An examination of these opinions would take us too far afield.

Margaret Macdonald

Art and Imagination

. . . the notion of Imagination enters differently into different aesthetic (and critical) theories according to other notions with which it is contrasted. Moreover, some of these differences connect more directly than others with ordinary uses of the words "imagination", "imagine" and their cognates. I am not at present prepared to say that these differences themselves represent different uses of such words. But certainly some theories about art and imagination are more "metaphysical" than others. Secondly, such theories may differ in width. At least, some of them may be more narrowly expounded and applied though it is not certain that nevertheless they do not have wider implications. For example, the most popular doctrines of the relation between art and imagination in English are confined to literature and particularly to poetry. I refer to the doctrines of Coleridge and other poets and critics of the romantic movement which have been continued by their modern followers.[1] Nevertheless, none of these writers explicitly denies that what is true of imagination in literature is true of it also in other arts. But if applied to those other arts, the doctrines would seem much less plausible without much modification. But even less explicit theorists make a similar restriction. For Shakespeare, *e.g.,* it is the *poet,* not the painter, sculptor or musician, who is, like the lunatic and the lover "of Imagination all compact".[2] This may be due to the fact that Englishmen are

---

[1] *Cf.* D. G. James, *Scepticism and Poetry* (1937) and R. L. Brett, *The Third Earl of Shaftesbury* (1951).

[2] *A Midsummer Night's Dream,* Act 5, Scene 1.

[Reprinted from *Proceedings of the Aristotelian Society,* 53: 208–218 (1952). Footnotes have been renumbered.]

more interested in literature than any other art. When Bacon, e.g., divided the human mind into the Faculties of Sensation, Reason, Memory and Imagination, he allotted Philosophy to Reason, History to Memory (*whose* memory, one wonders?) and Poesy, not art in general, to Imagination [3]. He thus suggests either that poetry is the sole art or that other arts do not use imagination. But then it would be odd to describe music and painting as either philosophy or history, *i.e.*, as forms of analytic reasoning or remembering. Probably, if pressed, Bacon would have pushed these other arts into the pigeon-hole of Sensation. But they would not stay there quietly. For Sensation as the lowliest of the faculty hierarchy was invariably thought to provide by passive reception the "raw material" upon which the higher faculties worked. But painters and composers do not passively see and hear what is "given" but actively produce what may be seen and heard by themselves and others. So their works cannot simply be allotted to Sensation as their origin. Indeed, the mythical matings of faculty psychology are totally inadequate to explain any of their alleged progeny, including the arts. It does not, of course, follow that artists are not sometimes correctly called "imaginative" and that this is not aesthetically important. It is also much more natural to speak of an "imaginative writer" than of an "imaginative painter" or an "imaginative composer" and this may also be important.

Examples of the wider doctrine which does define all works of art as works of imagination are the theories of R. G. Collingwood [4], Jean-Paul Sartre,[5] both influenced by Croce. According to them a work of art must be distinguished from all physical objects, even from such objects as the picture on the gallery wall, the sounds filling the concert hall, the printed volume from which the novel is being read. One reason given for this is that although a work of art cannot be communicated to others without a physical vehicle it can be imagined, and thus internally produced, by an artist who did not choose to manifest it exter-

[3] *Advancement of Learning*, Bk. II.
[4] *Principles of Art*. Oxford University Press, 1938.
[5] *The Psychology of Imagination*, trans. Philosophical Library, N.Y., 1948, Conclusion, Sec. 2, "The Work of Art".

nally. I think the relation is somewhat complex between works of art and physical objects, or, rather, between what is correctly said about works of art and the physical world.[6] But this is not elucidated by this metaphor popular with certain aesthetic philosophers of a work of art as a mysterious message transmitted by an intrinsically worthless instrument, the physical medium. The very notion of a *medium* suggests the spiritualist séance rather than the study or studio. Nevertheless, it does make sense (though it may be false) to say that Shakespeare made up a play which he did not write down or get performed and that no-one but he knew of this. So, it is argued, this situation may be generalised. Every work of art might similarly exist privately and remain uncommunicated. Physical labour is, therefore, not essential to a work of art which must be an imaginary object, a mental creation or private fantasy. But none of these consequences follow. There may, indeed, be good evidence to show that an artist had contemplated and even thought out a work which he never committed to word, paint, sound or other material. He may have described the work in a letter, diary or orally. But I doubt if an ordinary person would unhesitatingly assert that he had thereby *produced* the work. If the work were of one of the plastic arts I think this would certainly be denied. For it seems absurd to say of someone that he had painted a picture or carved a statue without the use of tools or materials. An imaginary picture or statue just isn't a picture or statue because these words stand for works which need hands as well as heads to bring them into existence. This may not be quite so clear for other works of art. I have said that Shakespeare might have made up a play which he did not write down or get performed. Similarly, Mozart might have composed a melody, say a setting for a song, which was never sung and for which he did not produce a score. Would one say that these works had existed and been lost to the world? Perhaps. Normally, a lost literary or musical work is one of which the text or score has disappeared or been forgotten, not one of which no text or score, written or oral, existed. But while no-one

---

[6] Cf. "*Art and the 'Object of Art'* " by Paul Ziff, Mind, N.S., vol. LX, 1951, pp. 466–480, but I think Mr. Ziff simplifies the problem by confining his remarks to objects of the plastic arts.

would say that a picture which had not been painted however clearly a painter had imagined or even described it, had existed and been lost one might hesitate to deny that a poem or a song had existed because it was known only to its author and had never been spoken or sung aloud. For if this had been done, only once, and had been overheard there would be no good reason to deny the existence of the work though it were never heard again. This seems to attribute an exaggerated artistic importance to the mechanical processes of making visible and audible. An imaginary picture is not a picture and is of an entirely different logical type because the *work* of producing a picture cannot be done or, at least, completed without physical labour. But the task of making up a poem or story or composing a tune may sometimes be over before these are spoken, sung or written down. Moreover, there seems to be no substantial difference between what is imagined and what is uttered, heard, written and read. I do not think these facts justify the conclusions of idealist aesthetic philosophers but they may give some excuse for them and do also show discrepancies between the works of different arts which are important for aesthetics. Yet although one may sometimes wonder whether an unrevealed poem or tune may properly be called a poem or tune, it does not follow that every literary and musical work still less every work of art is imaginary. For the circumstances I have described in which one might ask this question include the fact that it is asked of the work of an established artist. Of one who had never produced a public work it would be absurd to ask whether he might be a silent rival to all known artists. One who never exhibits his artistic skill is not a very "pure" artist but a fraud. Of a reputable author or composer, however, it might be sensible to ask whether all his works were known and there might be reason to believe they were not. I do not assert that we positively should add an imagined sonnet to the Shakespearean corpus but only that we might, rightly, hesitate and be inclined to do so as we should not hesitate to exclude an imagined statue from the works of Rodin. The hesitation would be due to a strong conflicting tendency to call works of art only certain public objects. This is, I am sure the primary use of the word for all and the sole use for some, works. Works of art

are, primarily, public, perceptual objects made by someone using
technical skill. There may be a distinction between artists and
craftsmen, as Collingwood insisted [7], but the borderland is wide
and all artists, as makers, are also craftsmen. What they make and
with what kind of skill, however, varies widely. In the plastic arts
(painting and sculpture), the finished work is, normally, a physical object of the same sort as stones and stars. If asked to count
the number of objects in a room one would include the Ming jar
and the Turner as well as the rest. These works are enduring,
particular objects each with its spatio-temporal position. They
are, moreover, distinguished, as originals, from all replicas or
copies [8]. They are made in the comparatively simple sense of
being constructed from physical materials and only attention by
a spectator is needed to perceive them as they were created [9]. In a
fairly straightforward sense one now "sees" the same picture or
statue as the artist painted or modelled. The situation is less
simple for literary and musical words of art. To revert to the
room already mentioned. One would probably include in the
collection of its objects the books in the bookcase and the scores
on the music stand. It would not, however, be so clear that one
had thereby included Shakespeare's plays or Verdi's operas. First,
because no author or composer directly produces a printed volume. Secondly, though he might produce a pile of written or
typewritten manuscript and this might be referred to as the work,
it would also, and perhaps more correctly, be called the text or
score of the work. More correctly, because written or printed
texts and scores are not necessary to the existence of literature
and music. The primary form of such works is vocal and their
survival formerly depended entirely upon memory and oral transmission. Spoken narratives, recitations, songs are not, however,

---

[7] *Principles of Art,* Pt. I, Ch. 2. O.U.P. 1938.

[8] It has been pointed out to me that such works as etchings and woodcuts
are exceptions to this. What the artist directly produces in these is an
engraved plate or worked block. These, however, are not identified with or
exhibited as the etching or woodcut but only prints taken from them of
which they may be many, each an original. They would not be so called,
however, unless taken from the object prepared by the artist.

[9] I ignore for this purpose such later operations as the cleaning of an old
work, the emending of a text or score, etc.

physical objects. They are rather physical events which begin, continue and then cease to exist. They are more like flashes of lightning and showers of rain than rocks and planets. But such events are public to all observers while they last. So are literary and musical performances. If, however, the corresponding work is identified with any one such performance it is obvious that compared with pictures and statues literary and musical works have a very brief existence. Well, it is possible that some have. A work might never be repeated after its first performance and be forgotten. Many thrilling camp fire stories and epic poems must have so perished. True, a picture or statue might be completed and immediately destroyed. The difference is that this need not happen whereas it is (I think, logically) impossible that the performance of a literary or musical work should continue for more than a very limited time. It would be absurd, *e.g.*, to suppose a play or symphony whose performance lasted a year. Yet there are many works of literature and music which have out-lasted many works of the plastic arts.

> "Not marble, nor the gilded monuments
> Of princes, shall outlive this powerful rhyme" [10]

(An optimistic remark in view of the author's well-known habit of leaving his offspring for players and patrons to preserve.) How does this happen? The poem (or symphony) outlives its competitors if at some time or place there is, or could be, a physical presentation of it. Such occurrences are not copies, replicas or reproductions of an original. A performance of *Hamlet* now is not a reproduction of the first or any other production. Nor is it a copy of the text. To say that would be absurd. Nor are these performances many but related to a single source as the etching to its incised plate. Yet they are each and all manifestations of "the same work". Thus works of literature and music lack the definite spatio-temporal position of most works of the plastic arts. They exist wherever and whenever they are physically mani-fested. One cannot sensibly ask for the whereabouts of Shake-speare's plays and Beethoven's symphonies as one can for that of the Mona Lisa and St. Paul's Cathedral.

[10] W. Shakespeare. *Sonnet 55.*

This distinction between the sense of "play" (and any comparable term) in which Shakespeare wrote only one play called *Hamlet* and that in which *Hamlet* has been played one hundred times this season has been likened to that between particular and universal and between type and token in the use of words. The first is wrong. The relation between a performance of *Hamlet* and the play may seem, superficially, to resemble that between the colour of this paper and "whiteness". The paper with its colour may be destroyed, but not whiteness; the performance ends but *Hamlet* remains. But differences make the comparison more misleading than helpful. It would be nonsense to talk of a performance of the play as an "instance" of *Hamlet* as the colour of this paper is an instance of whiteness. Universals are qualities and relations. *Hamlet* does not characterize the performances of the play nor does it relate any objects. Finally, universals are timeless. It makes no sense to ask when whiteness and equality began to exist. Yet it is both sensible and true to say that Shakespeare's *Hamlet* came into existence about 1600, has continued to exist, in the manner already suggested, since that date and may cease to exist.[11] The comparison with the type-token distinction in the use of "word" is less misleading. Words in the type sense have a beginning, a history and sometimes a decease—they become obsolete. Nor do they characterize or relate. For the sense of "the" in which there is only one word THE in the English language—the type word—does not characterize the token "the", which has just been printed, as does, *e.g.*, blackness. But the function of this, and every similar token, is to present the type-word. Tokens of the same type are related by similarity plus a convention which associates certain noises with certain marks as being of the "same" word. So, too, the performances of *Hamlet* or the Ninth Symphony are of those works if they resemble each other in certain fundamental respects. They will also differ, but if too eccentric they will be excluded from those which present these works. Perhaps the chief difference between "work of art" in this sense and "word" is that individual presentations of a work of art may have their own independent artistic value, while

[11] *Cf.* Wellek and Warren, *Theory of Literature*, London, 1949, p. 154.

token-words do not fulfil independent grammatical and stylistic functions. The performance of a great actor or violinist may be a work of art in its own right, apart from being yet another version of *Hamlet* or the Brahms Concerto, for acting and musical execution are also arts.

That a distinction must be made between some works of art and their manifestations may have led some aesthetic philosophers, especially those chiefly interested in literature, into bad metaphysics. For this looks like a distinction between two kinds of objects. Then it is tempting to construe a work of art as type as something above or behind its perceptible token occurrences, *e.g.*, a platonic Idea, a Norm [12], a private mental state. Or, alternatively, with the phenomenalists, to identify the work with the set of its occurrences. Neither alternative will do. For by the ordinary use of the term "literature" or "music" the ultimate test of whether works of these arts exist is sensory observation and not introspection or super-sensuous intuition. But neither did Shakespeare and Beethoven produce, nor do we see and hear, a *class* of occurrences when enjoying a play or symphony. The solution is to emphasize that because a word has two uses it does not follow that it is used for two different objects. "Work of art" is just used ambiguously in the manner described without implying any expansion or contraction of the universe.

As for the process of making or creating a work of art. I have suggested, somewhat crudely, that in some arts this is more physically laborious than in others. I wanted to show that there might be an excuse for saying that some composition, *e.g.*, in literature and music, is internal. That it occurs "in the mind" or "in imagination". I have said that this may sometimes happen. I also think that whether it happens or not is an unimportant accident. What is done "in the head" could have been done as well on paper, vocally or with a musical instrument. There is, however, a more fundamental answer to idealist and subjectivist conclusions drawn from the peculiarities of these arts. I have said that one cannot separate the making of a work of the plastic arts from the skilful handling of physical materials. There seem to be no

---

[12] Wellek and Warren, *loc. cit.*, p. 154.

comparable public materials and exhibitions of skill in literature and music. One may always watch a person painting, drawing, sculpting; one may not, even in his presence, be able to observe that someone is composing a novel or symphony. Hence aesthetic philosophers have supposed that musicians and authors, and, more particularly, authors [13] use more refined methods and materials to produce their aetherial works. The fact of occasional unrecorded composition is used to support this view. Authors are conceived to compose, like spiders, by each spinning his web of private fancies from his Imagination. These may then, if their author so chooses, be externalized, by an almost mechanical operation, in written or spoken words, for public appraisal. But this is a totally misleading picture. There is one physical element common to both literature and music, which is sound. Works of both arts are manifested in audible performances. But the sounds in literature are not mere physical noises but words of a particular language. The material with which the literary artist creates is certainly not crude physical sound, comparable to stone, marble or paint, but neither is it private fancies or images. What an English writer uses is the English language. I shall not discuss whether this is part of the physical world, but it is certainly not a private invention by an individual. A writer inherits his native language as the independent, public system of words and meanings of the society into which he is born. He absorbs and accepts it perhaps even more completely than the plastic artist receives his materials from nature. It is in this system that he learns to prattle, discourse and finally to create. If he is a good writer he may slightly modify the system; he will do that with the material which has not been done before. If he is a great writer, such as Shakespeare, appearing at the right historical moment, he may effect a major transformation, leaving his successors an incomparably more powerful and delicate instrument. Still, it will be the English language, not the language of Shakespeare. Not even the greatest literary genius creates an entirely new language. The work of a literary artist is thus a construction of words, the words

---

[13] I have considered literature and music together as in many ways similar and different from the plastic arts. But this is not general. Indeed, most aesthetic philosophers practically ignore music.

of an established language most of which are in common use and all of which may be understood by others and adopted into the language. His labour is

> "the intolerable wrestle
> With words and meanings" [14]

which are public, not private, and where,

> "Words strain
> Crack and sometimes break, under the burden,
> Under the tension, slip, slide, perish,
> Decay with imprecision, will not stay in place,
> Will not stay still".[15]

I said that whether some literary composition was unrecorded was unimportant and did not support idealist conclusions. The reason should now be clear. If what is done, externally or internally, audibly or silently, is literary composition, it will be a construction from the words of an established language. For this is what we mean by the term "literary composition". But if all that happens is the passage of a series of private images, feelings or symbols, this is not literary composition nor its result a work of art.

Much of this applies also to music. The material of the composer, too, is not mere physical sound or noise. Nor is it sounds used with the rules of significance which makes language a medium of communication about all topics. Musical sounds are notes of a scale and musical composition the arrangement of such notes according to further conventions of melody, harmony and the like which are common to a musical community [16]. These the composer finds and accepts as the writer accepts his native language. Like language, too, they change and develop and may even be revolutionised by great composers but are never entirely superseded. No more than literature is music a series of private feelings, sensations, images; it is a structure of sounds ordered by common conventions and addressed to a suitably trained audi-

[14] T. S. Eliot. *The Four Quartets: East Coker*, Sec. 2.
[15] *Loc. cit. Burnt Norton*, Sec. 5.
[16] *Cf.* E. Hanslick. *The Beautiful in Music*, pp. 144–145.

ence. As with literature, composition, whether external or internal, must follow this pattern if it is to be correctly termed "musical composition" and its result a musical work.

I have tried to show that the aesthetic theories of Croce, Collingwood, Sartre and other idealists who equate works of art with works of imagination and these with what is mental or physically unreal do not satisfactorily elucidate our use of the term "work of art". They confuse the indubitable fact that in composing a work of art an artist may imagine more than he now perceives or can remember, with the admission of imaginary objects and fictitious entities. *The Tempest* is a work of imagination, it shows great imaginative and creative power, but it is certainly not an imaginary or fictitious object. Shakespeare's play is as real as its author. True, it "contains" or is "about" imaginary objects, Prospero, Caliban, Ariel, a magic island. These require other treatment. I will say here only that their logical status differs from that of the work of art, for it is very obvious that we talk of them differently. . . .

Robert Hoffman

Conjectures and Refutations on the Ontological Status of the Work of Art

In this paper, I examine certain theses advanced in reply to the question, "What is the ontological status of the work of art?" Scrutinizing what has been written on the subject has convinced me that theories of the ontological status of the art work are rarely refuted; usually, they are merely opposed by counter-theses or shown to be awkward in some way or other. What I attempt to do is to state the theses (hence "conjectures") and then to refute them by demonstrating inconsistencies or other serious defects in them (hence "refutations").

Consider the following statements about particular works of art:

1. Shelley's *The Cenci* was dedicated to Leigh Hunt, Esq.
2. Shelley's *The Cenci* is shorter than his *The Revolt of Islam*.
3. Beethoven's *Op. 13* is shorter than his *Op. 111*.
4. Beethoven's *Op. 13* is in three movements.
5. Beethoven's *Op. 13* expresses a youthful conception of tragedy.
6. Serkin's *Pathétique* is superior to Rubinstein's.
7. Rubinstein's *Pathétique* is coupled with the *Appassionata*.
8. My *The Cenci* is torn.

Statement "1" refers to a series of marks on paper, indeed, to the first such series published under the name "*The Cenci* by Percy Bysshe Shelley" or under some synonymous designation; state-

[Reprinted from *Mind*, 71: 512–520 (1962). Footnotes have been renumbered. Robert Hoffman is in the Department of Philosophy, Kent State University, Kent, Ohio.]

ment "2" refers to any and all sign-events of the sign-design, "The Cenci"; statement "3" refers to (*a*) an ideal performance of that sonata, (*b*) the mean performance of it, (*c*) the mode performance of it, (*d*) the critically permissible mean performance of it or (*e*) the critically permissible mode performance of it; statement "4" refers to (*a*) the original manuscript of that sonata, (*b*) any accurate copy of that manuscript or (*c*) any critically acceptable version of that manuscript; statement "5" refers to (*a*) the projected experience of a particular listener, (*b*) the projected experience (s) of most listeners, (*c*) the projected experience (s) of most qualified listeners, (*d*) the projected experience of an ideal listener or (*e*) an ascribed regional quality of the object, conceived as a potentiality or a disposition to cause the experience (s) mentioned in " (*a*) " through " (*d*) "; statement "6" refers to (*a*) some particular performance by each of the pianists, (*b*) the usual performance by the pianists or (*c*) the best actual performance by them; statement "7" refers to (*a*) a particular recorded performance or (*b*) a performance at a particular concert; and statement "8" refers to a certain copy of the poem, *i.e.* to a particular sign-event. Which sort of the rather diverse sorts of object referred to by the statements listed above is the work of art? In other words, what is the ontological status of the work of art?

I shall begin my investigation by examining a theory sketched ever so briefly by Abercrombie, according to whom the work of art is constructed by and inheres in the spectator's self-consciousness.[1] Thus, a poetical work of art is understood as being the succession of experiences—sensations, images, feelings and ideas —that he has when he is reading the poem. The work of art is "the same thing as his self-consciousness".[2] But this view is faced with two overwhelming difficulties. First, since the experiences of different spectators who are confronted by the same object differ, there are on this view as many art works associated with a given poem as there are spectators reading it. From this it follows that no two persons ever do talk about the same work of art, for the

[1] Lascelles Abercrombie, *An Essay towards a Theory of Art* (London: Martin Secker, 1922) , especially pp. 42–43.
[2] *Ibid.* p. 43.

work of art would be purely private. It would be an epistemological, not an ontological, object.[3] But, in fact, we do communicate when we talk about art works. When, on page one, I wrote "Beethoven's *Op. 13*", you were able thereby to know to which of that composer's works I was referring: and should I go to a piano and begin playing another of his sonatas you will say, "No, that's not it"; and should I then begin playing *Op. 13*, you will signal recognition by saying, "Yes, that's the one". Second, how do the successive experiences constitute one work of art? Suppose, for example, that a person has the same succession of experiences when he reads Shakespeare's *Sonnet XXIX* as when he reads Shakespeare's *Sonnet XXX*. Should we say that there is but one work of art? To do so would be inconsistent with what we perfectly well do know, namely, that there are two sonnets, each a work of art in its own right. Nor can we escape the inconsistency by arguing that since the visual sensation caused by the printed page is different in the case of one sonnet from what it is in the case of the other, the same succession of experiences cannot in fact be had. For in that event, we should also have to say that a reader who thrice reads only *Sonnet XXIX*, but who reads it once in roman, once in gothic and once in cursive type and who therefore has different visual sensations at each reading, apprehends a different work of art each time. But this is plainly nonsensical: he is reading *Sonnet XXIX* and whether its sign-design or something associated with it constitutes the art work, surely the style of type is irrelevant to the ontological status of that work.[4]

Although we may not be able to equate the work of art with the experience (s) of a spectator (s), perhaps we can equate it with that of the artist who created it. Accordingly, we may say that the work of art is an imaginative experience had by the

---

[3] *Cf.* C. D. Broad, *The Mind and its Place in Nature* (London: Routledge & Kegan Paul Ltd. 1925), especially pp. 140–142.

[4] Were this theory not unsound for these reasons, it would present an obvious difficulty, namely, that we should be uncertain as to whether the experience in question is that of (*a*) just any spectator at all, (*b*) any qualified spectator or (*c*) an ideal spectator, *i.e.* one who makes no mistakes. This difficulty is representative of the sort that suggests a certain awkwardness in a theory but does not refute it.

artist.[5] Thus, a poem is not what is printed on paper; the marks on paper are merely means by which a spectator, if he reads intelligently, can reconstruct that experience for himself. The poem that is enjoyed as an art work is never sensuously seen (or heard) at all; it is something imagined.

But this view is no more sound than the one we have just rejected. Since no one but the artist himself ever has his experience, to equate the poem with that experience means that only the artist himself can be said ever to be acquainted with the poem. To be sure, it may be suggested, *per contra,* that this objection is based on a too literal reading of "the artist's experience"—that although a spectator cannot have the artist's experience, he can have an experience very like the artist's in content. And to the extent that he does have such an experience, he too is acquainted with the art work. There are, that is to say, degrees of knowing a work of art; and only the artist knows it fully. But this reply merely replaces one difficulty with another. The reply states, in effect, that if and only if the content of a spectator's experience overlaps that of the artist's does the spectator know the art work. The more extensive the overlap, the greater the degree of knowledge. But in order to verify that there is such an overlap, we should have to know what the artist's experience is. Yet since he alone is in a position to know this, no one can say whether or not a spectator's experience does in fact approximate his own. Nor can the artist himself say whether or not it does, for he is in the same position with respect to the spectator's experience as everyone else is with respect to his. Thus, on the view being criticized, we should be incapable even in principle of knowing whether or not someone has "read" a poem at all, to say nothing of whether or not he has "read" it correctly.

Can our rejoinder be obviated by arguing that the artist can tell the spectator whether or not the latter's statements allegedly describing his reconstruction of the former's imaginative experience are correct? Assertions by the spectator—so the argument runs—are *for him* about another mind, but the artist, about whom they are made, is able to say whether they are true or false

[5] R. G. Collingwood, *The Principles of Art* (Oxford: The Clarendon Press, 1938), especially pp. 139–151.

because he can directly inspect his own imaginative experience and determine whether or not he does experience what he is claimed to experience. But there is a telling objection to this rejoinder. According to the theory in question, the artist's imaginative experience is itself the art work and the poem is merely the most accurate record of that experience. Consider these lines:

> And on the water, like to burning coals
> On liquid silver, leaves of roses lay.

The spectator can describe his reconstruction of the poet's imaginative experience by saying, "You saw a scatter of red rose leaves floating on water". Yet this description, although not wholly so, is woefully inadequate. The poet would reject it and then quite sincerely and honestly describe his experience by repeating the lines in question. "When I write poetry", he might say in Humpty Dumpty-like fashion, "it means just what I choose it to mean—neither more nor less". And the spectator would thereby be reduced to repeating the poet's lines and hoping that they call up in his mind a vision exactly corresponding with the poet's. But because the content of each mind is private, he is doomed never to know whether his vision does correspond with the poet's. At best, by comparing his language to the poet's, the spectator can discover that they use the same words in all situations and that the structure of their languages is the same, but he cannot validly infer that their words signify their having exactly the same or even similar imaginative experiences. Hence, we cannot identify the work of art with the artist's imaginative experience.

At this point, another view of the ontological status of the art work recommends itself, namely, that the work is a construct out of the spectator's aesthetic experience.[6] According to this view, we must distinguish three categories when we talk about an art work: there are (a) the physical vehicle, *e.g.* the poem printed on the page, that acts as a control object and determines certain limits within which fall, (b) the aesthetic perceptions or appear-

---

[6] A theory of this sort is proposed in Stephen C. Pepper, *The Basis of Criticism in the Arts:* "Supplementary Essay" (Cambridge, Massachusetts: Harvard University Press, 1949) and *The Work of Art* (Bloomington: Indiana University Press, 1955).

ances that constitute the content of felt givenness had on stimulation by the control object; and out of these perceptions is constructed, (c) the object of critical and interpretative evaluation or the work of art.

But this view raises several difficulties. First, since different persons construct the art work on the basis of different perceptions—the perceptions being private—it follows that each person in talking about a construct out of his own perceptions is talking about something capable in principle of being apprehended only by him. Moreover, if at time t_0 I construct the work of art on the basis of perceptions p_1, p_2 and p_3, and at time t_1 construct it on the basis of these perceptions and perception p_4, then I am talking about two different constructs and *ipso facto* about two different art works. Second, if the name of any particular work of art signifies merely a construct out of the perceptions had by someone on a particular occasion, then there is no subsistent art work. That x be a work of art would mean merely that there be some person z for whom, at some time t_0, being presented in an appropriate manner with the vehicle y (associated with x) is a necessary and sufficient condition for z's having an aesthetic appearance or a set of such appearances. The symbolization of this is:

$$Wx = df[\,(\exists y)\,(\exists z)\,(t_0):\,(\,(Vyx)\cdot(Pyz \equiv zA_1 \vee zA_1,$$
$$zA_2,\ldots zA_n \vee \ldots.)\,)\,]\quad (I)$$

The expression, "the work of art" would be an incomplete symbol, not a designator. Third, if the name of an art work refers merely to the perceptions had by someone on a particular occasion, then we should be unable to speak of right or wrong with respect to any statement of the form, "x is a work of art", where "x" designates a construction out of someone's perceptions and "is" is identificational. This is so because we should have no independent standard or criterion by appeal to which we could determine the correctness of such a statement. This has been pointed out by Wittgenstein in another context:

> Let us imagine a table (something like a dictionary) that exists only in our imagination. A dictionary can be used to justify the translation of a word X by a word Y. But are we also to call it

justification if such a table is to be looked up only in the imagination?—"Well, yes; then it is a subjective justification"—But justification consists in appealing to something independent.—"But surely I can appeal from one memory to another. For example, I don't know if I have remembered the time of departure of a train right and to check it I call to mind how a page of the time-table looked. Isn't it the same here?"—No; if this process has got to produce a memory which is actually *correct*. If the mental image of the time-table could not itself be tested for correctness, how could it confirm the correctness of the first memory? (As if someone were to buy several copies of the morning paper to assure himself that what it said was true.)

Looking up a table in the imagination is no more looking up a table than the image of the result of an imagined experiment is the result of an experiment.[7]

In the case in point, once the perceptions have passed, there is nothing to which to point to justify someone's statement, "X is a work of art". Nor can it be argued in rebuttal that he might have the same perceptions again. For as Wittgenstein writes (again in another context) :

Let us imagine the following case. I want to keep a diary about the recurrence of a certain sensation. To this end I associate it with the sign "S" and write this sign in a calendar for every day on which I have the sensation.—I will remark first of all that a definition of the sign cannot be formulated.—But still I can give myself a kind of ostensive definition. How? Can I point to the sensation? Not in the ordinary sense. But I speak, or write the sign down, and at the same time I concentrate my attention on the sensation—and so, as it were, point to it inwardly.—But what is this ceremony for? for that is all it seems to be! A definition surely serves to establish the meaning of a sign.—Well, that is done precisely by the concentrating of my attention; for in this way I impress on myself the connexion between the sign and the sensation.—But "I impress it òn myself" can only mean: this process brings it about that I remember the connexion *right* in the future. But in the present case I have no criterion of correctness. One would like to say: whatever is going to seem right to me is right. And that only means that here we can't talk about 'right' (I. 259) .

[7] Ludwig Wittgenstein, *Philosophical Investigations,* trans. G. E. M. Anscombe, 2nd edn. (Oxford: Basil Blackwell, 1958) , I. 265.

This shows that speaking of correct and incorrect identification of something as an art work would be possible if and only if the aesthetic object were somehow public, for only on that condition could there be an independent criterion. But, on the construct theory, this condition, *ex hypothesi,* does not obtain.

Professor Pepper also suggests an alternative account of the art work within the framework of the construct theory. For he writes that the work of art "is in the nature of a potentiality or dispositional property of the vehicle. It is the full potentiality of aesthetic perception available to the aesthetic vehicle." [8] Now, first of all, it is misleading to use the concepts *potentiality* and *disposition* interchangeably, for the former involves merely that there are possible conditions under which a vehicle will appear such-and-such, whereas the latter involves that there are certain actually *specifiable* conditions under which it will do so. I shall assume that he means that a particular work of art is a specific dispositional property of a particular vehicle and that, speaking generally, the work of art is a potentiality of the vehicle to cause aesthetic perceptions.[9] Thus, individual control objects have the same potentiality by virtue of having different dispositions.

Although this view is somewhat more sophisticated than those we have already rejected, it is no more acceptable than they. It asserts that the art work is the class of potential aesthetic perceptions caused by the vehicle. But if we hark back to " (I) " we notice that the class of such perceptions or appearances is open; its membership is never fully determinate. It follows that we can never know "the full potentiality of aesthetic perception available to the aesthetic vehicle"—that we can never know the work of art. But to say that there is a work of art implies that it is knowable, *i.e.* is an object of knowledge, for an assertion about existence leaves one open to the question, "How do you know?" This question is unanswerable here, for we are in principle

---

[8] Stephen C. Pepper, *The Work of Art*, pp. 30–31.

[9] *Cf.* Wilfrid Sellars, "Aristotelian Philosophies of Mind", in Roy Wood Sellars, V. J. McGill and Marvin Farber, eds., *Philosophy for the Future* (New York: The Macmillan Company, 1949) , especially pp. 545 f; and C. D. Broad, *Examination of McTaggart's Philosophy* (Cambridge, England: The University Press, 1933) , I. 264–278.

incapable of knowing the full potentiality of the aesthetic vehicle; and it is with the full potentiality that the work of art is equated.

A view similar to the first account suggested by Professor Pepper has been advanced by Professor C. I. Lewis in his Carus Lectures.[10] An art work, according to this view, is an abstraction actualized by presentation through the medium of some physical vehicle. But the abstractness, contends Lewis, is not like that of triangularity or honesty or incompatibility: "It has the literal character of esthesis." [11] But in what sense can the abstraction have that character? Although the conceptual element of the abstraction is at a minimum—in contrast to what it is when we are concerned with triangularity or honesty or incompatibility— the interpretative and constructional elements are prominent. Indeed, Lewis himself recognizes that the interpretative element of the abstraction is prominent, for he remarks that "the aged man and the child by his side may both read the same responses from the prayer-book; but these words cannot have the same meaning for the two, because in the one case they are freighted with a lifetime of experience".[12] But he passes off the difference by insisting that this consideration holds for any language-presented phenomenon. But, although this is to some extent true, it is unreasonable to conclude, as Lewis seems to, that interpretation is no more significant in aesthetic than in non-aesthetic experience. Aesthetic perception, more than any other, involves not merely having experiences, but how they are had. When a spectator comes to an aesthetic vehicle, he comes freighted with particular perceptual sets, either momentary or long-standing, that affect his selection from among the elements that constitute the purely sensuous datum. The interpretation is not even temporally separate from the givenness of the datum. How the object is experienced is a function of the spectator's prevailing set: as Wittgenstein emphasizes, he perceives the object as he interprets

---

[10] Clarence Irving Lewis, _An Analysis of Knowledge and Valuation_ (La Salle, Illinois: The Open Court Publishing Company, 1946), especially pp. 469–478.

[11] _Ibid._ p. 475.

[12] _Ibid._ p. 473.

it.[13] Lewis's contention that the abstraction has the character of esthesis seems to me to be unsound; and since it is cardinal in his account of the aesthetic object, I am constrained to reject the account itself.

Professor C. J. Ducasse advances a view quite unlike any we have considered. He claims that the work of art is identical with the one and only physical product of artistic activity, in short, that the work of art is nothing else than the object that Professors Pepper and Lewis call the aesthetic vehicle.[14] But this view will not do. Consider, for example, the case of a poem. Is the art work the sign-design of the printed poem or is it the sign-events that constitute the several occurrences of the sign-design? If the latter, then there are as many works of art associated with a given poem as there are copies of it; if the former, then we are faced with a contradiction. For the sign-design is not a physical object or event; it is a class of printed marks to which belong all sign-events of a particular kind. Since, according to Ducasse, the work of art is a physical object, not an abstraction, he must reject the thesis that the poetical work of art is a sign-design. But the alternative entails that one poem comprehends a host of art works. This contradicts Ducasse's contention that the art work is identical with the one and only physical product of artistic endeavour.

None of these six theories, then, is free from serious defect; none satisfactorily explicates the concept of *the ontological status of the art work*. Perhaps these theories fail to do so because they seek to answer the wrong question. Rather than asking, "What is the ontological status of the work of art?" (as though there might be some sort of existence beyond either physical, sensory or perceptual existence), they might more profitably inquire, "How do the names of particular art works and the designator 'the work of art' and its synonyms function in the concrete contexts of art history, criticism and evaluation?" It may be that the concept of

[13] For a more detailed discussion of this point, see Wittgenstein, *op. cit.* pp. 193 ff.

[14] Curt John Ducasse, *The Philosophy of Art* (New York: The Dial Press, 1929) and *Art, the Critics, and You* (New York: Hafner Publishing Company, 1944).

an art work's ontological status has no sharp boundary; that among the various uses for the aforementioned names and designators there is merely the sort of kinship that Wittgenstein calls "a family resemblance". It may be that we actually use names and designators of the sort in question without their having precisely fixed meanings, for the varied application of the concept *work of art* to particular bases permits, so to speak, a whole series of bases upon one type of which we may lean if another should be taken away.[15] But a full discussion of this point is beyond the purpose of this paper, which is merely to demonstrate the inadequacy of an approach of the sort that characterizes the six theories hereinabove rejected.

[15] Wittgenstein, *op. cit.* I. 68, 76, and 79; Stephan Körner, *Conceptual Thinking: A Logical Inquiry* (Cambridge, England: The University Press, 1955), especially ch. IV.

Three

The Nature and Role
of Aesthetic Theory

Part Three. Selected Readings

Ashenbrenner, Karl. "Aesthetic Theory—Conflict and Conciliation," *Journal of Aesthetics and Art Criticism,* 18: 90–108 (1959).

Beardsley, Monroe C. "The Definition of the Arts," *Journal of Aesthetics and Art Criticism,* 20: 175–187 (1961).

D'Azevedo, W. L. "Structural Approach to Aesthetics: Toward a Definition of Art in Anthropology," *American Anthropologist,* 60: 702–714 (1958).

Gallie, W. B. "The Function of Philosophical Aesthetics," *Mind,* 57: 302–321 (1948).

Kahler, Erich. "What Is Art?" *Problems in Aesthetics,* ed. Morris Weitz. New York, 1959.

Kemp, J. "Generalization in the Philosophy of Art," *Philosophy,* 33: 147–157 (1958).

Morgan, Douglas. "Art Pure and Simple," *Journal of Aesthetics and Art Criticism,* 20: 187–196 (1961).

Introduction

The material in this section is logically connected to most of the material in the two preceding sections. Here the writers discuss not only some of the problems of defining art, but also whether art can be defined at all in any absolute sense.

When Véron, for example, says that ". . . art is the manifestation of emotion, obtaining external interpretation, now by expressive arrangements of line, form or colour, now by a series of gestures, sounds, or words governed by particular rhythmical cadence," he is attributing to art certain features—necessary and sufficient ones. That is, if and only if a painting has features A, B, and C, then it is a work of art, its painter an artist, and his activity art. Such absolutism in aesthetic theory is often attacked by people who believe the theory is either altogether or partially wrong or else it is too narrow. For example, Morris Weitz (who has his own critics) claims that art has no necessary and sufficient properties: Art does not necessarily have to be an expression of emotion nor does a work of art necessarily have to be a manifestation of emotion via external signs. The history of the use of the word "art" clearly shows this use, Weitz says.

As an adjunct to his study of such problems as this one, the reader could confront various works generally called art or works of art and try to discover a common property (or properties) among them. Such practical exercise will show him some of the problems connected with a definition of art.

W. B. Gallie

Art as an Essentially Contested Concept

One of the most welcome achievements of recent philosophy in this country and America has been the rehabilitation of aesthetics. To explore the relationships of the various arts and theories of art, and to seek to unravel the puzzles and paradoxes with which art-criticism is constantly beset, are once again perfectly respectable philosophical pursuits. Gone, let us hope for ever, are the days (which I can remember) when the subject of art was likely to evoke in serious philosophical circles looks of irritation and embarrassment—such as might greet the mention of mothers at a prep. school or of sex at Lords.

Two groups of philosophers have contributed to this change of attitude: those who, while denying the possibility of any over-all theory of art, yet insist on the importance of aesthetics as meta-criticism—a piece-meal investigation of the puzzles and conflicts that frustrate much of our critical discussion of works of art; and those who, while propounding an over-all theory, do so with a wholesome sense of the difficulties involved; and of the special character of the puzzles and conflicts that make it necessary. As examples of the first group I shall consider some of the contributions to Mr. William Elton's composite volume *Aesthetics and Language* [1]; and as examples of the second group two recent books on aesthetics by Mr. Harold Osborne. Both sets of examples seem to me to fall short at a crucial point: but from a

---

[1] In particular those of Dr. Helen Knight, Dr. Margaret Macdonald, Professor J. A. Passmore, Mr. Stuart Hampshire, and in a lesser degree my own.

[Reprinted from *The Philosophical Quarterly*, 6: 97–114 (1956).]

consideration of their respective short-comings I think we can see a possible line of development of real promise.

II

Mr. Elton's writers are at one in rejecting that kind of definition or over-all 'theory' of art which, traditionally, philosophical aestheticians have sought to provide. The case against these definitions and 'theories' can be resumed very briefly as follows:—Either they mislead us, by circumscribing the idea of art too narrowly, in that they exclude some universally acknowledged works or *genres* of art, or at least some necessary features of these. Or else—and this is particularly true of those metaphysical theories which pretend to tell us how art is 'possible' as a mode of experience or creation of value—they are couched in language so general and so vague that they can do nothing to illuminate the crucial difficulties, in particular those conflicts of standards, upon which our actual discussions of art generally come to grief. These criticisms seem to me in the main well justified, and I shall say nothing more on this negative head at the moment.

What, then, is meant by 'meta-criticism', which Mr. Elton's writers take to be the only proper function of philosophical aesthetics? In dealing with this question, it is necessary to bear in mind the general view of the function and method of philosophy to which anyhow most of Mr. Elton's authors adhere; since both the value and the limitations of what they tell us are due as much to the philosophical method they follow as to their perceptiveness (and the limits of their perceptiveness) regarding the arts and art-criticism. Luckily this view of the function and method of philosophy is now so well known, and so widely accepted in England to-day, that here again only the briefest outline is necessary.

Its starting-point is the long-recognised truth that philosophy is concerned with the elucidation of meanings, not with the discovery of new facts. The question, then, is how meanings are to be elucidated. On the view to be discussed, the meaning of, say, some perplexing highly abstract word (or formula or concept) is to be 'shown' or 'displayed' simply by a consideration of how it and its derivatives are used in a range of familiar contexts, and by a comparison of these uses with the uses of other abstract words (or formulae or concepts) with which our original word is more or less—more or less illuminatingly or more or less deceptively—analogous. A necessary assumption in this procedure is that there are many uses of any abstract word (or formula or concept), particularly in the way of the inferences which it permits, about whose propriety no one will disagree: and it is through these uses (and the partial parallels which we find for them) that the problem of the perplexing word or concept is resolved. The solution of any philosophical problem, therefore, lies in the recognition of how certain words are properly used, i.e. the answer is always already there *in the words as properly used*. Any attempt to go 'beyond' or 'behind' these uses is to be abjured. To seek to explain or justify what we ordinarily (and properly) say—save by comparing and contrasting it with other things we ordinarily say in similar or relevantly connected contexts—betrays a fundamental misconception of what philosophy, as opposed to other more positive or creative forms of enquiry, can do.

Clearly the value of philosophising to this pattern can be decided only by a consideration of its detailed elucidations of special problems. Nevertheless I think that the main achievements of Mr. Elton's authors can be usefully and fairly suggested under the following two heads— (i) They reiterate and re-enforce with many well-chosen examples the old truth that, since every work of art is prized for its own unique self, there can be no general rules or recipes for the creation and appreciation of works of art. Thus Dr. Margaret Macdonald points out that art-criticism is never in the nature of proof or persuasion in the scientific sense: it does not proceed by applying rules or formulae derived from observation of a selected number of 'standard works'. Perhaps the most helpful analogy, in displaying the relation of a critic to a work of art, is that of the executant to the music which he interprets and presents. The main point of any good criticism, Dr. Macdonald suggests, is similarly to 'present' what is of value in the original work, and no general rules can prescribe or delimit the executant's task. (ii) In the second place, Mr. Elton's authors emphasise the remarkable diversity and variety of the criteria we employ in assessing the value of works of art

—even of works that fall within a single *genre* or that, within one *genre,* might appear to have a closely similar subject-matter or theme. For example, we prize one painting solely or at least chiefly on the grounds of colour, another solely or at least chiefly for its line-drawing. To demand one single set of what Dr. Helen Knight calls 'criterion characters' for the evaluation of works of art in any *genre* is to be guilty of crude doctrinaire philistinism: and this is true *a fortiori* of a demand for a single set of criteria characters for *all* works of art. It is hardly necessary to add how powerfully these two conclusions re-enforce the rejection, by Mr. Elton's authors, of all general (in particular metaphysical) accounts of what art *is.* As Mr. Hampshire puts it, 'When in Aesthetics one moves from the particular to the general, one is travelling in the wrong direction'.

Yet despite these (to-day highly characteristic) efforts to move away from vacuous or misleading generalisations about the nature of art, the three writers I have quoted inevitably let slip a number of statements (some of them very interesting and controversial statements) about 'art in general' and our attitudes towards it.[2] I say *inevitably;* for how otherwise could the field of

---

[2] To specify this point. (i) Dr. Knight in the first part of her paper (*Aesthetics and Language,* p. 147 ff.) discusses the important distinction between the belief (*a*) that art in general—cf. knowledge or discussion in general—is a good thing, and the belief (*b*) that this or that particular work of art is good, in the sense of being a good instance of its kind. This obviously implies that we have an attitude or attitudes towards art in general, and one would like to know a lot more about what this highly generalised attitude to art amounts to. (ii) Professor Passmore (*Aesthetics and Language,* p. 36 ff.) is extremely suspicious—and to my mind rightly so—of so-called aesthetic experience, any how when this is taken to stand for some distinctive introspectible experience; and he is equally suspicious, and no doubt equally rightly, of so-called 'aesthetic properties'—if these are taken to stand for isolable and describable qualities which we can point to in any and every work of art. But he realises that if we are to make even this kind of negative criticism of traditional philosophical aesthetics, we must be able in some degree to circumscribe the field within which these probably bogus concepts have been applied. Thus he is led to the suggestion that 'although there are not "aesthetic properties" common to all good works of art, there is what we may call an aesthetic approach to works of art, just as there is a scientific way of considering things, without it being the case that things have scientific characters . . .' (*Aesthetics and Languages,* p. 52). Once again one would like to know much more about this approach or category, and about how its limits are to be determined. (iii) Mr. Hampshire's general thesis about works of art and aesthetic experience are discussed at p. 102–3 below.

their discussion be understood? How otherwise could they succeed, as they do, in illuminating the peculiar point and force of many of the things we say in artistic criticism, e.g., by contrasting them with superficially and misleadingly similar things that we say in the course of ethical or scientific theorising? To put this objection, which is of course as old as philosophy itself, in more polemical form: Unless these writers possess 'a concept of art' how can they tell us so much about the criticism of art—about what it is and what it is not? We must not forget, however, that previous attempts to define the 'concept of art' appear to have been uniformly unsuccessful. The situation might therefore be put in the form of a dilemma: Either we have a concept of art—and then it is useless for critical purposes, and usually misleading if applied to particular cases: or else we have no concept of art—in which case we have no adequate idea of the field of objects and activities to which we are so strenuously denying certain bogus metaphysical properties.

But I imagine that few if any of Mr. Elton's writers would be much worried by this dilemma: for one of the main claims commonly made for the philosophical method they follow is that it can provide us with reliable escape-routes from just this kind of Platonic puzzle. How can an escape be effected in this instance? How can it be shown that possession of a 'concept of art' is in no wise necessary to intelligent and even highly sophisticated (e.g. meta-critical) discussion of the arts?

It might be said: meta-criticism aims at solving certain problems that arise, sporadically and as it were locally, in the well-recognised field of art-criticism. But although this field is well-recognised, it is not therefore definable: its boundaries are in fact hopelessly hazy and our uses of it show no uniform or coherent logical structure; hence the wearisome failures of all philosophical aestheticians who have sought to define it. The words 'art' and 'work of art' do not express clear concepts any more than the words 'farming' or 'farming-job' do. In some of its uses, 'work of art' is probably a sheer blanket term, standing either for paintings *or* for poems *or* for musical composition and so on, without any suggestion of an *important* community of 'artistic nature' between these different kinds of production. In other cases, no doubt, it might be said to express a concept, but one of a very slippery and dangerous kind, resting—unsteadily—on our recognition of a 'family resemblance' or a perceptible overlap between a number of lines of resemblance running through a wide 'family' of instances. Think, for instance, of the very different ways in which comparisons are most naturally drawn between, say, a poem, a novel, a jest, a sketch from life, and a tune. The jest and the novel may have 'point'—in a sense in which the poem may not: the poem and the tune alone have rhythm: in the novel and the sketch there is in some a 'representation of things' as there certainly is not in the tune, and so on. Nevertheless, despite the shapelessness or incoherence of our uses of the expression 'work of art'—or, as some would urge, despite the fact that it does not express a genuine concept at all—it has proved perfectly possible for criticism to get on with its proper business of interpreting and assessing particular works of art: and it is equally possible for meta-criticism to get on with its business too. Imagine, for instance, two critics discussing the merits or failings of a particular picture. They will point to and try to describe in words certain special features of it which, in their opinions, are among the 'criterion-characters' (in Dr. Knight's phrase) of success or failure in paintings of this kind; they will recall other (relevantly similar) paintings, and so on. The special force of everything that they say is of a kind that could be 'shown' or 'displayed' (in the philosophical sense) in terms of the immediate context—picture facing men—or of other recalled or imagined relevantly similar contexts. The two critics may agree or disagree, may get entangled in irritating knots that call for meta-critical unravelling or may succeed in avoiding them; but whatever way their discussion goes, one thing that will not enter into it is the question of the 'artiness' of the picture they are assessing.

There are two main points to the above argument— (i) that the word 'art' expresses at most a fact of family resemblance, and (ii) that in any case criticism in no way requires or makes use of a 'concept of art'—both of which used to seem true to me, but do so no longer.[3] No doubt the family resemblance account applies to a number of features of works of art with which criticism is concerned. But until it is worked out in detail I cannot see that it

[3] Cf. the present writer's *'The Function of Philosophical Aesthetics,'* reprinted in *Aesthetics and Language,* pp. 13 ff.

provides any grounds for rejecting the view that certain highly general features may in conjunction be found necessary and peculiar to the heads of object or performance that are commonly regarded as works of art. Moreover, the family resemblance account offers no explanation of why, among all the conceivable sets of over-lapping resemblance that could be traced between and among, say, printed books, vocal performances, rhythmic bodily movements and pictorial representations, *one particular line of resemblances,* or one set of such lines, has been picked out and valued under the rubric 'work of art'. In sum, I now want our uses of that phrase *explained* in a manner in which Mr. Elton's writers did not choose, or did not think it possible, to explain them.

Now for the second point:—that criticism has no need of a concept of art, that the special force of any piece of criticism can be shown in terms of its immediate context and of other relevantly similar contexts. The crucial question here is: how *widely* can the sense of this last phrase be stretched? or, what is the criterion of *'relevantly* similar contexts'? Let it be granted that a critic, in discussing a particular picture, may not use the word 'art' or any of its derivatives, and is most unlikely to make any reference to, or any use of, any philosophical theory or definition of art. Let it be further assumed that even in his leisure hours our critic never bothers to read the 'abstract stuff' of philosophical aestheticians. Still, perhaps, he once *did* read a book by an obscure German idealist, or perhaps, say, Tolstoy on art. No doubt, when he did so, he entirely rejected (if he succeeded in understanding) the theory of art which Schiller, or Schelling, or Solger, or Schlegel (or the other Schlegel) or Schleiermacher or Schopenhauer . . . or even Tolstoy propounded. Yet the book he read may have done something to—and for—him; may have affected however slightly his view and practice of the critic's calling, may have modified his handling of current critical terminology in a way that considerably affected his power and consistency as a critic. This seems to me perfectly *possible;* and in point of fact nothing is easier than to find in the least philosophically minded critics the unmistakable traces of past philosophical doctrines.

On each of its main theses, therefore, I now find the above

defence of 'criticism and meta-criticism *without* a concept of art' quite unsatisfactory. To be sure, this defence brings out the fact that the concept of art (if it exists) must be a very queer concept —one of a kind whose structure has never been adequately explored. It may even be simply an embryonic, as yet unarticulated, concept, in which case its beneficent effects upon criticism must be hard to evaluate or may for the most part be yet to come. But these are not reasons for ignoring it or for dismissing its effects as unimportant.

At this point the reader may complain: why so much fuss about a hypothetical concept which might in certain hypothetical cases prove of importance to criticism and to meta-criticism? My answer is that the case is far from hypothetical: for Mr. Elton's volume provides us with a most arresting example of why further clarification of the concept of art is vitally necessary to both criticism and meta-criticism. The example consists in the marked disagreement between at least two of his writers, Dr. Helen Knight and Mr. Hampshire, upon no less a question than the proper function of artistic criticism. Dr. Helen Knight, basing her view very properly on what critics actually say and do, assumes that an important part of the critic's job is to assess works of art in the sense of grading them, or, at the very least, of classifying them as 'good' and 'bad' [4] Mr. Hampshire, if I understand him aright, denies this; and since he appears to be the heretical party here, we shall do well to concentrate upon him.

Mr. Hampshire asserts that the art-critic's attitude is that of the pure spectator: his job is simply to help us to see what is there— there for aesthetic enjoyment—in this or that work of art. Indeed the critic's main difficulty is to sustain this pure spectator's attitude, as opposed to that of the moralist or the practical man. Hence it is no part of his job to tell us that we should *prefer* one work of art to another. In so far as he engages upon this task he will in effect become a moralist; for he will now be advising us to *do* certain things, e.g. read certain books or buy certain pictures

[4] Other writers in Mr. Elton's volume would appear to agree with Dr. Helen Knight, e.g. Professor Passmore. The present writer's paper hovers, with unhappy inconsistency, between the views of Miss Knight and Mr. Hampshire on this issue.

in preference to other things, and such advice must take us far beyond the specifically artistic sphere into 'the whole economy of human needs and purposes'.[5]

Here then is a straight enough issue: how is it to be decided? On the view that aesthetics is simply meta-criticism, it can presumably be decided in only one way, viz., by the careful collation and comparison of a sufficient number of the different kinds of context in which the phrase 'criticism of the arts' (or its equivalents), or in which a sufficient number of standard usages and methods of art-criticism, are to be found. This task would be a very long and laborious one; but worse still, it might well prove to be one from which no definite decision could emerge. At first sight no doubt it would seem that Mr. Hampshire is just plainly wrong. Literary and artistic critics as a rule give us—as we should all expect them to give us—assessments in the sense of gradings of different works of art. But to this there is an obvious rejoinder: are these adjudications and gradings part of that job which makes the critic a *critic of works of art*—as opposed to a social critic or moralist, or literary adviser, or artistic stockbroker or advertiser? It would be a very long and laborious task to go through instance after instance of critical usage in an attempt to answer this last question. Moreover, in this attempt would we not be compelled to grade some of the specimen instances as more or less to our purpose, or as more or less authoritative? And, if we did this, surely we should have let certain extraneous considerations enter into, and indeed decide for us, a problem which, on modern views, should be decided simply by an examination of *what is said* in the relevant kinds of context?

A more natural and profitable approach would be to ask: what is the main general premiss upon which Mr. Hampshire's heretical conclusion is hinged? And the answer to this question is not hard to find. The required premiss is that every work of art is 'gratuitous': it is a 'free creation', there to be enjoyed (or neglected) simply for what it is. The canons of its success or failure are internal to itself, and if we choose to grade it—to express our preference as between it and other works of art—we are adding

---

[5] *Aesthetics and Language*, p. 169.

nothing essential to that for which we regard (and perhaps prize) it as art. Now I am not sure that I understand fully the special force which Mr. Hampshire gives to the key word 'gratuitous': but the general attitude to art which he uses it to describe is surely familiar enough. For all that Mr. Hampshire gives it an engagingly original twist and expresses it in the plain common-sense style of mid-twentieth century philosophy, it is a view of art for which many nineteenth century artists and critics, particularly in France, have pleaded, and which forms one central theme in the philosophical aesthetics of both Bergson and Croce.

I will not discuss here whether Mr. Hampshire is right or wrong, as against Dr. Helen Knight and others, in his account of what art-criticism is and is not, can and cannot do: an answer to that question would require a frame of reference, an interpretation of the phrase 'work of art' which I have still to give. All I want to stress at the moment is that here, on a question that is crucial for the whole programme of meta-criticism, we find one very persuasive writer expressing opinions which appear to be based on a general view (philosophy?) of art, however incompletely formulated. Nor, for reasons we have already stated, is it easy to see how this general view of art could be contraverted by the methods which meta-criticism is meant to employ. This suggests that it is time to reconsider more carefully the possibility of an over-all theory of art, and for this purpose I turn to Mr. Osborne.

III

To read Mr. Osborne's books is to recognise that aesthetic problems have a far wider interest and far greater urgency than a reading of Mr. Elton's volume would lead us to suppose. Aesthetic problems, for Mr. Elton's writers, begin from the occasional logical perplexities of serious critics and readers of criticism; for Mr. Osborne they begin from the utterly anarchic babel of voices that—as it seems to him—greets the simple art-lover when he turns in search of guidance to art-criticism as it is practised to-day. Mr. Osborne has been led to construct his philosophy of art in the face of the apparently endless conflicts which the history of criticism discloses: conflicts not simply between particular judgments on particular works of art, but in respect of the basic points of view from which such judgments are made. 'In fact', he writes, 'most criticism as it is now written is, in the strict sense of the word, unintelligible. We may gather that the critic esteems this work of art above that, that he considers this one good and that one bad; but we remain in ignorance of what he intends to mean when he says that any work of art at all is good or bad. Criticism is, to this extent, no more than an autobiographical record of unexplained and unjustified preferences and prejudices. This has often been said, but the reason why it is so, and the remedies for it, have seldom been exposed'.[6]

To remedy this situation, Mr. Osborne puts forward in his first book, *A Theory of Beauty*, what seems to him the one and only general aesthetic acceptance of whose principles would enable criticism to become 'a science'—i.e., a body of doctrines and of particular judgments to which all serious and properly trained people could broadly agree. Beauty, or the proper excellence of any work of art, consists, he claims, in its possession of the formal property of being an 'organic whole' or a 'configurational unity'. This property, he maintains, is at once common to all works of art and ·possessed by different works of art in varying but comparable degrees. Hence it is always possible, in terms of this formal property, to answer the primary question: 'Is this a work of art or not?' and then to proceed to make intelligible and justifiable judgments as to the relative excellence which the work in question possesses. Mr. Osborne offers some illuminating logical analyses of the notion of 'configurational wholeness', which he further elucidates in terms of the kind of psychological state that is necessary for the apprehension and appreciation of it.

It is difficult, in reading Mr. Osborne, not to admire the spirit with which he sets about his task. He is one who has had philosophy thrust upon him: who has been impelled to work out his own theory to meet what he feels to be an urgent need. By contrast, too many of Mr. Elton's writers seem to be offering us modish, philosophical five-finger exercises applied to a new key; in particular these writers would seem to have assumed too

---

[6] *Aesthetics and Criticism,* p. 37.

lightly that the diversity of criteria which we find used in art-criticism is something that every intelligent person can cope with,
without difficulty, for himself—something which requires neither
rectification nor explanation of any kind. Nevertheless, Mr. Osborne's programme seems open to all the familiar objections that
have been raised against theories which seek to define the characteristic excellence of works of art in terms of a single essential
property. Is he not indeed guilty of the extreme error of seeking
for a general recipe or formula for judging works of art? Or, if he
claims simply to have supplied a useful negative rule, by which
critics would do well to test their intuitive judgments, then at
best he has been describing one necessary condition of artistic
excellence; and in that case where and what are the others? [7]

These objections, however, do not apply so obviously to Mr.
Osborne's second book, *Aesthetics and Criticism*. Here his approach is less direct, but much more penetrating and persuasive.
He now lays aside the claim that 'the configurational point of
view' is the only possible one in general aesthetics (for all that he
still clearly believes this to be the case). He presents his own view
as one among other possible alternatives—e.g., the point of view
which he calls Realism (Representationalism in its various
forms), the hedonistic point of view, and the point of view of
communication and expression theories of art. He then tries to
show the nature and limits of the kinds of criticism which adher-
ence to each of these aesthetic points of view will allow; and he
has little difficulty in showing that much criticism shows a shocking disregard for such limits, and in fact romps with happy
inconsistency from the kind of evaluation permissible from one
point of view to a kind only permissible from another. Moreover,
he argues that for various reasons a number of aesthetic points of
view, for example, the hedonistic, cannot possibly be used to
justify criticism claiming objective validity, whereas his own configurational point of view can do so. [8] Undoubtedly in performing

[7] See the very able criticism of Mr. Osborne's *A Theory of Beauty* by Mr. P.
F. Strawson in *Mind*, N.S. Vol. LXIII, pp. 413 ff.
[8] This suggests how the difference between Mr. Hampshire and Dr. Helen
Knight can be resolved, or at least explained.

this task Mr. Osborne has taught any critic who reads his book some very valuable lessons.

Nevertheless, I am not at all satisfied with the *rationale* of Mr. Osborne's revised programme, salutary though many of its practical effects may be. In the first place, there is the question: How has he selected the various possible points of view which he discusses? Or, more accurately, on what principle has he grouped together different aesthetic theories under the rubrics Realist, Expressionist, and so on? I have found no satisfying answer to this question in Mr. Osborne's otherwise admirably argued pages; and it seems to me important to press it for the following reason. Despite the notorious (and apparently endless) conflicts of philosophical aestheticians there is inevitably a good deal of agreement—agreement at the 'commonsense level'—to be found in their respective theories. Nothing could be more natural, therefore, than to try to group them together: to abstract from them the five or six really important different things that philosophical aestheticians have had to say. But it is all too possible, in proceeding thus, to lose sight of the distinctive, original and valuable thing that any one aesthetician has had to say. And it is therefore essential that our principles of selection and grouping, in any collative task of this kind, shall be designed to ensure, so far as possible, that the distinctive merits of each theory under discussion shall be brought to light. Now, despite their great interest, Mr. Osborne's surveys of his alternative possible aesthetic points of view do not meet this requirement. They give us excellent accounts of the successive 'salvaging operations' that have proved necessary as each aesthetic point of view has been subjected to searching, detailed criticism. But for none of these points of view—save his own 'configurational' one—does Mr. Osborne possess much sympathy. He is too eager (at heart) to correct, to be able to understand: at any rate in that sense of understanding which is peculiar and necessary to the historian of thought. For unless a given theory is to be treated simply as a pathological specimen (for logical excision or correction) then it is incumbent upon the historian, not indeed to show that its tenets are right or justifiable, but at least to show that they are intelligible—are of a kind that quite intelligent men could naturally find persuasive and, up to a point, sensible and illuminating. If he fails to do this, the historian's criticisms of the theories he has examined will not simply be unfair: they are very likely to be useless.

Closely connected with this criticism is the following. Mr. Osborne entirely neglects (anyhow in the main body of his book) [9] the possibility that each of the alternative points of view he mentions may have something of essential importance to contribute to our understanding of the concept of art: that each succeeds in emphasising—with a one-sidedness which is intelligible if not logically justifiable—some facet or feature of works which is a necessary, and perhaps easily neglected condition of artistic excellence. I shall try to show that this is the case, anyhow for a number of aesthetic points of view, in what follows. In the meantime, we can see the plausibility of this suggestion if we consider how much we should lose if all critics swallowed Mr. Osborne's medicine and proceeded to produce good consistent criticism from the 'configurational point of view'. Would it not be a real loss if the peculiarly individual points of view and voices of Samuel Johnson and Coleridge, of Reynolds and Ruskin, of Venturi and Fry, were denied to us? The diversity of point of view which bedevils art criticism and which frequently leaves the layman at a loss what to think, has its valuable side as well.

These two lines of criticism are, I believe, complementary. If we had a properly sympathetic historical account of how the concept of art *came to be*—of how and why different and to all appearances radically opposed aesthetic standpoints have been favoured by, to all appearances, equally intelligent and knowledgeable people—then we should be in a position to appreciate the peculiar structure of the concept of art: to see that it is one of a fairly wide and important class of concepts which are, as I like to put it, *essentially complex,* and, chiefly for this reason, *essentially contested.* Conversely, if we have a proper grasp of the structure of the concept of art—if we see the grounds of its essential complex-

[9] But see his very interesting footnote to p. 44 of *Aesthetics and Criticism.*

ity and contestedness—we should thereby be enabled to make some sense of, to read with some appreciation and sympathy, the otherwise apparently futile history of conflicting aesthetic schools.

IV

What light is thrown on the concept of art by the *history* of the concept of art? Or, to simplify this Crocean mouthful of a question, let us begin by considering it in terms of one particular brand of art and of art-criticism. Let us imagine the case of a simple man who likes many recent and contemporary paintings, and who seeks guidance in the formation of his taste from the judgment of professional art critics. And let us suppose that he is rather unlucky in his initial readings and inquiries: that he hits, not upon the kind of critics—and of course there are many such —who go out of their way to emphasise the one-sidedness of their own sympathies and their own characteristic approach to painting, but upon a number of those critics—and there are many such —who either openly or deviously give the innocent reader to understand that there is *one* style or method of painting (the one which the critic in question happens to prefer) which *alone* gives us real paintings—paintings which sustain and advance the great traditions of the past and herald the unborn masterpieces of to-morrow. And of course the trouble is that a number of critics will be saying this about a number of different (and often radically conflicting) styles or movements in recent and contemporary painting. In this situation, deafened and confused by the confident voices and commanding jargons of some half-dozen different camps, our simple art-lover will be utterly discouraged and at a loss. Whom can he trust? Had he not better rely on his own untutored taste, wobbly and diffident though it may be? But suppose that at this point a friendly and modest voice speaks in his·ear: 'God alone knows which, if any, of these conflicting voices is right, or how, if at all, their different points of view could be reconciled. But I think I can tell you how this separation of points of view came to be. I cannot solve your problem, but I can tell you how it all happened'. If he is wise, our simple

art-lover will grasp at this offer of aid from the historian of art
and art-criticism, limited and not quite directly to his purpose
though it may be.

We need not go into any of the details of the story which the
art-historian would unfold. No doubt it would take as its base-
line that deep division in artistic aims and standards that was
effected by the Romantic movement. The reasons for further
splinterings within, in particular, the art of painting as practised
in France, will then be (as far as possible sympathetically) dis-
closed. Some of these reasons will be of a kind that would arise
naturally from the experience of practising artists in a society in
which there is no longer a single authoritative conception of the
aims of art or of the standards of artistic excellence; others would
arise from the increasing availability of specimens of art of the
most diverse ages and cultures; others from the teachings of
popularised science—as with the first Impressionists; yet others
from political and social pressures—as with the Social Realists.

Throughout this explanation one point of great importance
would continually be stressed: the spokesman of *most* of the rebel
movements or schools would claim, with some show of justice,
that the style of painting which they defended was the true
inheritor and advancer of the great tradition of painting which
had preceded them. But how, it may be asked, could this claim
have been made with any show of plausibility from so many
different, and often radically conflicting quarters? Simply, I
would answer, because painting is a highly complex affair, admit-
ting, in different circumstances, of a number of different but
genuinely helpful and illuminating descriptions. Painting *is* the
placing of colour on canvas: it *is* the expression of how a given
artist sees things—whether in nature or in his imagination: moreover, simply in virtue of this medium, this expression is given an
essentially communicative form: finally, any successful painting is
the source, for the spectator, of so-called aesthetic enjoyment. It is
natural and useful to describe paintings—and to encourage or
applaud or criticise painters—sometimes in terms of one of the
above descriptions, sometimes in terms of another. One of the
above styles of description will be best suited to the discussion
and interpretation of one school or movement in painting, while

a second style of description will be suited to other schools or movements. To put the same point in another way. Painting has a number of aspects; and the relative importance of any of these aspects will be differently assessed according to the beliefs of any painter or critic as to the best way in which the traditional values of painting can be developed or sustained. But there is no certain way in which the correctness or incorrectness of any such belief can be established in advance or on principle. The result is that, so long as there is painting as we know it, there will always be a number of ways (or at least of alleged ways) in which the traditional values of paintings can best be kept alive. The lion and the unicorn—classicists and romanticists, impressionists and post-impressionists, abstractionists and expressionists—will always be fighting for the crown. 'Painting', when used as it often is to-day as an 'achievement word', meaning 'real painting', 'genuine painting', 'painting which reminds us of what painting can do', etc., is the expression of an essentially contested concept.[10]

When our simple art-lover has listened to the historian's explanatory narrative, and has appreciated the aesthetic moral or gloss which I have attached to it, he should at least feel some lightening of his previous bewilderment. He will understand that the situation in contemporary criticism (in so far as this does consist of a babel of conflicting voices) is a perfectly natural one: irritating, no doubt, but not therefore altogether deplorable, any more than the rival and often contradictory claims of competing political parties are altogether deplorable. If political welfare can be advanced by the device of party government, why should not art and the appreciation of art be assisted by a somewhat analogous competition between different schools of artists and their critical interpreters and cheer-leaders?

Now I want to suggest that we should regard the four or five most important classic theories or definitions of art in a closely similar way: i.e., that we should regard them as highly abstract—and often quite unplausibly over-generalised—attempts to make certain current preferences in criticism conform to the framework

[10] The same is true of such ostensibly neutral terms of criticism as 'coloration', 'unity', 'depth', in so far as these are used by critics writing from radically different aesthetic points of view.

of particular philosophical systems. In support of this suggestion, we may recall that the most interesting developments in aesthetics have usually been due to writers who were not primarily philosophers at all, but were men of great insight into some two or more of the arts and very forceful exponents of some new movement of feeling and aspiration in the critical appreciation of these arts. Examples would be Addison, Burke, Vico, Coleridge, Baudelaire, Nietzsche, Péguy, and in our day Mr. Eliot and M. André Malraux. Such men as these voice new standards and aims in some group of the arts so powerfully that they exert a considerable influence upon critics of yet *other* arts, so that their teachings and preachings are eventually stretched to apply—often with much decreased plausibility—to the arts in general. At this point, it might be suggested, the philosophic aesthetician picks them up, and proceeds to pack a dehydrated version of some great critic's message into the framework of his system of philosophy.

Whatever the shortcomings of this account of the genesis of philosophical aesthetics, it does not err by being over-flattering. This is all to the good; since I suspect that the vehemence with which philosophical aestheticians have recently been trounced by their critics is due to the fact that these critics, in their secret hearts, have held too high hopes of what a general aesthetic could conceivably accomplish. Let us make it quite clear, then, how little we can properly expect from any general, over-all theory of art. The propositions must be confined to the few, and perhaps not very exciting, respects in which *all* works and *genres* of art can fruitfully be compared.[11] Now no one will wish to deny that fruitful comparisons can be made between instances of a number of different art-forms: no one will wish to deny the close kinship of painting with sculpture or with abstract design, of some music with the dance and with certain kinds of poetry: the possibility of *combinations* of these usually separate art-forms speaks for itself.

---

[11] Less widely generalised reflection (by poets and others) on, e.g. the 'mystery of the word', or on the peculiar evocative capacity of colours and tones, or on the 'correspondence' of these with other sense-qualities, are likely to be deeper, to be more metaphysically toned, and certainly to be more capable of deepening our responses to the arts, than any of the general propositions of philosophical aesthetics.

Similarly, much of the best criticism of the last two hundred years forces us to recognise a looser, but for interpretative purposes still useful, 'cousin-age' between e.g. the literary and the plastic arts. But the grounds of any fruitful comparison between *all* the arts can be only of a very abstract kind: there can be no question of comparison, in respect of observable or indicatable properties, between them all. Indeed it would seem that the only possible comparison between all successful works of art must be in respect of such things as their originality, their achievement or advancement of traditional standards, their 'organic wholeness', their communicative effect. All these, pretty clearly, are species of the general category of 'success' or 'achievement': but they are all of them sub-categories that apply to plenty of other things besides works of art. Hence the most characteristic difficulty of every classic aesthetic theory: to specify some sense of one of these categories so that it applies to all works of art and to nothing else. And the results are familiarly disappointing: failure to specify sufficiently narrowly gives us a hopelessly vague theory: stricter specification means the exclusion of something essential to at least *some* works of art. A fairly obvious way out of this difficulty would be to suggest—as I shall do—that a certain combination of the above species of achievement applies to all works of art and to nothing else. But this suggestion leaves unexplained the surprising fact that almost all philosophical aestheticians (and almost the great creative critics who lie at the back of them) have sought to define art by means of one key notion or category. This point, however, can be explained if we can show that the concept of art, as well as being essentially complex, is also essentially contested.

Let us, then, try to see through the history of the concept of art (fortunately it is a relatively short and simple history) how its essential complexity and contestedness came to be. Philosophical aesthetics—apart from the brilliant proem supplied for it by Plato—is a creation of the eighteenth century. What successes, since that period, has it to record? One thing would perhaps generally be claimed for it: its vindication of the autonomy or uniqueness of artistic values. Yet this claim, as just stated, is liable to prove very misleading; for it suggests either that artistic excellence consists in one single unique thing or property (intuition-expression *or* communication *or* configurational unity or whatever you please) or else, if it is complex, that its ingredients are one and all confined to the sphere of art: and both these contentions are, I think, certainly false. What is valid in this first claim on behalf of philosophical aesthetics could, I think, be better expressed by saying: its history discloses a growing recognition of the fact that the word 'art' is most usefully employed, not as a descriptive term standing for certain indicatable properties, but as an appraisive term accrediting a certain kind of achievement. This truth (though, of course, differently phrased) seems to me to be made progressively clearer in the writings of idealist aestheticians, from Kant through Hegel to Croce and Collingwood. At the same time none of the idealists, with the exception of Kant, showed any appreciation of the essential complexity of every artistic achievement; and we have still to see how the history of the concept of art forces recognition of this complexity upon us.

Eighteenth century aesthetics inherited a traditional naive aesthetic which was already of at least two-fold character. It combined an element of representationism (illusionism, imitation of nature) with an element of idealisation (sometimes conceived in terms of 'correct' formal relationships). The first of these elements did not survive long in the history of aesthetics: there are some arts which are manifestly *not* representational. But the second may be regarded as the prototype of later 'configurationist' theories. Now according to almost all 'configurationist' theories artistic excellence is an inherent or resident property in the work of art itself. The artist must work to get it there; the spectator finds it there; but there it emphatically is—and not in anybody's imaginings or perceivings or judgings. Evidently, on this view, to say of any (presumed) 'good' work of art, that it will therefore be admired by competent judges, is to make a *synthetic* statement. Eighteenth century subjectivist aesthetic theories denied this, urging very persuasively that any excellence we attribute to a work of art can be more properly described and valued in terms of the states of mind, e.g. certain pleasurable responses, of the suitably situated and cultivated spectator. Thus the first important step in the history of aesthetics was to shift attention from the thing, the work of art, to the spectator who enjoys it. The second step is the work of the Romantic movement: attention is shifted from the cultivated spectator to the creative artist. Ludicrously excessive, useless for all critical purposes though the Romantic cult of individual genius may have been, it nevertheless served to enforce an all-important lesson. Eighteenth century aesthetics had set up the spectator-critic as the proper locus of aesthetic value. But the critics' taste, as such, is for the already achieved, the *déjà fait*. Hence the justification of Wordsworth's 'Every great and original writer . . . must *create* the taste by which he is relished'. Freshness, originality, spontaneity—creation itself—were admitted to be artistic excellences before the Romantics sang and spluttered: but the Romantics gave to these values an emphasis which they had never before enjoyed and are never likely now to lose. The third important step to be noticed may also be traced to the Romantic movement—to its recognition of the validity of many *different* traditions—for all that the full development of this insight had to wait until the present century. The inadequacy of the individual artist (who may be either unrecognised originative genius or self-intoxicated ass *bombinans in vacuo*) as locus or source of artistic value is to be made good by reference to the traditionally accepted values, in any one style or *genre* of art, with and from which—to sustain or develop or reform or revolutionise which—every genuine artist, every genuine work of art, begins. Only by reference to such values can the original (or the conservative) value of any work of art be appraised. Meanwhile the fourth step had already been taken by the one truly titanic figure in our history. With Tolstoy, attention is shifted—from the object, from the spectator-critic, from the individual artist, and the tradition within which he works—to the proper relationship between artist and public. Art is an achieved communication; and its peculiar value is simply that a certain elementary kind of communication takes place. Art is no longer to be valued as a commodity, as an object of cupboard love, as a display of original virtuosity or traditional discipline. It is proclaimed as an essential bond of union between man and man, as a necessity of human life.

In this abstract of aesthetic history we see the main grounds—
and the very real justification—of some five of the main types of
aesthetic theory: configurationist theories, theories of aesthetic
contemplation and response (usually couched in psychological
terms, usually—though not necessarily—hedonistic), theories of
art as expression, theories emphasising traditional aims and
standards, and communication theories. Each in its own highly
abstract way gave expression to powerful and justifiable movements in the preceding (or in Tolstoy's case the succeeding)
history of the Arts and of art-criticism. Each, since it was first
propounded, has been a contestant for the title of the true, the
only satisfying, the only plausible theory of art. Each is still
capable of exercising a certain pull on our sympathies. But each,
in respect of its exclusive claims to define or clarify the concept of
Art, is utterly unacceptable. The historical evidence makes good
this conclusion, which a direct 'phenomenological' analysis of our
appraisive attitude to the arts could equally well have suggested.

Could we not, however, attempt to combine these theories to
give a single compendious definition of art—or, more accurately,
of the ways in which the characteristic achievements of the different arts can fruitfully be compared? Well, there is nothing to stop
us, and nothing is easier.

We may write:

(1) 'Any successful work of art is an achievement (usually
individual though sometimes collective), in relation to certain
traditionally accepted standards, of an original configurational
unity, that is by its very nature communicable and fitted to be
received and contemplated, for its own sake, by a certain kind of
audience at that audience's pleasure'.

This is, of course, a very clumsy sentence, and it is an interesting exercise to try and remove its clumsiness by re-arranging its
component phrases. But this experiment has the interesting result that changes in order effect changes in emphasis. The above
statement emphasises the element of achievement—personal or
collective—in relation to traditional standards. Suppose, however, we wrote:

(2) 'Any successful work of art is the communication, to an
audience that is fitted to receive it, for its own sake, at that

audience's pleasure, of an original configurational unity . . .
etc.',

then evidently we shall give pride of place, and special emphasis, to the element of communication. And so we could proceed
(though I cannot pretend to have completed the experiment) for
all the hundred-and-twenty possible arrangements of the component phrases in our definition.

Now this illustrates a fact of the first importance for our
discussion. The different aspects of artistic achievement which
different aesthetic theories emphasise [12] are very *naturally* graded
in different orders of importance, not so much because of different personal preferences among critics and aestheticians as because of the general condition of the arts (or of any one importantly advancing art) and of art-criticism at any particular time.
It was natural—and in a sense justifiable—that the Romantics
should have turned their cult of genius into an expressionist
aesthetic: natural and justifiable as a kind of complement and
corrective to the eighteenth century's excessive cult of taste. And
just the same claim—or excuse—could be made for Tolstoy's
identification of artistic value with the value of a certain kind of
communication, and even for the very questionable practical
conclusion he went on to draw from this identification. To be
sure, as philosophical analysts we must try to do justice to the
many-sidedness, the intrinsic complexity, of artistic excellence;
and when we are thinking as philosophers we must condemn the
claims of the Romantics or of Tolstoy as hopelessly one-sided.
But it is not only as philosophers that we think and speak of Art,
i.e. of the field of fruitful comparison between the different arts.
We also think and speak of it in this sense, as art-lovers and
enthusiasts, as protagonists or camp-followers in some movement
of critical opinion. In this capacity we apply the term Art in

[12] To be sure, philosophical aestheticians usually go far beyond this and
exclude from consideration *all but one* of the different aspects of artistic
achievement that we have discussed. In fact, however, they are less 'one-idea'd'
in the working out of their theories than in their formal definitions. Time
and again we find them letting in, as it were anonymously and by the back
door, 'subordinate considerations' (i.e. additional aspects of artistic excellence) which their formal definitions exclude, but without reference to which
their theories would be patently one-sided and unplausible.

particular arguments aimed, say, to show the justification of some new development within or between certain classic art-forms. In general, the special form of the concept of art that we favour will widen the range of our aesthetic sympathies in certain directions, and curtail it in others. But when we use, or rely upon, our concept of art in live criticism, when we press or resist the claim of a particular work or genre or style to be regarded as 'art', we will inevitably be using the term in a contestable (and often as not in an immediately contested) way. What we say can easily be recognised as appreciation or criticism from the (excessively one-sided) 'configurationist' or 'expressionist' or 'communicationist' point of view.

My thesis has been that this situation should neither surprise nor shock us; that, the arts being the kinds of activity that they are—ever expanding, ever reviving and advancing values inherited from a long and complex tradition—the character which I have ascribed to the concept of art is exactly what we should expect. Indeed, I fancy that if we should hear about or happen upon a society whose aesthetic valuations showed as high a degree of uniformity, in respect both of particular assessments and general point of view, as do, say, our valuations of scientific achievement, we should be inclined to say that, however *artistically gifted* some of its members might be, its artistic life—its production and enjoyment of works of art—was of an unhappily stinted kind. The question might even arise whether, in our sense of the term, they had an adequate appreciation of works of art at all. At any rate this supposition helps us to recognise that uniformity of judgment and appraisal, although so necessary in many fields of activity, is by no means necessary or even desirable in all. In any field of activity in which achievements are prized because they renew or advance a highly complex tradition, the point of view from which our appraisals are made—our concept of the achievement in question—would seem always to be of the kind I have called 'essentially contested'.[13]

[13] For a fuller account of concepts of this kind see my *Essentially Contested Concepts* in the Aristotelian Society Proceedings, N.S., Vol. lvi, March 1956.

William E. Kennick

Does Traditional Aesthetics Rest on a Mistake?

It rests, I think, on at least two of them, and the purpose of this paper is to explore the claim that it does.

By 'traditional aesthetics' I mean that familiar philosophical discipline which concerns itself with trying to answer such questions as the following: What is Art? What is Beauty? What is the Aesthetic Experience? What is the Creative Act? What are the criteria of Aesthetic Judgement and Taste? What is the function of Criticism? To be sure, there are others, like: Are the aesthetic object and the work of art the same? or, Does art have any cognitive content?—but these questions are commonly taken to be subordinate to those of the first group, which might be called the 'basic questions' of traditional aesthetics.

1. *The Basic Questions as Requests for Definitions.* If someone asks me 'What is helium?' I can reply: 'It's a gas' or 'It's a chemical element' or 'It's a gaseous element, inert and colourless, whose atomic number is 2 and whose atomic weight is 4·003'. A number of replies will do, depending upon whom I am talking to, the aim of his question, and so on. It is a pretty straightforward business; we get answers to such questions every day from dictionaries, encyclopedias, and technical manuals.

Now someone asks me 'What is Space?' or 'What is Man?' or 'What is Religion?' or 'What is Art?' His question is of the same form as the question 'What is helium?' but how vastly different! There is something very puzzling about these questions; they

[Reprinted from *Mind,* 67: 317–334 (1958). Footnotes have been renumbered.]

cannot be answered readily by appealing to dictionaries, encyclopedias, or technical manuals. They are philosophical questions, we say, giving our puzzlement a name, although we should not think of calling 'What is helium?' a philosophical question. Yet we expect something of the same sort of answer to both of them. There's the rub.

We say that questions like 'What is Space?' or 'What is Art?' are requests for information about the nature or essence of Space or of Art. We could say that 'What is helium?' is a request for information about the nature or essence of helium, but we rarely, if ever, do; although we do use questions like 'What is helium?' as analogues of questions like 'What is Space?' to show the sort of reply we are looking for. What we want, we say, is a definition of Space or of Art, for as Plato and Aristotle taught us long ago, "definition is the formula of the essence". So, just as the traditional metaphysicians have long sought for the nature or essence of Space and of Time, of Reality and of Change, the traditional aesthetician has sought for the essence of Art and of Beauty, of the Aesthetic Experience and the Creative Act. Most of the basic questions of traditional aesthetics are requests for definitions; hence the familiar formulae that constitute the results of traditional aesthetic inquiry: 'Art is Expression' (Croce), 'Art is Significant Form' (Clive Bell), 'Beauty is Pleasure Objectified' (Santayana), and so on. Given these definitions we are supposed to know what Art is or what Beauty is, just as we are supposed to know what helium is if someone tells us that it is a chemical element, gaseous, inert, and colourless, with an atomic number of 2 and an atomic weight of $4 \cdot 003$. F. J. E. Woodbridge once remarked that metaphysics searches for the nature of reality and finds it by definition. We might say that traditional aesthetics searches for the nature of Art or Beauty and finds it by definition.

But why should it be so difficult to discern the essence of Art or Beauty? Why should it take so much argument to establish or defend such formulae as 'Art is Expression'? And once we have arrived at such formulae or have been given them in answer to our question, why should they be so dissatisfying?

To come closer to an answer to these questions, we must look at what it is the aesthetician expects of a definition of Art or

Beauty. De Witt Parker has stated with unusual clarity the "assumption" of the aesthetician in asking and answering such questions as 'What is Art?'; at the beginning of his essay on "The Nature of Art" (note the title) he says:

> The assumption underlying every philosophy of art is the existence of some *common nature* present in all the arts, despite their differences in form and content; something the *same* in painting and sculpture; in poetry and drama; in music and architecture. Every single work of art, it is admitted, has a unique flavour, a *je ne sais quoi* which makes it incomparable with every other work; nevertheless, there is some mark or set of marks which, if it applies to any work of art, applies to *all* works of art, *and to nothing else*—a common denominator, so to say, which constitutes the definition of art, and serves to separate . . . the field of art from other fields of human culture.[1]

What we are after, it should be clear, is what the traditional logic texts call a 'definition *per genus et differentiam*' of Art and Beauty.

2. *The Assumption Questioned; the First Mistake.* The assumption that, despite their differences, all works of art must possess some common nature, some distinctive set of characteristics which serves to separate Art from everything else, a set of necessary and sufficient conditions for their being works of art at all, is both natural and disquieting, and constitutes what I consider to be the first mistake on which traditional aesthetics rests. It is natural, because, after all, we do use the word 'art' to refer to a large number of very different things—pictures and poems and musical compositions and sculptures and vases and a host of other things; and yet the word is one word. Surely, we are inclined to say, there must be something common to them all or we should not call them all by the same name. *Unum nomen; unum nominatum.*

Yet the assumption is disquieting when we come to search for the common nature which we suppose all works of art to possess. It is so elusive. We ought to be able to read a poem by Donne or

[1] De Witt H. Parker, "The Nature of Art", *Revue Internationale de Philosophie*, July 1939, p. 684; reprinted in E. Vivas and M. Krieger, eds., *The Problems of Aesthetics* (New York, 1953) , p. 90. Italics mine.

by Keats, a novel by George Eliot or Joseph Conrad, or a play by Sophocles or Shakespeare, to listen to Mozart and Stravinsky, and to look at the pictures of Giotto and Cezanne and the Chinese masters and *see* what Art is. But when we look we do not see what Art is. So we are inclined to suppose that its essence must be something hidden, something that only an aesthetician can see, like the sounds that only a dog can hear, or else, as Parker, for example, supposes, that it must be something very complex, involving many characteristics (*op. cit.* p. 93) . This explains why an adequate definition of Art is so hard to arrive at, why it is so much harder to answer questions like 'What is Art?' than it is to answer questions like 'What is helium?' Perhaps this also explains why there is a Philosophy of Art when there is no Philosophy of Helium?

But this explanation will not do. It will not do, that is, to suppose simply that the essence or nature of Art is elusive, very hard to detect, or very complex. It suggests that what we are faced with is a problem of scrutinizing, that what we have to do is to look long and hard at works of art, examine them carefully and diligently and, *voila!* we shall *see*. But no amount of looking and scrutinizing gives us what we want. All we see is this poem and that play, this picture and that statue, or some feature of them that catches our attention; and if we find some resemblances between poems or plays or pictures, or even between poems *and* pictures, pictures *and* musical compositions, these resemblances quickly disappear when we turn to other poems and plays and pictures. That is why in aesthetics it is best not to look at too many works of art and why, incidentally, aesthetics is best taught without concrete examples; a few will do. We can readily believe that we have seen the essence of Art when we have selected our examples properly; but when we range farther afield we lose it.

Despite the temptation to think that if we look long enough and hard enough at works of art we shall find the common denominator in question, after all the fruitless scrutinizing that has already been done, it is still more tempting to think that we are looking for something that is not there, like looking for the equator or the line on the spectrum that separates orange from red. No wonder that in aesthetics we soon begin to feel the frustration of St. Augustine when he asked himself 'What is Time?': "If I am not asked, I know; if I am asked, I know not". Something must be wrong.

What is wrong, as I see it, has nothing to do with the nature or essence of Art at all; that is, there is neither anything mysterious nor anything complicated about works of art which makes the task of answering the question 'What is Art?' so difficult. Like St. Augustine with Time, we do know quite well what Art is; it is only when someone asks us that we do not know. The trouble lies not in the works of art themselves but in the concept of Art. The word 'art', unlike the word 'helium', has a complicated variety of uses, what is nowadays called a complex 'logic'. It is not a word coined in the laboratory or the studio to name something that has hitherto escaped our attention; nor is it a relatively simple term of common parlance like 'star' or 'tree' which names something with which we are all quite familiar. As Professor Kristeller has shown us,[2] it is a word with a long, involved, and interesting history; a complicated concept indeed, but not for the reasons which the aestheticians suppose. Any good dictionary will indicate some of its many meanings, some of the variety of uses which the word 'art' has; but no dictionary will give us the kind of formula which the aestheticians seek. That is why we suppose that the nature of Art is a philosophical problem and why there is a Philosophy of Art but no Philosophy of Helium. It is the complicated concepts like those of Space, Time, Reality, Change, Art, Knowledge, and so on that baffle us. Dictionaries and their definitions are of use in making short shrift of questions of the form 'What is X?' only in relatively simple and comparatively trivial cases; in the hard and more interesting cases they are frustrating and disappointing.

Doubtless there is an answer to this, and it might run somewhat as follows: "We know that the word 'Art' has a variety of uses in English. Most commonly it is used to refer to pictures alone; when we visit an art museum or consult an art critic, we expect to see pictures or to hear pictures talked about. We say

---

[2] P. O. Kristeller, "The Modern System of the Arts: A Study in the History of Aesthetics", *Journal of the History of Ideas,* xii (1951), 496–527; xiii (1952), 17–46.

that painting, painting pictures, *not* painting houses or fences, is *an* art, that cooking and sewing and basket-weaving, bookbinding and selling are *arts,* but only some pictures do we call *works* of art, and rarely do we refer to dishes or garments or baskets as works of art, except honorifically. We speak of the liberal arts and the industrial arts and of the art of war. But all of this is beside the point. As aestheticians we are interested only in what are sometimes called the 'fine arts', or what Collingwood calls 'art proper'—works of art. Surely all of these have something in common, else how should we be able to separate those paintings and drawings and poems and plays, musical compositions and buildings which are works of art from those which are not?"

To answer the last question first and make a long story short: we are able to separate those objects which are works of art from those which are not, because we know English; that is, we know how correctly to use the word 'art' and to apply the phrase 'work of art'. To borrow a statement from Dr. Waismann and change it to meet my own needs, "If anyone is able to use the word 'art' or the phrase 'work of art' correctly, in all sorts of contexts and on the right sort of occasions, he knows 'what art is', and no formula in the world can make him wiser".[3] "Art proper" is simply what is properly called 'art'. The 'correctly' and 'properly' here have nothing to do with any 'common nature' or 'common denominator' of all works of art; they have merely to do with the rules that govern the actual and commonly accepted usage of the word 'art'.

Imagine a very large warehouse filled with all sorts of things— pictures of every description, musical scores for symphonies and dances and hymns, machines, tools, boats, houses, churches and temples, statues, vases, books of poetry and of prose, furniture and clothing, newspapers, postage stamps, flowers, trees, stones, musical instruments. Now we instruct someone to enter the warehouse and bring out all of the works of art it contains. He will be able to do this with reasonable success, despite the fact that, as even the aestheticians must admit, he possesses no satisfactory definition of Art in terms of some common denominator, because no such definition has yet been found. Now imagine the same

[3] See F. Waismann, "Analytic-Synthetic II", *Analysis,* 11 (1950), p. 27.

person sent into the warehouse to bring out all objects with Significant Form, or all objects of Expression. He would rightly be baffled; he knows a work of art when he sees one, but he has little or no idea what to look for when he is told to bring an object that possesses Significant Form.

To be sure, there are many occasions on which we are not sure whether something is a work of art or not; that is, we are not sure whether to call a given drawing or musical composition a work of art or not. Are "Nearer My God to Thee" and the political cartoons of Mr. Low works of art? But this merely reflects the systematic vagueness of the concepts in question, or what Dr. Waismann on another occasion has called their 'open texture'; a vagueness, note, which the definitions of the aestheticians do nothing at all to remove. On such occasions we can, of course, tighten the texture, remove some of the vagueness, by making a decision, drawing a line; and perhaps curators and purchasing committees of art museums are sometimes forced for obvious practical reasons to do this. But in doing so, they and we are not discovering anything about Art.

We do know what art is when no one asks us what it is; that is, we know quite well how to use the word 'art' and the phrase 'work of art' correctly. And when someone asks us what art is, we do *not* know; that is, we are at a loss to produce any simple formula, or any complex one, which will neatly exhibit the logic of this word and this phrase. It is the compulsion to reduce the complexity of aesthetic concepts to simplicity, neatness, and order that moves the aesthetician to make his first mistake, to ask 'What is Art?' and to expect to find an answer like the answer that can be given to 'What is helium?'

What I have said about Art in this section applies, *mutatis mutandis,* to Beauty, the Aesthetic Experience, the Creative Act, and all of the other entities with which traditional aesthetics concerns itself.

Where there is no mystery, there is no need for removing a mystery and certainly none for inventing one.

3. *Common Denominators and Similarities.* Is the search for common characteristics among works of art, then, a fool's errand?

That depends upon what we expect to find. If we expect to find some common denominator in Parker's sense, we are bound to be disappointed. We shall get ourselves enmeshed in unnecessary difficulties, and the definitions which we hope will free us from the net will be specious at best. If we say 'Art is Significant Form' we may feel momentarily enlightened; but when we come to reflect upon what we mean by 'significant form' we shall find ourselves entangled again. For the notion of Significant Form is clearly more obscure than is that of Art or Beauty, as the example of the warehouse above amply illustrates; the same holds for Expression, Intuition, Representation, and the other favoured candidates of the aestheticians. Nor will it do to say, as Professor Munro does,[4] that "art is skill in providing stimuli to satisfactory aesthetic experience". This has merely a scientific *sound,* and this sound is about as close as the effort to make aesthetics scientific comes to science. The notion of aesthetic experience is fraught with the same difficulties as the notion of art. To put it dogmatically, there is no such thing as *the* Aesthetic Experience; different sorts of experiences are properly referred to as aesthetic. Do not say they must all be contemplative. Does that really help at all?

There is, however, a fruitful and enlightening search for similarities and resemblances in art which the search for the common denominator sometimes furthers, the search for what, to torture a phrase of Wittgenstein's, we can call 'family resemblances'. When we squint we can sometimes see features of an object which otherwise we should miss. So in aesthetics, when we narrow our view, when in the search for the common denominator we carefully select our examples and restrict our sight, we may not see what we are looking for, but we may see something of more interest and importance. The simplifying formulae of the aestheticians are not to be scrapped merely because they fail to do what they are designed to do. What fails to do one thing may do another. The mistake of the aestheticians can be turned to advantage. The suspicion that aesthetics is not nonsense is often justified. For the idea that there is a unity among the arts, properly employed, can lead to the uncovering of similarities which, when

[4] Thomas Munro, *The Arts and Their Interrelations* (New York, 1949), p. 108.

noticed, enrich our commerce with art. Croce's supposed discovery that Art is Expression calls our attention to, among other things, an interesting feature of some, if not all, works of art, namely, their indifference to the distinction between the real and the unreal.

Or, to take examples from critics, when F. R. Leavis says of Crabbe, "His art is that of the short-story writer",[5] and when Professor Stechow compares the fourth movement of Schumann's "Rhenish" Symphony with certain features of the Cologne Cathedral,[6] we have something of interest and importance. Our attention is refocused on certain works, and we see them in a new light. One of the offices of creative criticism, as of creative aesthetics, is the finding and pointing out of precisely such similarities.

4. *Aesthetic Theories Reconsidered.* Philosophical mistakes are rarely downright howlers; they have a point. What I have said is, I think, correct, but it neglects an important facet of the quest for essences, a by-product of that search, so to speak, which we should not ignore. An aesthetic theory, by which I mean a systematic answer to such questions as 'What is Art?' 'What is Beauty?' and the like, frequently does something quite other than what it sets out to do. The assumption underlying traditional aesthetics, as Parker states it in the passage quoted above, is wrong, and I hope I have shown why it is wrong. It does not follow from this, however, that aesthetic theories are wholly without point, that they are merely mistaken, that formulae like 'Art is Significant Form' are worthless, useless, or meaningless. They do serve a purpose, but their purpose is not that which Parker assigns them. Considered in context, in the historical or personal context, for example, they are frequently seen to have a point which has nothing to do with the philosophical excuses that are made for them.

Take Bell's famous dictum that 'Art is Significant Form'. It does not help us to understand what art is at all, and to that

---

[5] F. R. Leavis, *Revaluation: Tradition and Development in English Poetry* (London, 1936), p. 125.

[6] Wolfgang Stechow, "Problems of Structure in Some Relations Between the Visual Arts and Music", *The Journal of Aesthetics and Art Criticism*, xi (1953), 325.

extent it is a failure; its shortcomings in this direction have been exposed on numerous occasions. It is easy to beat Bell down; he is so vulnerable. But when we stop to consider that he was an Englishman and when he wrote his book on art (1913) and what the taste of the English was like then and of his association with Roger Fry, the statement that 'Art is Significant Form' loses some of its mystifying sound. It has a *point*. Not the point that Bell thinks it has, for Bell was also looking for the common denominator; another point. We might put it this way. The taste of Edwardian Englishmen in art was restricted to what we pejoratively call the 'academic'. Subject-matter was of prime importance to them—portraits of eminent persons, landscapes with or without cows, genre scenes, pictures of fox hunts, and the rest. Bell had seen the paintings of Cezanne, Matisse, and Picasso, and he was quick to see that subject-matter was not of prime importance in them, that the value of the paintings did not rest on realism or sentimental associations. It rested on what? Well, 'significant form'; lines and colours and patterns and harmonies that stir apart from associations evoked by subject-matter. He found also that he could look at other paintings, older paintings, paintings by the Venetian and Dutch masters, for example, and at vases and carpets and sculptures in the same way he looked at Cezanne. He found such looking rewarding, exciting. But when he turned to the pictures of the academicians, the thrill·disappeared; they could not be looked at profitably in this way. What was more natural, then, than that he should announce his discovery by saying 'Art *is* Significant Form'? He *had* discovered something for himself. Not the essence of Art, as the philosophers would have it, although he thought that this is what he found, but *a new way of looking at pictures*. He wanted to share his discovery with others and to reform English taste. *Here* is the point of his dictum; 'Art is Significant Form' is a slogan, the epitome of a platform of aesthetic reform. It has work to do. Not the work which the philosophers assign it, but a work of teaching people a new way of looking at pictures.

When we blow the dust of philosophic cant away from aesthetic theories and look at them in this way, they take on an importance which otherwise they seem to lack. Read Aristotle's

Poetics, not as a philosophical exercise in definition, but as instruction in one way to read tragic poetry, and it takes on a new life. Many of the other dicta of the aestheticians can also be examined in this light. We know that as definitions they will not do; but as instruments of instruction or reform they will do. Perhaps that is why they have had more real weight with practising critics than they have had with philosophers. The critics have caught the point, where the philosophers, misguided from the start by a foolish preoccupation with definition, have missed it.

5. *Aesthetics and Criticism; the Second Mistake.* One of the prime reasons for the aesthetician's search for definitions of Art, Beauty, and the rest, is his supposition that unless we know what Art or Beauty is, we cannot say what good art or beautiful art is. Put it in the form of an assumption: Criticism presupposes Aesthetic Theory. This assumption contains the second mistake on which traditional aesthetics rests, namely, the view that responsible criticism is impossible without standards or criteria universally applicable to all works of art. The second mistake is in this way closely related to the first.

To see more clearly how this assumption operates, we can turn to a recent book by Mr. Harold Osborne,[7] *Aesthetics and Criticism*. Osborne believes that "a theory of the nature of artistic excellence is implicit in every critical assertion which is other than autobiographical record", and he thinks that "until the theory has been made explicit the criticism is without meaning" (p. 3). By a 'theory of the nature of artistic excellence' Osborne means a theory of the nature of Beauty (p. 3).

Osborne examines several theories of the nature of Beauty and finds them all wanting. His moves against them are instructive. Take, for example, his move against a version of the Realistic Theory in Chapter V, that theory holding that artistic excellence consists in 'truth to life'—or so Osborne states it. He correctly notes that practising critics have rarely insisted that verisimilitude is a necessary condition of artistic excellence, and we should all agree that it is not. "But", says Osborne, "if correspondence with real or possible actuality is not a necessary condition of

[7] Routledge and Kegan Paul Ltd., London, 1955.

artistic excellence, then most certainly it is not and cannot be of itself an *artistic* virtue, or an aesthetic merit, in those works of literature where it happens to occur" (p. 93). This is a curious argument. It seems to contain a glaring non-sequitur. But what leads Osborne from his protasis to his conclusion is the assumption that the only acceptable reason offerable for a critical judgement of a work of art is one framed in terms of a characteristic which all works of art, *qua* works of art, must possess. Since we admit that not all works of art must possess truth to life or verisimilitude, we cannot use their adventitious possession of this property as a reason for praising, judging, or commending them as works of art.

Now surely this is mistaken. We can agree that correspondence with real or possible actuality, whatever that may mean, is not a *necessary* condition of artistic excellence; that is, it is *not* necessary that it appear among the reasons offerable for the judgement that a given work of art is good or beautiful. But it does not follow that therefore it does not and cannot appear as *a* reason for such a judgement. We can and do praise works of art, *as* works of art, whatever the force of that is, for a variety of reasons, and not always the same variety. Osborne's reply here is that in doing so we are being 'illogical and inconsistent'. Attacking the users of the Hedonistic Criterion, he says, "In so far as he [the critic] also uses other criteria [than the hedonistic one] for grading and assessing works of art, he is being illogical and inconsistent with himself whenever he does introduce the hedonistic—or emotional —assumption" (p. 139). But why? There is nothing whatever illogical or inconsistent about praising, grading, or judging a work of art for more than one reason, unless we assume with Osborne that one and only one reason is offerable on pain of inconsistency, which is clearly not the case in art or anywhere else.

Osborne, true to the assumptions of traditional aesthetics, is looking for that condition which is both necessary and sufficient for artistic excellence or merit. His own candidate for that condition is what he calls "configurational coherence". But if anything pointed were needed to convince us of the emptiness of the search, it is the unintelligibility of Osborne's account of "beauty

as configuration". If what I have said above about the concepts of
Art and Beauty is true, we should not be surprised by this. For
'art' and 'beauty' do not name one and only one substance and
attribute respectively; no wonder we cannot find the one thing
they name or render intelligible the felt discovery that they do
name one thing. We can *make* each of them name one thing if we
wish. But why should we bother? We get along very well with
them as they are.

6. *Ethics and Criticism; the Second Mistake Again.* 'But
surely', someone will say, 'this cannot be the whole story. We can
and do say that this work of art, this picture, for example, is
better than that, or that this is a good one and that one is not. Do
we not presuppose certain standards or criteria when we make
such judgements? And isn't this really all that Osborne and other
aestheticians have in mind when they insist that criticism presupposes aesthetic theory? They are looking for the standards of
critical judgement and taste in the nature of art, just as many
moralists have looked for the standards of right conduct in the nature of man. They may be looking in the wrong place, but clearly
they are right in assuming that there must be something to find.'

My reply is this: they are not looking in the wrong place so
much as they are looking for the wrong thing. The bases of
responsible criticism are indeed to be found *in* the work of art
and nowhere else, but this in no way implies that critical judgements presuppose any canons, rules, standards, or criteria applicable to all works of art.

When we say that a certain knife is a good knife, we have in
mind certain features of the knife, or of knives in general, which
we believe will substantiate or support this claim: the sharpness
of the blade, the sturdiness of the handle, the durability of the
metal, the way it fits the hand, and so on. There are a number of
such considerations, all of which refer to characteristics of the
knife and not to our feelings about or attitudes towards it, which
may be said to constitute the criteria of a good knife. Special
criteria may be adduced for fishing knives as opposed to butcher
knives, and so on, but this does not affect the issue in question.
Note first that there is no definite or exhaustively specifiable list
of criteria in common and universal employment; it does not

make sense to ask how many there are or whether we have considered them all. But there are generally accepted criteria with which we are all familiar which we use to support our judgements, though in cases of special instruments or implements, like ophthalmoscopes, only specialists are acquainted with the criteria. Secondly, note how the criteria are related to the purposes or functions of knives, to the uses to which we put them, the demands we make upon them. 'Knife', we might say, is a function-word, a word that names something which is usually defined by its function or functions. The criteria, we can say loosely, are derivable from the definition. This second consideration has led some aestheticians to look for the standards of taste and criticism in the function of art.

Now take apples. They have, of course, no function. We use them, we do things with them—eat them, use them for decoration, feed them to pigs, press cider from them, and so on—but none of these things can be said to constitute the function of an apple. Depending, however, on how we use them or what we use them for, we can frame lists of criteria similar to the lists for knives. The best apples for decoration are not always the best for eating, nor are the best for making pies always the best for making cider. Now take mathematicians. A mathematician, unless he is assigned a particular work to do, again has no function. There are certain things a mathematician does, however, and in terms of these we can again frame criteria for judging, praising, grading, and commending mathematicians. Finally, take men in general. We often praise a man, *as* a man, as opposed to as a plumber or a mathematician, and we call this sort of praise moral praise. Here again, we have criteria for assessing the moral worth of men, although, theological considerations aside, we do not frame them in terms of man's function, purpose, or task, even if some moralists, like Aristotle, have tried to frame them in terms of man's end. But we make demands on men, moral demands on all men, and our criteria reflect these demands.

Let us turn now to art. The question we have to raise is this: Are critical judgements of pictures and poems logically symmetrical to the sorts of judgements we have been considering? I think they are not, or not entirely. Not because they are somehow more subjective or unreliable than other value judgements (this issue is as false as an issue can be!), but because the pattern of justification and support which is appropriate to them is of a different sort. Any critical judgement, to be justified, must be supported by reasons; this goes without saying, for this is what 'justification' means. But must the reasons offerable and acceptable in cases of critical appraisal be of the same order or type as those offerable and acceptable in cases of instruments, implements, useful objects, professional services, jobs, offices, or moral conduct? In particular, must there be any general rules, standards, criteria, canons, or laws applicable to all works of art by which alone such critical appraisals can be supported? I think not.

In the first place, we should note that only a man corrupted by aesthetics would think of judging a work of art *as* a work of art in general, as opposed to as this poem, that picture, or this symphony. There is some truth in the contention that the notions of Art and Work of Art are special aestheticians' concepts. This follows quite naturally from the absence of any distinguishing feature or features common to all works of art as such, and from the absence of any single demand or set of demands which we make on all works of art as such. Despite the occasional claim that it has, Art has no function or purpose, in the sense in which knives and ophthalmoscopes have functions, and this is an insight to be gained from the 'art for art's sake' position. This does not mean that we cannot use individual works of art for special purposes; we can and do. We can use novels and poems and symphonies to put us to sleep or wake us up; we can use pictures to cover spots on the wall, vases to hold flowers, and sculptures for paper weights or door stops. This is what lends point to the distinction between judging something *as* a work of art and judging it *as* a sedative, stimulant, or paper weight; but we cannot conclude from this that Art has some special function or purpose in addition to the purposes to which it can be put.

Similarly there is no one thing which we *do* with all works of art: some we hang, some we play, some we perform, some we read; some we look at, some we listen to, some we analyse, some we contemplate, and so on. There is no special aesthetic use of works of art, even though it may make sense, and even be true, to say that a person who uses a statue as a door stop is not using it as a work of art; he is not doing one of the things we normally do with works of art; he is not treating it properly, we might say. But the proper treatment of works of art varies from time to time and from place to place. It was quite proper for a cave man to hurl his spear at the drawing of a bison, just as it was quite proper for the Egyptians to seal up paintings and sculptures in a tomb. Such treatment does not render the object thus treated not a work of art. The attempt to define Art in terms of what we do with certain objects is as doomed as any other. From this and the first consideration it follows that there is no way by which we can derive the criteria of taste and criticism from the function of art or from its use.

The remaining parallel is with moral appraisal, and this is the most interesting of them all. It has been, and perhaps still is, a common view among philosophers that Beauty and Goodness are two species of the same genus, namely, Value, and that therefore there are at least two classes of value judgements, namely, moral judgements and aesthetic judgements. For this reason there is a tendency further to suppose that there is a logical symmetry between the two. But the supposition of symmetry is a mistake, and I am led to suspect that it does little but harm to suppose that Beauty and Goodness are two species of the same genus at all. There are clearly certain similarities between the two, that is, between the logic of statements of the form 'This is good' and the logic of statements of the form 'This is beautiful'—they are used in many of the same ways—but this must not blind us to the differences. Criticism suffers from a very natural comparison with ethics.

Moral appraisal is like the other forms of appraisal, in this respect; it expresses a desire for uniformity. It is when we are interested in uniformity of size, milk producing capacity, conduct, and so on, that standards or criteria become so important. We maintain standards in products and in workmanship; we enforce them, hold ourselves up to them, teach them to our children, insist on them, and so on, all for the sake of a certain uniformity.

In morals we *are* interested in uniformity, at least in what we expect men not to do; that is one reason why rules and laws are necessary and why they play such an important rôle in moral appraisal. But in art, unless, like Plato, we wish to be legislators and to require something of art, demand that it perform a specified educational and social service, we are not as a rule interested in uniformity. Some critics and aestheticians are, of course, interested in uniformity—uniformity in the works of art themselves or uniformity in our approach to them. For them it is quite natural to demand criteria. For them it is also quite natural to formulate theories of Art and Beauty. Remember what we said about aesthetic theories above: the definitions in which they issue are often slogans of reform. As such they are also often devices for the encouragement of uniformity. But this merely betrays the persuasive character of many aesthetic theories, and the peculiar legislative posture of some critics and aestheticians is no warrant for the assumption that the criteria in question are necessary for responsible criticism. Nor should it blind us to the fact that we do quite well without them. Criticism has in no way been hampered by the absence of generally applicable canons and norms, and where such norms have been proposed they have either, like the notorious Unities in the case of tragedy, been shown to be absurd, or else, like the requirements of balance, harmony, and unity in variety, they have been so general, equivocal, and empty as to be useless in critical practice. Ordinarily we feel no constraint in praising one novel for its verisimilitude, another for its humour, and still another for its plot or characterization. We remark on the richness of Van Gogh's impasto, but we do not find it a fault in a Chinese scroll painting that it is flat and smooth. Botticelli's lyric grace is his glory, but Giotto and Chardin are not to be condemned because their poetry is of another order. The merits of Keats and Shelley are not those of Donne and Herbert. And why should Shakespeare and Aeschylus be measured by the same rod? Different works of art are, or may be, praiseworthy or blameworthy for different reasons, and not always the same reasons. A quality that is praiseworthy in one painting may be blameworthy in another; realism is not always a virtue, but this does not mean that it is not sometimes a virtue.[8]

Mr. Hampshire has put the reason why the criteria sought by the aestheticians are so 'elusive' and why the parallel with ethics is a mistake in this way: "A work of art", he says, "is gratuitous. It is not *essentially* the answer to a question or the solution of a presented problem" (*op. cit.* p. 162). There is no one problem being solved or question answered by all poems, all pictures, all symphonies, let alone all works of art. If we set a number of people to doing the same thing, we can rate them on how well they do it. We have, or can frame, a criterion. But not all artists are doing the same thing—solving the same problem, answering the same question, playing the same game, running the same race. Some of them may be, we do group artists together by 'schools', and in other ways, to indicate precisely this kind of similarity; but only in so far as they are does it make sense to compare and appraise them on the same points. It is no criticism of Dickens that he did not write like Henry James. Writing a novel or a lyric poem may, in some interesting respects, be like playing a game or solving a problem, we in fact speak of artists as solving problems. But it is also different; so that if we wish to retain the analogy we must call attention to the differences by saying that not all poets or novelists are playing the *same* game, solving the *same* problems. There is indeed a certain gratuitousness in art which destroys the parallelism or symmetry between moral and aesthetic appraisal.

But there is also a gratuitousness in aesthetic criticism. Moral appraisal, like legal judgement, is a practical necessity; aesthetic appraisal is not. That is why the claim that in art it is all a matter of taste is tolerable, even if it is false, when this sounds so shocking in morals. We can live side by side in peace and amity with those whose tastes differ quite radically from our own; similar differences in moral standards are more serious. And yet, of course, aesthetic criticism is not merely a matter of taste, if by taste we mean unreasoned preferences. Taste does play an impor-

---

[8] I owe much in this section to Helen Knight's "The Use of 'Good' in Aesthetic Judgments", *Aesthetics and Language,* William Elton edn. (Oxford, 1954), pp. 147 ff., and to Stuart Hampshire's "Logic and Appreciation", *ibid.* pp. 161 ff.

tant part in the differences among critical appraisals, but we are clearly not satisfied when, in answer to our question 'Why is it good?' or 'What's good about it?', we are told 'It's good because I like it'. Mrs. Knight correctly notes that "my *liking* a picture is never a criterion of its goodness" (*op. cit.* p. 154). That is, my liking a picture is no reason for its *being* good, though it may be a reason for my *saying* that it is good.

But if it is not all a matter of liking and disliking, why is it that a certain feature is a virtue in a given work of art? If someone tells me that a certain work of art is good for such and such reasons, how can I tell whether the reasons he offers are good reasons or not, or even if they are relevant? These questions are not easily answered, for in practice we adduce many considerations for saying that a work of art is good or that a certain feature of it is a virtue. I will make no attempt to canvass these considerations but will close with some observations on a logical feature of the problem.

We are confronted, I think, with a problem that is really two problems: there is the problem of saying why a given work of art is good or bad, and there is the problem of saying why our reasons are good or bad, or even relevant. We may praise a picture, say, for its subtle balance, colour contrast, and draughtsmanship; this is saying why the picture is good. We may now go on to raise the more 'philosophical' question of what makes balance, or this sort of colour contrast, or this kind of draughtsmanship an artistic virtue. The first sort of question, the question of why the work of art is good or bad, is decided by appeal to the 'good-making characteristics' or 'criterion-characters' of the work of art in question, that is, by an appeal to certain objectively discriminable characteristics of the work under discussion. These characteristics are many and various; there is a large variety of reasons offerable for a work of art's being a good or bad work of art. The second sort of question, the question of the worth or relevance of the reasons offered in answer to the first question, is settled by appeal either to custom or to decision. In this respect aesthetic criticism is very like moral appraisal. We either simply praise what is customarily praised and condemn what is customarily condemned or we *decide* what the criteria shall be. This does not mean that the criteria, that is, the reasons offerable for a work of art's being good or bad, are arbitrary. There may be plenty of reasons why one feature is a 'criterion-character' and another is not. Part of the reason may be psychological, part sociological, part metaphysical, or even religious and ethical. Only an aesthete ignores, or tries to ignore, the many relations of a poem or picture to life and concentrates on what are called the purely 'formal' values of the work at hand; but in doing so he *determines* what he will accept as a reason for a work of art's being good or bad. That a work of art assists the cause of the proletariat in the class struggle *is* a reason for its being a good work of art to a convinced Marxist, but it is not a reason, let alone a good reason, to the bourgeois aesthete. That a picture contains nude figures is a reason, to the puritan and the prude, for condemning it, though no enlightened man can be brought to accept it. Thus morals and politics and religion do enter into our critical judgements, even when we claim that they should not.

I noted above that there is no one use which we make of all works of art, nor is there any one demand or set of demands which we make on them. This is, I think, important, and serves to explain, at least in part, the actual relativity of aesthetic criteria. What one age looks for in painting or in literature, another age may neglect. What one group demands, another forbids. We are not always consistent in even our own demands on art, and I can see no reason why we should be. We can be interested in works of art for many reasons, and some of these reasons may be more decisive at one time or in one set of circumstances than they are at another time or in another set of circumstances. This affects the very logic of critical appraisal by determining the relevance and merit of the reasons we offer for our judgements. We are well aware of the fact that the estimate of a given poet or painter changes from period to period. El Greco's or Shakespeare's reputation has not always been what it is, and no one should be surprised if it should change in the future. But if we examine the reasons that have been offered for the different estimates, we find that they too are different. Different reasons are persuasive at different times and in different contexts. The same explanation is operative: the needs and interests that art gratifies are different from time to time and, to a lesser extent perhaps, from person to person. But as the needs and interests vary, so also will the criteria and the weight we place on them. This is a vicious relativism only to those who are morally disposed to insist on the uniformity of taste.

Summary: I have tried to show (1) that the search for essences in aesthetics is a mistake, arising from the failure to appreciate the complex but not mysterious logic of such words and phrases as 'art', 'beauty', 'the aesthetic experience', and so on. But (2) although the characteristics common to all works of art are the object of a fool's errand, the search for similarities in sometimes very different works of art can be profitably pursued, and this search is occasionally stimulated by the formulae of the aestheticians. (3) Although the definitions of the aestheticians are useless for the role usually assigned to them, we must not ignore the live purpose they frequently serve as slogans in the effort to change taste and as instruments for opening up new avenues of appreciation. (4) If the search for the common denominator of all works of art is abandoned, abandoned with it must be the attempt to derive the criteria of critical appreciation and appraisal from the nature of art. (5) Traditional aesthetics mistakenly supposes that responsible criticism is impossible without a set of rules, canons, or standards applicable to all works of art. This supposition arises from an uncritical assimilation of the pattern of critical appraisal to that of appraisal in other areas, particularly morals, and from a failure to appreciate the gratuitousness of art and the manner in which reasons are operative in the justification of critical judgements.

Morris Weitz

The Role of Theory in Aesthetics

Theory has been central in aesthetics and is still the preoccupation of the philosophy of art. Its main avowed concern remains the determination of the nature of art which can be formulated into a definition of it. It construes definition as the statement of the necessary and sufficient properties of what is being defined, where the statement purports to be a true or false claim about the essence of art, what characterizes and distinguishes it from everything else. Each of the great theories of art—Formalism, Voluntarism, Emotionalism, Intellectualism, Intuitionism, Organicism—converges on the attempt to state the defining properties of art. Each claims that it is the true theory because it has formulated correctly into a real definition the nature of art; and that the others are false because they have left out some necessary or sufficient property. Many theorists contend that their enterprise is no mere intellectual exercise but an absolute necessity for any understanding of art and our proper evaluation of it. Unless we know what art is, they say, what are its necessary and sufficient properties, we cannot begin to respond to it adequately or to say why one work is good or better than another. Aesthetic theory, thus, is important not only in itself but for the foundations of both appreciation and criticism. Philosophers, critics, and even artists who have written on art, agree that what is primary in aesthetics is a theory about the nature of art.

Is aesthetic theory, in the sense of a true definition or set of necessary and sufficient properties of art, possible? If nothing else does, the history of aesthetics itself should give one enormous

[Reprinted from *The Journal of Aesthetics and Art Criticism*, 15: 27–35 (1956) . Footnote 7 has been omitted.]

pause here. For, in spite of the many theories, we seem no nearer our goal today than we were in Plato's time. Each age, each art-movement, each philosophy of art, tries over and over again to establish the stated ideal only to be succeeded by a new or revised theory, rooted, at least in part, in the repudiation of preceding ones. Even today, almost everyone interested in aesthetic matters is still deeply wedded to the hope that the correct theory of art is forthcoming. We need only examine the numerous new books on art in which new definitions are proffered; or, in our own country especially, the basic textbooks and anthologies to recognize how strong the priority of a theory of art is.

In this essay I want to plead for the rejection of this problem. I want to show that theory—in the requisite classical sense—is *never* forthcoming in aesthetics, and that we would do much better as philosophers to supplant the question, "What is the nature of art?," by other questions, the answers to which will provide us with all the understanding of the arts there can be. I want to show that the inadequacies of the theories are not primarily occasioned by any legitimate difficulty such e.g., as the vast complexity of art, which might be corrected by further probing and research. Their basic inadequacies reside instead in a fundamental misconception of art. Aesthetic theory—all of it—is wrong in principle in thinking that a correct theory is possible because it radically misconstrues the logic of the concept of art. Its main contention that "art" is amenable to real or any kind of true definition is false. Its attempt to discover the necessary and sufficient properties of art is logically misbegotten for the very simple reason that such a set and, consequently, such a formula about it, is never forthcoming. Art, as the logic of the concept shows, has no set of necessary and sufficient properties, hence a theory of it is logically impossible and not merely factually difficult. Aesthetic theory tries to define what cannot be defined in its requisite sense. But in recommending the repudiation of aesthetic theory I shall not argue from this, as too many others have done, that its logical confusions render it meaningless or worthless. On the contrary, I wish to reassess its role and its contribution primarily in order to show that it is of the greatest importance to our understanding of the arts.

Let us now survey briefly some of the more famous extant aesthetic theories in order to see if they do incorporate correct and adequate statements about the nature of art. In each of these there is the assumption that it is the true enumeration of the defining properties of art, with the implication that previous theories have stressed wrong definitions. Thus, to begin with, consider a famous version of Formalist theory, that propounded by Bell and Fry. It is true that they speak mostly of painting in their writings but both assert that what they find in that art can be generalized for what is "art" in the others as well. The essence of painting, they maintain, are the plastic elements in relation. Its defining property is significant form, i.e., certain combinations of lines, colors, shapes, volumes—everything on the canvas except the representational elements—which evoke a unique response to such combinations. Painting is definable as plastic organization. The nature of art, what it *really* is, so their theory goes, is a unique combination of certain elements (the specifiable plastic ones) in their relations. Anything which is art is an instance of significant form; and anything which is not art has no such form.

To this the Emotionalist replies that the truly essential property of art has been left out. Tolstoy, Ducasse, or any of the advocates of this theory, find that the requisite defining property is not significant form but rather the expression of emotion in some sensuous public medium. Without projection of emotion into some piece of stone or words or sounds, etc., there can be no art. Art is really such embodiment. It is this that uniquely characterizes art, and any true, real definition of it, contained in some adequate theory of art, must so state it.

The Intuitionist disclaims both emotion and form as defining properties. In Croce's version, for example, art is identified not with some physical, public object but with a specific creative, cognitive and spiritual act. Art is really a first stage of knowledge in which certain human beings (artists) bring their images and intuitions into lyrical clarification or expression. As such, it is an awareness, non-conceptual in character, of the unique individuality of things; and since it exists below the level of conceptualization or action, it is without scientific or moral content. Croce singles out as the defining essence of art this first stage of spiritual life and advances its identification with art as a philosophically true theory or definition.

The Organicist says to all of this that art is really a class of organic wholes consisting of distinguishable, albeit inseparable, elements in their causally efficacious relations which are presented in some sensuous medium. In A. C. Bradley, in piece-meal versions of it in literary criticism, or in my own generalized adaptation of it in my *Philosophy of the Arts,* what is claimed is that anything which is a work of art is in its nature a unique complex of interrelated parts—in painting, for example, lines, colors, volumes, subjects, etc., all interacting upon one another on a paint surface of some sort. Certainly, at one time at least it seemed to me that this organic theory constituted the one true and real definition of art.

My final example is the most interesting of all, logically speaking. This is the Voluntarist theory of Parker. In his writings on art, Parker persistently calls into question the traditional simple-minded definitions of aesthetics. "The assumption underlying every philosophy of art is the existence of some common nature present in all the arts." [1] "All the so popular brief definitions of art—'significant form,' 'expression,' 'intuition,' 'objectified pleasure'—are fallacious, either because, while true of art, they are also true of much that is not art, and hence fail to differentiate art from other things; or else because they neglect some essential aspect of art." [2] But instead of inveighing against the attempt at definition of art itself, Parker insists that what is needed is a complex definition rather than a simple one. "The definition of art must therefore be in terms of a complex of characteristics. Failure to recognize this has been the fault of all the well-known definitions." [3] His own version of Voluntarism is the theory that art is essentially three things: embodiment of wishes and desires imaginatively satisfied, language, which characterizes the public medium of art, and harmony, which unifies the language with the layers of imaginative projections. Thus, for Parker, it is a true

[1] D. Parker, "The Nature of Art," reprinted in E. Vivas and M. Krieger, *The Problems of Aesthetics,* (N.Y., 1953), p. 90.
[2] *Ibid.,* pp. 93–94.
[3] *Ibid.,* p. 94.

definition to say of art that it is ". . . the provision of satisfaction through the imagination, social significance, and harmony. I am claiming that nothing except works of art possesses all three of these marks." [4]

Now, all of these sample theories are inadequate in many different ways. Each purports to be a complete statement about the defining features of all works of art and yet each of them leaves out something which the others take to be central. Some are circular, e.g., the Bell-Fry theory of art as significant form which is defined in part in terms of our response to significant form. Some of them, in their search for necessary and sufficient properties, emphasize too few properties, like (again) the Bell-Fry definition which leaves out subject-representation in painting, or the Croce theory which omits inclusion of the very important feature of the public, physical character, say, of architecture. Others are too general and cover objects that are not art as well as works of art. Organicism is surely such a view since it can be applied to *any* causal unity in the natural world as well as to art.[5] Still others rest on dubious principles, e.g., Parker's claim that art embodies imaginative satisfactions, rather than real ones; or Croce's assertion that there is non-conceptual knowledge. Consequently, even if art has one set of necessary and sufficient properties, none of the theories we have noted or, for that matter, no aesthetic theory yet proposed, has enumerated that set to the satisfaction of all concerned.

Then there is a different sort of difficulty. As real definitions, these theories are supposed to be factual reports on art. If they are, may we not ask, Are they empirical and open to verification or falsification? For example, what would confirm or disconfirm the theory that art is significant form or embodiment of emotion or creative synthesis of images? There does not even seem to be a hint of the kind of evidence which might be forthcoming to test these theories; and indeed one wonders if they are perhaps honorific definitions of "art," that is, proposed redefinitions in terms of

---

[4] *Ibid.*, p. 104.

[5] See M. Macdonald's review of my *Philosophy of the Arts, Mind,* Oct. 1951, pp. 561–564, for a brilliant discussion of this objection to the Organic theory.

some *chosen* conditions for applying the concept of art, and not true or false reports on the essential properties of art at all.

But all these criticisms of traditional aesthetic theories—that they are circular, incomplete, untestable, pseudo-factual, disguised proposals to change the meaning of concepts—have been made before. My intention is to go beyond these to make a much more fundamental criticism, namely, that aesthetic theory is a logically vain attempt to define what cannot be defined, to state the necessary and sufficient properties of that which has no necessary and sufficient properties, to conceive the concept of art as closed when its very use reveals and demands its openness.

The problem with which we must begin is not "What is art?," but "What sort of concept is 'art'?" Indeed, the root problem of philosophy itself is to explain the relation between the employment of certain kinds of concepts and the conditions under which they can be correctly applied. If I may paraphrase Wittgenstein, we must not ask, What is the nature of any philosophical x?, or even, according to the semanticist, What does "x" mean?, a transformation that leads to the disastrous interpretation of "art" as a name for some specifiable class of objects; but rather, What is the use or employment of "x"? What does "x" do in the language? This, I take it, is the initial question, the begin-all if not the end-all of any philosophical problem and solution. Thus, in aesthetics, our first problem is the elucidation of the actual employment of the concept of art, to give a logical description of the actual functioning of the concept, including a description of the conditions under which we correctly use it or its correlates.

My model in this type of logical description or philosophy derives from Wittgenstein. It is also he who, in his refutation of philosophical theorizing in the sense of constructing definitions of philosophical entities, has furnished contemporary aesthetics with a starting point for any future progress. In his new work, *Philosophical Investigations,*[6] Wittgenstein raises as an illustra-

---

[6] L. Wittgenstein, *Philosophical Investigations*, (Oxford, 1953), tr. by E. Anscombe; see esp. Part I, Sections 65–75. All quotations are from these sections.

tive question, What is a game? The traditional philosophical, theoretical answer would be in terms of some exhaustive set of properties common to all games. To this Wittgenstein says, let us consider what we call "games": "I mean board-games, card-games, ball-games, Olympic games, and so on. What is common to them all?—Don't say: 'there *must* be something common, or they would not be called "games"' but *look and see* whether there is anything common to all.—For if you look at them you will not see something that is common to *all,* but similarities, relationships, and a whole series of them at that . . ."

Card games are like board games in some respects but not in others. Not all games are amusing, nor is there always winning or losing or competition. Some games resemble others in some respects—that is all. What we find are no necessary and sufficient properties, only "a complicated network of similarities overlapping and crisscrossing," such that we can say of games that they form a family with family resemblances and no common trait. If one asks what a game is, we pick out sample games, describe these, and add, "This and *similar things* are called 'games'." This is all we need to say and indeed all any of us knows about games. Knowing what a game is is not knowing some real definition or theory but being able to recognize and explain games and to decide which among imaginary and new examples would or would not be called "games."

The problem of the nature of art is like that of the nature of games, at least in these respects: If we actually look and see what it is that we call "art," we will also find no common properties—only strands of similarities. Knowing what art is is not apprehending some manifest or latent essence but being able to recognize, describe, and explain those things we call "art" in virtue of these similarities.

But the basic resemblance between these concepts is their open texture. In elucidating them, certain (paradigm) cases can be given, about which there can be no question as to their being correctly described as "art" or "game," but no exhaustive set of cases can be given. I can list some cases and some conditions under which I can apply correctly the concept of art but I cannot list all of them, for the all-important reason that unforeseeable or novel conditions are always forthcoming or envisageable.

A concept is open if its conditions of application are emendable and corrigible; i.e., if a situation or case can be imagined or secured which would call for some sort of *decision* on our part to extend the use of the concept to cover this, or to close the concept and invent a new one to deal with the new case and its new property. If necessary and sufficient conditions for the application of a concept can be stated, the concept is a closed one. But this can happen only in logic or mathematics where concepts are constructed and completely defined. It cannot occur with empirically-descriptive and normative concepts unless we arbitrarily close them by stipulating the ranges of their uses.

I can illustrate this open character of "art" best by examples drawn from its sub-concepts. Consider questions like "Is Dos Passos' *U.S.A.* a novel?," Is V. Woolf's *To the Lighthouse* a novel?," "Is Joyce's *Finnegan's Wake* a novel?" On the traditional view, these are construed as factual problems to be answered yes or no in accordance with the presence or absence of defining properties. But certainly this is not how any of these questions is answered. Once it arises, as it has many times in the development of the novel from Richardson to Joyce (e.g., "Is Gide's *The School for Wives* a novel or a diary?"), what is at stake is no factual analysis concerning necessary and sufficient properties but a decision as to whether the work under examination is similar in certain respects to other works, already called "novels," and consequently warrants the extension of the concept to cover the new case. The new work is narrative, fictional, contains character delineation and dialogue but (say) it has no regular time-sequence in the plot or is interspersed with actual newspaper reports. It is like recognized novels, A, B, C . . . , in some respects but not like them in others. But then neither were B and C like A in some respects when it was decided to extend the concept applied to A to B and C. Because work N + 1 (the brand new work) is like A, B, C . . . N in certain respects—has strands of similarity to them—the concept is extended and a new phase of the novel engendered. "Is N 1 a novel?," then, is no factual, but rather a decision problem, where the verdict turns on whether or not we enlarge our set of conditions for applying the concept.

What is true of the novel is, I think, true of every sub-concept of art: "tragedy," "comedy," "painting," "opera," etc., of "art" itself. No "Is X a novel, painting, opera, work of art, etc.?" question allows of a definitive answer in the sense of a factual yes or no report. "Is this *collage* a painting or not?" does not rest on any set of necessary and sufficient properties of painting but on whether we decide—as we did!—to extend "painting" to cover this case.

"Art," itself, is an open concept. New conditions (cases) have constantly arisen and will undoubtedly constantly arise; new art forms, new movements will emerge, which will demand decisions on the part of those interested, usually professional critics, as to whether the concept should be extended or not. Aestheticians may lay down similarity conditions but never necessary and sufficient ones for the correct application of the concept. With "art" its conditions of application can never be exhaustively enumerated since new cases can always be envisaged or created by artists, or even nature, which would call for a decision on someone's part to extend or to close the old or to invent a new concept. (E.g., "It's not a sculpture, it's a mobile.")

What I am arguing, then, is that the very expansive, adventurous character of art, its ever-present changes and novel creations, makes it logically impossible to ensure any set of defining properties. We can, of course, choose to close the concept. But to do this with "art" or "tragedy" or "portraiture," etc., is ludicrous since it forecloses on the very conditions of creativity in the arts.

Of course there are legitimate and serviceable closed concepts in art. But these are always those whose boundaries of conditions have been drawn for a *special* purpose. Consider the difference, for example, between "tragedy" and " (extant) Greek tragedy." The first is open and must remain so to allow for the possibility of new conditions, e.g., a play in which the hero is not noble or fallen or in which there is no hero but other elements that are like those of plays we already call "tragedy." The second is closed. The plays it can be applied to, the conditions under which it can be correctly used are all in, once the boundary, "Greek," is drawn. Here the critic can work out a theory or real definition in which he lists the common properties at least of the extant Greek tragedies. Aristotle's definition, false as it is as a theory of all the plays of Aeschylus, Sophocles, and Euripides, since it does not cover some of them, properly called "tragedies," can be interpreted as a real (albeit incorrect) definition of this closed concept; although it can also be, as it unfortunately has been, conceived as a purported real definition of "tragedy," in which case it suffers from the logical mistake of trying to define what cannot be defined—of trying to squeeze what is an open concept into an honorific formula for a closed concept.

What is supremely important, if the critic is not to become muddled, is to get absolutely clear about the way in which he conceives his concepts; otherwise he goes from the problem of trying to define "tragedy," etc., to an arbitrary closing of the concept in terms of certain preferred conditions or characteristics which he sums up in some linguistic recommendation that he mistakenly thinks is a real definition of the open concept. Thus, many critics and aestheticians ask, "What is tragedy?," choose a class of samples for which they may give a true account of its common properties, and then go on to construe this account of the chosen closed class as a true definition or theory of the whole open class of tragedy. This, I think, is the logical mechanism of most of the so-called theories of the sub-concepts of art: "tragedy," "comedy," "novel," etc. In effect, this whole procedure, subtly deceptive as it is, amounts to a transformation of correct criteria for *recognizing* members of certain legitimately closed classes of works of art into recommended criteria for *evaluating* any putative member of the class.

The primary task of aesthetics is not to seek a theory but to elucidate the concept of art. Specifically, it is to describe the conditions under which we employ the concept correctly. Definition, reconstruction, patterns of analysis are out of place here since they distort and add nothing to our understanding of art. What, then, is the logic of "X is a work of art"?

As we actually use the concept, "Art" is both descriptive (like "chair") and evaluative (like "good"); i.e., we sometimes say, "This is a work of art," to describe something and we sometimes say it to evaluate something. Neither use surprises anyone.

What, first, is the logic of "X is a work of art," when it is a descriptive utterance? What are the conditions under which we would be making such an utterance correctly? There are no necessary and sufficient conditions but there are the strands of similarity conditions, i.e., bundles of properties, none of which need be present but most of which are, when we describe things as works of art. I shall call these the "criteria of recognition" of works of art. All of these have served as the defining criteria of the individual traditional theories of art; so we are already familiar with them. Thus, mostly, when we describe something as a work of art, we do so under the conditions of there being present some sort of artifact, made by human skill, ingenuity, and imagination, which embodies in its sensuous, public medium— stone, wood, sounds, words, etc.—certain distinguishable elements and relations. Special theorists would add conditions like satisfaction of wishes, objectification or expression of emotion, some act of empathy, and so on; but these latter conditions seem to be quite adventitious, present to some but not to other spectators when things are described as works of art. "X is a work of art and contains *no* emotion, expression, act of empathy, satisfaction, etc.," is perfectly good sense and may frequently be true. "X is a work of art and . . . was made by no one," or . . . "exists only in the mind and not in any publicly observable thing," or . . . "was made by accident when he spilled the paint on the canvas," in each case of which a normal condition is denied, are also sensible and capable of being true in certain circumstances. None of the criteria of recognition is a defining one, either necessary or sufficient, because we can sometimes assert of something that it is a work of art and go on to deny any one of these conditions, even the one which has traditionally been taken to be basic, namely, that of being an artifact: Consider, "This piece of driftwood is a lovely piece of sculpture." Thus, to say of anything that it is a work of art is to commit oneself to the presence of *some* of these conditions. One would scarcely describe X as a work of art if X were not an artifact, or a collection of elements sensuously presented in a medium, or a product of human skill, and so on. If none of the conditions were present, if there were no criteria present for recognizing something as a work of art, we would not describe it as one. But, even so, no one of these or any collection of them is either necessary or sufficient.

The elucidation of the descriptive use of "Art" creates little difficulty. But the elucidation of the evaluative use does. For many, especially theorists, "This is a work of art" does more than describe; it also praises. Its conditions of utterance, therefore, include certain preferred properties or characteristics of art. I shall call these "criteria of evaluation." Consider a typical example of this evaluative use, the view according to which to say of something that it is a work of art is to imply that it is a *successful* harmonization of elements. Many of the honorific definitions of art and its sub-concepts are of this form. What is at stake here is that "Art" is construed as an evaluative term which is either identified with its criterion or justified in terms of it. "Art" is defined in terms of its evaluative property, e.g., successful harmonization. On such a view, to say "X is a work of art" is (1) to say something which is taken *to mean* "X is a successful harmonization" (e.g., "Art *is* significant form") or (2) to say something praiseworthy *on the basis* of its successful harmonization. Theorists are never clear whether it is (1) or (2) which is being put forward. Most of them, concerned as they are with this evaluative use, formulate (2) , i.e., that feature of art that *makes* it art in the praise-sense, and then go on to state (1), i.e., the definition of "Art" in terms of its art-making feature. And this is clearly to confuse the conditions under which we say something evaluatively with the meaning of what we say. "This is a work of art," said evaluatively, cannot mean "This is a successful harmonization of elements"—except by stipulation—but at most is said in virtue of the art-making property, which is taken as a (the) criterion of "Art," when "Art" is employed to assess. "This is a work of art," used evaluatively, serves to praise and not to affirm the reason why it is said.

The evaluative use of "Art," although distinct from the conditions of its use, relates in a very intimate way to these conditions. For, in every instance of "This is a work of art" (used to praise) , what happens is that the criterion of evaluation (e.g., successful harmonization) for the employment of the concept of art is converted into a criterion of recognition. This is why, on its evaluative use, "This is a work of art" implies "This has P," where "P" is some chosen art-making property. Thus, if one chooses to employ "Art" evaluatively, as many do, so that "This is a work of art and not (aesthetically) good" makes no sense, he uses "Art" in such a way that he refuses to *call* anything a work of art unless it embodies his criterion of excellence.

There is nothing wrong with the evaluative use; in fact, there is good reason for using "Art" to praise. But what cannot be maintained is that theories of the evaluative use of "Art" are true and real definitions of the necessary and sufficient properties of art. Instead they are honorific definitions, pure and simple, in which "Art" has been redefined in terms of chosen criteria.

But what makes them—these honorific definitions—so supremely valuable is not their disguised linguistic recommendations; rather it is the *debates* over the reasons for changing the criteria of the concept of art which are built into the definitions. In each of the great theories of art, whether correctly understood as honorific definitions or incorrectly accepted as real definitions, what is of the utmost importance are the reasons proffered in the argument for the respective theory, that is, the reasons given for the chosen or preferred criterion of excellence and evaluation. It is this perennial debate over these criteria of evaluation which makes the history of aesthetic theory the important study it is. The value of each of the theories resides in its attempt to state and to justify certain criteria which are either neglected or distorted by previous theories. Look at the Bell-Fry theory again. Of course, "Art is significant form" cannot be accepted as a true, real definition of art; and most certainly it actually functions in their aesthetics as a redefinition of art in terms of the chosen condition of significant form. But what gives it its aesthetic importance is what lies behind the formula: In an age in which literary and representational elements have become paramount in painting, *return* to the plastic ones since these are indigenous to painting. Thus, the role of the theory is not to define anything but to use the definitional form, almost epigrammatically, to pin-point a crucial recommendation to turn our attention once again to the plastic elements in painting.

Once we, as philosophers, understand this distinction between the formula and what lies behind it, it behooves us to deal generously with the traditional theories of art; because incorporated in every one of them is a debate over and argument for emphasizing or centering upon some particular feature of art which has been neglected or perverted. If we take the aesthetic theories literally, as we have seen, they all fail; but if we reconstrue them, in terms of their function and point, as serious and argued-for recommendations to concentrate on certain criteria of excellence in art, we shall see that aesthetic theory is far from worthless. Indeed, it becomes as central as anything in aesthetics, in our understanding of art, for it teaches us what to look for and how to look at it in art. What is central and must be articulated in all the theories are their debates over the reasons for excellence in art—debates over emotional depth, profound truths, natural beauty, exactitude, freshness of treatment, and so on, as criteria of evaluation—the whole of which converges on the perennial problem of what makes a work of art good. To understand the role of aesthetic theory is not to conceive it as definition, logically doomed to failure, but to read it as summaries of seriously made recommendations to attend in certain ways to certain features of art.

Joseph Margolis

Mr. Weitz and the Definition of Art

Mr. Morris Weitz has recently written an extremely misleading essay on the problem of defining fine art.[1] He pleads, as he says, "for the rejection of" the problem of providing "a true definition or set of necessary and sufficient properties of art."[2] We must begin, he argues, not with "What is art?" but "What sort of concept is 'art'?"[3] And the ammunition for his present view (for he himself acknowledges that his earlier volume, *Philosophy of the Arts*,[4] was premised on the orientation he now considers a false one[5]) is provided by applying a distinction that Ludwig Wittgenstein proposed in his *Philosophical Investigations*.[6] Weitz summarizes the relevance of Wittgenstein's remarks for his own issue in the following way: "The problem of the nature of art is like that of the nature of games, at least in these respects: If we actually look and see what it is that we call 'art,' we will also find no common properties—only strands of similarities. Knowing what art is is not apprehending some manifest or latent essence but being able to recognize, describe, and explain those things we call 'art' in virtue of these similarities.

"But the basic resemblance between these concepts is their

[1] "The Role of Theory in Aesthetics," *Journal of Aesthetics and Art Criticism*, 15: 27–35 (September 1956); the essay is one of the Matchette Foundation prize essays for 1955.
[2] *Ibid.*, p. 27.
[3] *Ibid.*, p. 30.
[4] Cambridge: Harvard University Press, 1950.
[5] "The Role of Theory in Aesthetics," p. 29.
[6] Translated by G. E. M. Anscombe (New York: Macmillan, 1953); cf. I, sections 65–75, cited by Weitz.

[Reprinted from *Philosophical Studies,* 9: 88–95 (1958).]

open texture. In elucidating them, certain (paradigm) cases can be given, about which there can be no question as to their being correctly described as 'art' or 'game,' but no exhaustive set of cases can be given. I can list some cases and some conditions under which I can apply correctly the concept of art but I cannot list all of them, for the all-important reason that unforeseeable or novel conditions are always forthcoming or envisageable.

"A concept is open if its conditions of application are emendable and corrigible; i.e., if a situation or case can be imagined or secured which would call for some sort of *decision* on our part to extend the use of the concept to cover this, or to close the concept and invent a new one to deal with the new case and its new property. If necessary and sufficient conditions for the application of a concept can be stated, the concept is a closed one. But this can happen only in logic or mathematics where concepts are constructed and completely defined. It cannot occur with empirically-descriptive and normative concepts unless we arbitrarily close them by stipulating the range of their uses." [7]

I should like to make some systematic observations about Weitz's charge which, I trust, will show without requiring additional comment the logical suitability of attempting to define art.

1. On Weitz's view, the error involved in defining art (cf. the third paragraph quoted above) applies to *all* "empirically-descriptive" concepts and so is not peculiarly to be found in the theory of art. On this basis, the definition of "man" and "tree" and "stone" suffers from the same error. But this is surely a curious view. I suggest that what Weitz wishes to say is that the error, when it is found, is found exclusively in the "empirically-descriptive" and "normative" domains, though it need not occur in every case in those domains, that it never occurs in logic and mathematics where "concepts are constructed and completely defined."

2. I agree with Weitz's view of the "open character" of "art"; Weitz does show persuasively that an old-fashioned definition of the novel may exclude, contrary to our wishes, Joyce's *Finnegans*

[7] "The Role of Theory in Aesthetics," p. 31.

Wake or Dos Passos' *U.S.A.* or Virginia Woolf's *To the Lighthouse* [8] and that we therefore decide to adjust the definition to incorporate these.[9]

3. It may be true that the objects that we wish to call "novels" (any other subclass of fine art will serve as well, and even the generic class, art) do not have any enumerable properties that we should wish to call "necessary and sufficient properties" of the entire class but have only (following Wittgenstein) "strands of similarity." What I must insist on, however, is that to determine whether this is so is an *empirical* question and not a *logical* one. That it is an empirical question seems to be the intent of the first paragraph quoted above (it is also the intent of Wittgenstein's advice to "look and see") ; it is part of the equivocal intent of the second paragraph quoted above where Weitz says, "I *cannot* list all of them"; but it is not the intent of the third paragraph, where Weitz uses the word "only," nor is it the intent of the rest of the article. He states his most extreme view unambiguously: "What I am arguing, then, is that the very expansive, adventurous character of art, its ever-present changes and novel creations, makes it logically impossible to ensure any set of defining properties." [10] This remark of course tends to reinforce the point made in (1), namely, that the problem of definition Weitz is interested in appears in the empirical domain though it does not necessarily apply to every empirical concept; it is the peculiar properties of art that affect our effort at definition.

4. Weitz appears to confuse in his argument logical and merely practical reasons. For when he explains why it is that "art" is an "open" concept, he says: "We can, of course, choose to close the concept. But to do this with 'art' or 'tragedy' or 'portraiture,' etc., is ludicrous since it forecloses on the very conditions of creativity in the arts." [11] He may be right, though I suspect he is not; after all, we do not anticipate that the definition of "living organism" will "foreclose" on biological evolution, and yet we have reasonable hopes of defining the term (in Weitz's sense) so that it will

8 *Ibid.*, p. 31.
9 *Ibid.*, p. 32.
10 *Ibid.*
11 *Ibid.*

comprehend "forthcoming and envisageable" types of organisms. But more important even than this, the reason he supplies for demurring to definitions is very clearly a practical one; he is simply concerned that the effort to define an enormously complicated and creative domain like art is probably beyond the capacities of anyone, that every effort will probably (though he has no logical basis for saying "necessarily") fail because the theorists are ordinarily myopically committed to the special features of narrow art traditions they have studied, that commitment to a definition may have unfortunate consequences for the very practice of art.

5. That Weitz's objections are merely practical is obvious once again from his admission that "there are legitimate and serviceable closed concepts in art" for such as "have been drawn for a *special* purpose." [12] He goes on to show, and persuasively, that "a theory or real definition . . . at least of the extant Greek tragedies" can be given, that in fact Aristotle's definition is *false*.[13] But if this*is admitted (and it is difficult to see how it could be reasonably denied), it suddenly becomes obscure what the sense is in which such definitions *cannot* be given for "tragedy," "comedy," "art." We see now the implicit circle Weitz has unwittingly entered when he makes the extreme remark quoted above. For he speaks of the "adventurous character *of* art" when he wishes to say that a previous definition of art would probably (though again, he has no basis for saying "necessarily") not apply to the objects *he now wishes to be admitted as works of art*. The confusion in short rests here: there is a difference between noting the inadequacy of any formulated definition of art, *if* we wish to include as art certain objects that do not share the necessary and sufficient properties listed in that definition, and (on the other hand) proving logically impossible the enumeration of necessary and sufficient properties *for* any set of objects already agreed upon. It is our practical dissatisfaction with any empirical definition of this sort that urges us to revise it, to make a "decision" (as Weitz would put it).

6. Weitz must be wrong in denying that the same problem of

---

[12] *Ibid.*
[13] *Ibid.*

definition occurs in mathematics and logic (as he argues in the third paragraph quoted above). For even though the concepts there are "constructed," it is conceivable that, examining the empirical use of these constructions, we "decide" (again for practical reasons) to change the definitions of certain concepts. And this is all that is required to fulfill Weitz's criterion of an "open" concept (see the third paragraph quoted above). But we surely can imagine a definition of number, for example, made in a relatively early phase of the history of mathematics, that could not be applied to other invented entities of a later stage of development. We could, conceivably, "decide" that the manipulation of these latter entities constituted play with something other than "number" or we could even insist that "number" refers to "family resemblances" only. Or we could "decide" to revise our definition to accommodate the new development; and this would surely be the most reasonable thing to do. We must be clear, however, that the change is for a practical reason and that changes made on any given occasion do not argue that similar changes must be made for every innovation in a given domain.

7. There is something odd about Weitz's statement (third paragraph quoted above) that we cannot supply closed concepts in the "empirically-descriptive" domain "unless we arbitrarily close them by stipulating the ranges of their uses." This seems to suggest that there is a conceivable alternate procedure for securing closed concepts. But, on inspection, we see that there is none. For one thing, even the privileged domain of mathematics and logic, on Weitz's view, employs such stipulative definitions; in this respect, the logic of the empirical domain resembles that of mathematics and logic. For another, Weitz actually, as we have seen in (5), does not always treat such stipulative definitions in the empirical domain in a pejorative fashion; he merely insists that there must be an assignable practical reason for the use of such a definition. We are forced to a rather surprising conclusion: Weitz's entire argument presupposes in a subterranean way that we are, in some sense, able to grasp the eternal forms of things. We are to *recognize* that Joyce's *Finnegans Wake,* for example, *is* a novel just as Flaubert's *Madame Bovary* and hence are to reject, as *false,* definitions of the novel which fail to include *Finnegans*

Wake. Weitz himself of course would not subscribe to this reading of his view. But it is difficult to see how else such statements as the following may be understood:

"If we take the aesthetic theories literally, as we have seen, they all fail; but if we reconstrue them, in terms of their function and point, as serious and argued-for recommendations to concentrate on certain criteria of excellence in art, we shall see that aesthetic theory is far from worthless." [14]

None of the criteria of recognition is a defining one, either necessary or sufficient, because we can sometimes assert of something that it is a work of art and go on to deny any one of these conditions . . ." [15]

Either (a) the definition offered for an agreed set of objects is empirically inadequate, in which case we must try to better it; or (b) the new objects now to be called by the same name as the previous set (for which a definition was empirically adequate) are arbitrarily selected, in which case every definition may be struck down; or (c) we now wish, for practical reasons, to enlarge the set of objects to be grouped together, in which case we must attempt (and we cannot antecedently decide that it is impossible) to provide a definition of their necessary and sufficient properties. That is, either all definitions have some stipulative basis or we must hold to some version of the theory of forms (even if recognized only darkly through "family resemblances").[16] I hasten to remark that, even if Weitz's empirical findings on the definition of art were defensible, even if only "family resemblances" could be enumerated, it would not follow that empirical definition is logically impossible; C. L. Stevenson, it may be observed, has suggested a procedure for defining art based on this very notion (which appears to be logically sound).[17]

8. It is necessary to observe that both Weitz and Wittgenstein, in speaking of "family resemblances," use a categorical negative

[14] *Ibid.*, p. 35.
[15] *Ibid.*, p. 34.
[16] It is an interesting oddity that the appeal to ordinary usage may hide an incipient theory of forms.
[17] Cf. "On 'What Is a Poem?'" *Philosophical Review*, 66:329–62 (July 1957), esp. pp. 340–47.

regarding the enumeration of necessary and sufficient properties. This is simply unwarranted. All Weitz has done is show that specific well-known definitions are inadequate for a determined set of objects. The notion of "family resemblances" is at best an empirical compromise; having failed to arrive at a satisfactory definition, we are inclined to think none can be formulated (Weitz's own disappointment on his use of the organic theory of art is to the point). But this is to transform an empirical finding (and that a negative one) into the strongest logical objection. The use of "family resemblances" is inevitably a makeshift; it is never logically impossible that we may agree on a suitable definition at a later date, else the logical objections would apply as well to the use of "family resemblances." Surely, "family resemblances" between different kinds of energy, for example, has had to give way gradually to an empirically adequate definition of the necessary and sufficient properties of energy.

9. Weitz carries his argument to a disingenuous extreme when he asserts: "None of the criteria of recognition is a defining one, either necessary or sufficient, because we can sometimes assert of something that it is a work of art and go on to deny any one of these conditions, even the one which has traditionally been taken to be basic, namely, that of being an artifact: Consider, 'This piece of driftwood is a lovely piece of sculpture.' " [18]

There is no question that ordinary language supplies us with remarks such as the one Weitz has selected; but we are not required, even in ordinary language, to take every remark as a literal statement of fact. If anyone were pressed to explain such a remark, he would of course say that the driftwood looks very much like a sculpture, that it is as if nature were a sculptor, that we could imagine the driftwood actually fashioned by a human sculptor into its present form. And this means that, in making such a remark, we hardly wish to deny what is a necessary condition for an object's actually being a work of art, "namely, that of being an artifact." Disputes of this sort raise a question about what sort of evidence is to be supplied to support or defeat Weitz's thesis. Whether anyone (Weitz himself) really prefers

[18] "The Role of Theory in Aesthetics," p. 34.

the interpretation Weitz advances of the above remark seems to me to be utterly beside the point. It seems possible to accommodate the sense in which a piece of driftwood is called a piece of sculpture, to get agreement on the sense in which it differs fundamentally from the vast class of objects that ordinary usage calls sculptures or works of art, and thence to "decide," independently of, though not without attention to, ordinary usage, to define the term to cover the vast class rather than the marginal case of the driftwood. I cannot see how this stipulative feature of definition can be eliminated. Even if one were to ask, in an inductive sense, how do people define art and we were to find that "family resemblances" are probably the only traits we could enumerate, the finding would be quite irrelevant for any systematic effort to classify our knowledge; we would simply construct a concept which (in this instance) would accommodate at least an important part of ordinary usage and which, together with other distinctions, would allow us to classify empirical statements about any other related phenomena without contradiction. An immediately apparent analogy may be seen in considering ordinary references to porpoises or whales as interesting fish and the usage of science.

10. If we reconsider the quotation given in (3), we can pinpoint the fundamental weakness of Weitz's view. As Weitz puts it, the creative nature of art "makes it *logically* impossible to *ensure* any set of defining properties." I have italicized the clue words. In the very next sentence, Weitz admits that we "can . . . choose to close the concept," which shows that for him such a concept is not self-contradictory. It is not logically impossible to construct such a concept but only logically (*sic*) impossible to ensure it. If Wittgenstein's corresponding entry [19] is examined, we see that Wittgenstein's purpose was to draw attention to the fact that the usage of "family resemblances" is familiar and distinct from that of the use of deliberately closed concepts (it is interesting that Wittgenstein's, contrary to Weitz's, emphasis (as in the third paragraph quoted above) admits that even the concepts of mathematics may be used in an "open" sense). In

---

[19] *Philosophical Investigations*, I, section 68.

other words, Wittgenstein distinguishes between two types of usage and really examines the usage of "games" in the sense of that of "family resemblances." He expressly says that he *can* use mathematical concepts either in the "open" or "closed" sense, but he insists (and his argument is surely inconclusive here) that we *use* "games" in the "open" sense—as if to say, only in the "open" sense. Weitz consequently decides that we cannot *logically* ensure any "closed" sense of "art," though he only means to say that such a "closed" sense would be different from that of an "open" sense and *that we are not entitled somehow to prefer this "closed" sense to the "open."* What the priority of the "open" sense is, is left unexplained.

11. It may further be argued that the innovations Weitz has introduced (following Wittgenstein) are self-defeating. He fails (the passages cited from Wittgenstein's *Investigations* also fail) to discuss the need for distinguishing, and the distinction itself, between the "closed" and "open" senses even of concepts defined in terms of "family resemblances." Consider the concept "games." Is courtship a game? Is love a game? Is life a game? There seems to be a stipulative element required even here to give discipline to usage; else we run the risk of linguistic anarchy. But if a "closed" sense of "family resemblances" is allowed, why not a "closed" sense for "necessary and sufficient properties"? In short, the notion of an "open" concept is equivocally employed. It sometimes means a concept defined in terms of "family resemblances" and it sometimes means the opposite of a "closed" concept. On the argument advanced, the two are independent notions and "open" is best employed if restricted to the latter sense. Wittgenstein's concern, to summarize this as well, is to argue that concepts based on "family resemblances" are *usable* as such; he sometimes exceeds his argument when he appears to claim that some concepts, like "games," are usable *only* in terms of "family resemblances." This is clearly not so; but even with this restriction, the "openness" of the concept is not automatically decided. And therefore, the mere substitution of "family resemblances" for "necessary and sufficient properties" fails to eliminate the problem Weitz originally proposed, namely, of employing the concept of art in such a way as to avoid "foreclos-

ing" on artistic innovation. By the same token, the use of any formulated "necessary and sufficient properties" in an open sense need not prejudice such innovation.

I believe that Weitz's argument founders on the objections enumerated. And since the definitional effort in question is not self-contradictory and resembles other such efforts that are both meaningful and actually successful, I say let us simply try again.

Lewis K. Zerby

A Reconsideration of the Role of Theory in Aesthetics—A Reply to Morris Weitz

In the September 1956 issue of this *Journal,* Morris Weitz published a very important and controversial article about aesthetics. It was such a basic article that philosophers must either agree with it or criticize it. Since I am convinced that there are fundamental difficulties in Weitz's position, I feel obliged to answer it in print as I did verbally at the American Philosophical Association meeting where it was first read.

I

Professor Weitz proposes that we drop the theorist's question, "What is the nature of art?" and ask instead the more fruitful question, "What sort of concept is 'art'?" Following this comes the very important sentence, "Rather than a definition, let us try for a logical description of the actual employment of the concept."

In order to clarify the problem here illustrated, I should like to shift from aesthetics to the philosophy of science. Suppose we imagine a philosopher saying, "It is more fruitful to ask 'What sort of concept is probability?' than to ask 'What is the nature of probability?'" I do not think that we would be tempted to say to such a man, "Probability is not a word and not a concept, though we may refer to probability by means of the word 'probability' and conceive it."

[Reprinted from *The Journal of Aesthetics and Art Criticism,* 16: 253–255 (1957).]

It seems clear to me that Weitz is not concerned with the word "art" as a grammarian might be concerned with it, nor is he concerned with the concept "art" as a logician might be concerned with it. Rather Weitz is concerned with the word "art" as Carnap, for example, might be concerned with the word "probability." Weitz says he wants to try for a "logical description of the actual employment of the concept 'art.'" He does not want to call this a definition, because as he uses the word "definition" it means Aristotelian real definitions.

II

For some reason or other, Weitz insists that in aesthetics "definition, reconstruction, and patterns of analysis are out of place since they distort, and add nothing to our understanding of art." Let us look for a moment at this term "definition." Is it not the case that Weitz is making a kind of definition of art in his answer to the question, "What is the logic of 'x' as a work of art?" And just as it seems to me that definition is in place, not only in aesthetics in general, but even in this particular paper by Weitz, so it seems to me that analysis is similarly in place. When Weitz says that "art" is both descriptive (like "chair"), and evaluative (like "good"), it seems to me that he is clearly making an analysis.

But perhaps Weitz is really telling us that this definition and analysis is not *theory* in aesthetics but just plain aesthetics. If this is so, I am at a loss to know his justification for his somewhat Pickwickian nominal definition of *"theory,"* a definition that makes theory in aesthetics look very much like what we would ordinarily call art criticism. Perhaps I should ask what that part of aesthetics which is concerned with definition and analysis should be named, if we refuse to name it *theory*.

It would seem to me that much of our trouble is in our different conceptions of definition. It strikes me that Weitz has put forward the sort of real definition for the term "real definition" that he objects to having theorists in aesthetics put forward for the term "art." Is not the term "real definition" an open concept? Is it not indeed as expansive and as adventuresome as the concept "art"? Why, then, should we make it a closed concept by defining it as "the statement of the necessary and sufficient properties" of the definiendum? By doing this are we not distorting and adding nothing to our understanding of definition? Such a definition, I am afraid, radically misconstrues the logic of the concept of definition and is doomed to failure.

I am especially surprised to find Weitz taking this archaic view of real definition because in 1949 he was the author of a paper which took a very different view of the matter. This article, called "Analysis and Real Definition," contained the following passage:

> Of course, real definition, at least as it has been conceived and accepted by the whole Aristotelian tradition has experienced much abuse, and deservedly, since it has been so completely tied up with the metaphysical view that what is being defined is certain fixed essences. But there is another sense of real definition, the common sense one, which is *that kind of definition in which the properties of a given complex are enumerated;* by properties is meant the elements or terms of a complex, together with their characteristics and the relations that obtain among them, and by complex, a fact or group of facts.

Having written this in 1949, Weitz has strangely given up the common-sense notion of real definitions in order to return to the real-definition of the Aristotelian tradition.

It is my own persuasion that the role of theory in aesthetics is to provide *this* sort of real definitions and that such definitions are far more than "summaries of argued-for recommendations to attend in certain ways to certain features of art."

III

Since I am going to argue in this section that it is the role of theory in aesthetics to make definitions which clarify our understanding of art, I shall begin by discussing briefly several sorts of definition. The first sort, which Weitz calls real definitions, is of no help in modern aesthetics. But it is possible to think of real definitions as reported definitions or definitions in more or less general usage. In this sense of real definition we do not need to have a statement of the necessary and sufficient properties of the thing defined or a true claim about its essence. We need only have a definition actually in use. Contrasted with real definitions are nominal or stipulated definitions. Such definitions are state-

ments of the author's intent to use a term in the way the definition designates or stipulates.

In addition to real and nominal definitions there are complete
and incomplete definitions. Now I think Weitz is claiming rightly
that traditional definitions of art are incomplete. We do not have
any definition which completely defines the term 'art.' This is
part of what we mean by saying that "art" is an open concept.
However, I do not believe we should say that because we have no
complete definition of art's essence, we have no definition *at all*
of art. Certainly many definitions about art and other things in
aesthetics are nominal definitions; but I am inclined to think
that if all these definitions were *merely* nominal, we would not be
very interested in aesthetics; nor would we be very hopeful that a
study of aesthetics would increase our understanding of art.
While many of the definitions in aesthetics are nominal ones; I,
for one, find a number of definitions which are substantially
agreed upon and which I am willing to call real definitions, even
if they are not universally agreed upon or complete.

If we are to have any aesthetics at all, we must have some sort
of definitions. Unless we have an understanding of the signification of the term "art," how can we write histories, or sociologies,
or criticisms of art? To clarify the meaning of the term "art" is a
cognitive enterprise, and aesthetics insofar as it is a branch of
philosophy can justify its existence only to the extent that it
provides a unifying definition in terms of which art can be
organized. The definitions in aesthetics serve for writers about art
the sort of use served by theories in science. A theory in science is
the name for an organizing principle, unifying device, or intellectual hatrack upon which one can hang generalizations or laws.
Observations, hypotheses, and laws are made in terms of a physi-
calistic language or are reducible to such a language. No such
reduction is required in the case of theories. Theories have value
for science because they are useful in achieving structure and
organization. One does not speak of them as true or as false. One
judges them rather as useful or not insofar as they are capable or
incapable of providing unity to laws and observations contained
in science. Likewise in aesthetics, definitions are valuable only if
they provide a framework within which cognitive progress can
be made in the study of art.

Arnold Berleant

A Note on the Problem of Defining "Art"

Recent attempts at explicating the essential character of art [1] have given rise to discussions concerning the significance of this question for aesthetic theory and to skepticism in some quarters about the very possibility of defining 'art'. While this issues raises numerous difficulties, not the least of these revolves around the nature of the concept 'art' itself. Some (Weitz and Morgan, following Wittgenstein) term it an "open" concept, since its boundaries, by the very nature of an empirical concept, cannot be finally drawn. Others (Kahler) object to this manner of definition, maintaining, instead, that an empirical concept must be defined from its central feature, and that while this feature may be made clear, there will always occur borderline instances that are ambiguous. Still others (Beardsley, Pepper) have attempted to demarcate the aesthetic field so as to arrive at dependable aesthetic criteria.

It might be helpful in dealing with the problem of defining 'art' to look at the concept once more, going, as it were, not from a proposed definition (be it by boundaries or central notion) outward to the phenomena which it may be considered to denote, but from those phenomena commonly considered to exemplify art and from the experiences by which they are known and for

[1] Cf. Symposium in *Journal of Aesthetics and Art Criticism*, XX, 2 (Winter, 1961), 175–198 (Beardsley, Morgan, and Mothersill), and Pepper's comment, "Evaluative Definitions in Art and Their Sanctions," *ibid.*, XXI, 2 (Winter, 1962), 201–208. Also Morris Weitz, "The Role of Theory in Aesthetics," *ibid.*, XV, 1 (September, 1956), 27–35. Reprinted in Weitz's *Problems in Aesthetics* (New York, 1959), pp. 145–156, along with a reply by Erich Kahler, "What is Art?," pp. 157–171.

[Reprinted from *Philosophy and Phenomenological Research*, 25: 239–241 (1964–1965).]

which they are sought, inward to the concept. If we were to do this, that is, if we were to approach the problem of concepts, not as hypostatizations, each possessing its distinctive essence or its precise limits, but as conceptual constructs formed by people for the purpose of effectively dealing with their multitudinous similar and diverse experiences, we would come to realize that, apart from formal notions amenable to rigid delimitation, the search for a completely demarcated concept, unequivocal in its denotation, is an *ignis fatuus,* as impossible to attain as it is undesirable to possess. For concepts are employed and acquire their importance in the ordering of experience previously undifferentiated or indistinct, and the concept 'art' functions in the ordering of the experience of art and the objects which give rise to such experience. If we deal primarily empirically with experiences and not rationalistically with concepts, it takes little insight to recognize that the concept will depend upon the experiences from which it obtains its meaning and to which it refers. Consequently, it will vary in its connotation to the extent that the experiences vary; that is, it will be relative to the experiencer and will embody whatever constancy and variability lie in such experiences. Here is an instance in which the genetic account of the functional origin of concepts provides a healthier influence and a more satisfactory explanation than does abstract analysis, by redirecting our consideration back to essentials. Thus it can be seen that the use of the same term is no guarantee of identity of connotation or denotation. Rather, it reveals the poverty of language in attempting communication of a rich variety of experiences with a paucity of verbal means. And no mode of experience surpasses the richness and variety of the aesthetic.

Such an interpretation as this requires a review of our thinking about our conceptual tools. It demands a forthright repudiation of the Platonic-Aristotelian inheritance of completed concepts or ideas, each possessing its own essence. Indeed, it observes that any discussion of concepts, independently of or in isolation from our experiences, individual and social, is destined to be empty dialectics, perhaps absorbing as a kind of mental acrobatics, but ineffectual or even debilitating for the purpose of sharing experiences. Thus the skepticism of many toward the question of the definition of 'art' is a fitting conclusion to a disjoined inquiry. Let us better admit of a plurality of meanings to encompass a plurality of experiences, having perhaps some things in common (these being expressed in the conventional connotations of terms), but shading off imperceptibly into experiences inadmissible to some and eventually inadmissible to all. A language of experience is far more appropriate in dealing with experiences than is a language of things. The sooner we repudiate the rationalistic conception of a world of finished objects and turn to that one in which we live and act, the more effectively shall we be able to adapt our thinking and expressing to our experiencing.

The touchstone of all art is thus seen to be aesthetic experience and not a definition. Clearly, the experience of art is prior to its definition. If an object succeeds in evoking aesthetic experience, it, then, in that instance, becomes an aesthetic object. The problem, consequently, resolves into the description and clarification of the *experience* of art. Similarly, the assertion that "evaluations occur by way of definitions" [2] raises the question of whether a definition must be a prerequisite for evaluation or whether evaluation follows from the experience of art and then becomes formulated in a justificatory definition. The latter, if it were the case, would not necessarily mean subjectivism in evaluating art. It does insist, however, that art is never art by definition. A rule, in this case a definition, never made a painting or a piece of music beautiful. It is the intellectual, who strives for cognitive apprehension of what he has undergone in an art gallery or concert hall, who seeks to understand, to codify, to systematize and regularize, who may inadvertently discover himself upholding the contrary. Nor is there anything amiss in his cognitive activities, so long as the priority of experience to definition be acknowledged and deferred to.

[2] Pepper, *op. cit.*, 203.

Four

Standards of Evaluation

C. J. Ducasse
from *The Philosophy of Art*

L. A. Reid
Greatness

Cleanth Brooks and Robert Penn Warren
Joyce Kilmer's "Trees"

David Hume
Of the Standard of Taste

Morris Weitz
Criticism without Evaluation

Part Four. Selected Readings

Beardsley, Monroe C. *Aesthetics*. New York, 1958. Chs. X–XI.

Daiches, David. "The New Criticism: Some Qualifications," *College English*, 11: 242–250 (1950).

Fleece, Jeffrey. "Further Notes on a 'Bad' Poem," *College English*, 12: 314–320 (1951).

Green, T. M. *The Arts and the Art of Criticism*. Princeton, 1940, pp. 404–407.

Hampshire, Stuart. "Logic and Appreciation," *Aesthetics and Language*, ed. William Elton. Oxford, 1954.

Hungerland, Helmut. "Suggestions for Procedure in Art Criticism," *Journal of Aesthetics and Art Criticism*, 5: 189–195 (1947).

Isenberg, Arnold. "Critical Communication," *The Philosophical Review*, 58: 330–344 (1949).

Knight, Helen. "The Use of 'Good' in Aesthetic Judgments," *Aesthetics and Language*, ed. William Elton. Oxford, 1954.

Weitz, Morris. *Philosophy of the Arts*. Cambridge, Mass., 1950. Ch. VII.

Wimsatt, William K., and Monroe C. Beardsley. "The Intentional Fallacy," *Sewanee Review*, 54: 468–488 (1946).

Ziff, Paul. "Reasons in Art Criticism," *Philosophy and Education*, ed. I. Scheffler. Boston, 1958.

Introduction

After a critic has made up his mind about the nature of art, the nature and identity of a work of art, and the nature and role of aesthetic theory, he usually, and logically, eventually talks about standards of evaluation. X might be art, but is it good art? Such-and-such might be a novel, but is it a good novel? Decision making of this latter sort is often thought to be the ultimate goal of the whole critical process. Sometimes it is thought to be second in importance only to establishing the value of art to the lives of people. And sometimes it is thought to be not a proper part of the critical process at all.

As a whole, the writers in this section not only propose some standards of evaluation and argue against others, but they also discuss the qualities of a capable critic and the weaknesses of arguments about the goodness (or badness) of art and works of art.

C. J. Ducasse

from *The Philosophy of Art*

The principal standards of criticism that may be used in connection with works of art and aesthetic objects are as follows:

(a) A work of art may be considered as such, i.e., as the product of an endeavor on the artist's part to express objectively something he felt, and the question be raised whether or not it is good, in the sense of expressing that feeling adequately.

(b) The question may on the other hand be asked whether the work adequately expresses not so much the feeling that the artist originally attempted to express through it, but rather a feeling which on consideration he is willing to acknowledge as truly an aspect or part of himself.

(c) A work of art may, however, be considered also in the light of its capacity to communicate to others the feeling that the artist objectified in it, and be judged good or bad according to the measure of that capacity.

(d) Again, any aesthetic object, whether it be a work of art or a natural thing, may be criticized simply in respect to its beauty or ugliness.

(e) Any aesthetic object, whether natural or a product of art, may also be criticized in the light of the worth of the sort of action through which the particular feeling obtained in the contemplation of the object will tend to discharge itself, if, when that feeling has been obtained, the *practical* attitude is then allowed to replace the contemplative.

These various standards of criticism will now be examined in turn.

[Reprinted from *The Philosophy of Art*. New York: The Dial Press, 1929. Pp. 269–277.]

§3

Success of the attempt at self-expression, as standard. The most common form of criticism of works of art is criticism in terms of beauty and ugliness. The terms beautiful and ugly, however, have no meaning whatever in terms of the creating artist's point of view, but only in terms of the spectator or "consumer," whether he be the artist himself later contemplating and evaluating his creation, or someone else. That which is evaluated in terms of beauty and ugliness is therefore not at all the work of art as such, viz., as product of the artist's endeavor to give his feeling embodiment in an object, but only the object itself that the spectator contemplates, and wholly without reference to the question whether that object is a product of art or of nature.

On the other hand, criticism of a work of art considered as such, would be concerned solely with the measure of success or failure of the art, i.e., of the artist's attempt consciously to objectify his feeling. It is obvious, however, that no one but the artist himself is in a position to say whether, or how far, he has succeeded in creating an object adequately embodying his feeling. The test of the success of his attempt at objectification, as we have seen, is whether the object created does, in contemplation, mirror back the feeling which he attempted to express. What that feeling was, however, is something which is known to no one but himself; and therefore he alone is in a position to perform the test. If the artist is able to say: "Yes, this exactly reflects back to me the feeling I had," then the last word has been said *as to that,* i.e., as to the success of his attempt at objective expression of his feeling. It may quite properly be insisted, however, that success of that sort is something which is of interest to no one but himself, or, possibly, his mother or his wife. Conscious objectification of feeling, as defined by that test, may therefore be termed *private or individual objectification,* as distinguished from *social objectification,* the test of which would be the object's capacity to impart in contemplation the artist's feeling not merely back to himself, but on to others also. Criticism in terms of this test will be considered presently.

§4

Signability of the work of art by its creator. As already noted, however, the artist's *final* criticism at least, of his own work, is likely to be based not so much on the question whether the feeling which he finds he has objectified is exactly that which he attempted to objectify, as on the question whether, after thoroughly "tasting" (through contemplation of his work) the feeling he has actually objectified, he finds it to be one that he is *willing to own,* i.e., to acknowledge as being really a part or aspect of his emotional self at the time. In other words, the question is whether the work he has created is one which he honestly feels he can sign.

It is obvious that, again, no one but the artist himself is in a position to criticize his own work on that basis. Criticism of this sort would normally accompany criticism of the kind first mentioned, which passes on the question of the sameness of the feeling actually objectified, and of the feeling which was to be objectified.

As pointed out earlier, this sameness obviously cannot be sameness in every respect, but only *qualitative* sameness. Such qualitative identity of the two feelings, however, leaves room for gain in clearness and vividness of the given quality of feeling, as a result of the process of objectification. Such a gain in clearness and vividness beyond question occurs, but it is the only respect in which the feeling need become different through the process of objectification. Indeed, the qualitative identity of the feeling before and after objectification is an absolute prerequisite, if one is to be able to say that it is *that* feeling which has been clarified. That the feeling should be clear, however (in the sense in which it is possible for a feeling to become so), is in turn a prerequisite of criticism of one's work in terms of the second question mentioned above, namely, the question whether it constitutes objectification of an emotional self *truly one's own.*

It is perhaps unnecessary to point out in this connection that approving on this basis the object that one has created is quite a different thing from finding it beautiful. The pleasure which

such approval does express is pleasure found, *not in the feeling*
objectified by the work (which would be what would constitute
the work of art beautiful), but *in the success* of one's attempt to
objectify an aspect of one's emotional self; and this latter pleasure remains, whether the feeling objectified be a pleasurable or a
painful one, i.e., whether the object created be beautiful or ugly.
The difference is analogous to that between the pleasure of
having succeeded in stating accurately some thought that one
had, and the pleasure (or displeasure) of finding true (or false),
on reflection, the statement that one has made.

§5

Signability of the work of art by the beholder. Criticism of a
work of art (and equally of a natural object) on the basis of the
question whether one is willing to *own* the feeling which it
objectifies, is possible to others than the artist himself. The only
difference is this. When the artist answers that question in the
negative, he then proceeds to alter the object he has created until
he finds himself able to say: "Yes, the feeling which this now
objectifies is truly a part of myself." But when the critic on this
basis, is someone else than the artist, that critic is then not trying
to objectify his feeling himself, nor therefore is he called upon to
make alterations in the object before him. His problem is simply
to decide whether or not the thing before him objectifies a feeling
that was his, or one that perhaps he had not yet experienced but
that he is able and willing to call his. And once more, this
decision is one quite distinct from the question whether or not
the feeling objectified is pleasant and the object therefore beautiful. Most of us are quite able to obtain pleasure from various
sources of which we are ashamed; so that the self that experiences
pleasure from such sources is not one which we acknowledge as
truly our own, but only a self with which we find ourselves
saddled, and of which we cannot get rid.

§6

Capacity to transmit the artist's feeling to others. To say that a
given aesthetic object (whether natural or a work of art), objectifies a certain feeling means, we have agreed, simply that that

feeling is obtainable from it in contemplation, and we have just seen that, with regard to such a feeling, the question can be raised, by others as well as by the maker of the object (if it be man-made), whether the feeling objectified in it is a feeling that they are *willing to own*.

We saw too that another question distinct from this can be asked, namely, the question whether the feeling actually objectified, i.e., obtained from the object in contemplation, is qualitatively *the same as* that which the artist originally endeavored to objectify. We may now go on and point out that this question, like the preceding one, can be asked (if not, perhaps, answered) by others than the artist himself. When others than the artist ask it, what they do is to consider the work of art as a possible *means for the conveying to them* of the feeling which the artist endeavored to express.

Expression of a feeling in a manner adequate to impart it in contemplation not merely back to the artist himself, but also on to others, may be called *socially objective,* as distinguished from expression which is only *privately* or *individually objective.*

Whether an artist's expression of a feeling which he had, achieves private objectivity, is something which, as we have noted, cannot be decided by others; but *can* be decided by the artist, since both of the feelings the qualitative sameness of which is in question are facts of his own experience. Social objectivity of the expression of a feeling, on the contrary, is not something the achieving of which can ever be strictly proved or disproved either by the artist or by others, since God alone would be in a position to compare *directly* the two feelings experienced by two persons in contemplation of the same object. All that can be said is that the two feelings will be qualitatively the same (i.e., social objectification of the feeling will be a fact), if the two (or more) persons concerned are alike in their psycho-physical constitutions. Of this, however, we can make no direct observation either, or at least none that will be adequate. Any conclusion that we reach as to the sameness of the feeling that the two persons each have on the given occasion, has therefore no other status than that of an inference from their observable behavior, which here would be mainly verbal behavior, viz., their words. And any such conclusion, therefore, is reliable only so far as the two persons use their words in the same sense. But whether two people use their words in the same sense is something which, in *ultimate* analysis, can be checked up only through the act of pointing. This means that it can be checked up only in case a word signifies something that can be pointed to, and even in such cases, the sameness that is insured is sameness only so far as purposes of coöperation are concerned. For instance, if I say that by "green" I mean something which I actually point to, and another person accepts my use of the word, all that we then know is that we call by the same name whatever color we each perceive in the place pointed to. We do not in the least know that the *quality* of sensation which the one experiences when he looks there, is the same quality as that experienced by the other. It is quite conceivable, for instance, that all my sound sensations in response to given stimuli should be pitched one octave above those which another man has in response to the same stimuli. If this were so, all *relations* between sounds would be left unaltered by this difference, and the answers of each of us concerning questions of intervals, pitches, tone-color, etc., would agree perfectly although we never in fact would be hearing literally the same thing. The *literal* qualitative sameness of the subjective experiences of two persons, such as their sensations and feelings, could be ascertained only if we, or some third party, were in a position to compare the experience of the two in the same direct manner in which anyone of us can compare, for instance, two of his own sound sensations, or two of his own emotions.

Such literal qualitative sameness, of course, has no *practical* importance whatever. For all practical purposes the only thing important is the sameness of the relations, which can be checked up by pointing. But where the transmission of feeling for purely aesthetic purposes is concerned, the *literal qualitative sameness of the feeling* is on the contrary the only sort of sameness then relevant. Oratory, in probably the majority of cases, is primarily skilled work. That is, the orator is usually not primarily intent upon transmitting integrally his own feelings to his auditors, but rather upon inspiring them with any feeling that will express itself practically in the sort of behavior he desires of them,

—voting, fighting, subscribing to a fund, or what not. But with the artist it is otherwise. The poet, for instance, if he reads his verses to others at all, is not concerned to make them do anything, but only to have them reproduce in themselves the very feeling which he sought to objectify. Only literal sameness of the feeling will do here. The most enthusiastic praise of an artist's work by someone else is disappointing to the artist and makes him feel more alone than adverse but discriminating criticism would, if he believes the praise to be based upon a misperception of what he sought to express. Pragmatic sameness of feeling, i.e., sameness *of behavior* after contemplation of the object, has no relevance here except in so far as it may constitute evidence of literal qualitative sameness of feeling. And that it constitutes any evidence of it at all is ultimately nothing but a postulate, a fond hope of the gregarious heart, the fulfilment of which is never actually to be verified. But it is nevertheless a hope that the gregarious heart does entertain, and does stake upon.

Just this, viz., staking upon a hope, is what constitutes *making* a postulate, as distinguished from merely *stating* one. But when once is made the general postulate that sameness of behavior constitutes evidence of sameness of feeling, then under that postulate *the strength* of the evidence becomes a matter of the *degree* of sameness of the behavior, and of the *variety of respects* in which that sameness obtains. This theoretically precarious criterion of literal sameness of feeling being the only one available, it is the one we actually use to decide whether another person gets or (with more confidence) does not get from the contemplation of a given object the same feeling that we do. The same thing may be put in other words by saying that that criterion is the one we use to decide whether or not a given work of art is good, considered as a means of conveying some certain feeling from one person (who may or may not be the artist) to another.

*　　*　　*　　*

L. A. Reid

Greatness

What do we mean by greatness? Greatness is difficult to define, though as to what it is in actuality, there is a certain body of agreement. We all recognise to some degree the distinction between the great and the trifling, in art. We recognise that the passage where Samson cries,

> "O dark, dark, dark, amid the blaze of noon",

is 'greater' than the last lyric of Comus, that Beethoven's *Hammerklavier* Sonata is 'greater' than his first, that the reclining *Theseus* of Pheidias on the Parthenon is 'greater' than the Hermes of Praxiteles, that Shakespeare's *Macbeth* is 'greater' than his *A Midsummer Night's Dream*, or any lyric in it.

But can we say what we mean by the comparative 'greater'? In the first place, we seem to mean *at least* expressiveness of the 'great' values of life. As the question of greatness is easier to discuss in the case of an art like poetry, where ideas are more readily discernible, I shall select my examples mainly from poetry. This does not mean that, if true, our answers should not apply to arts like music and architecture. Certainly they ought. But for general reasons already made clear, the elements of greatness are always far harder to analyse in these cases.

It is very difficult, as has been said, and dangerous, to try to define greatness, to say exactly *why* what we call the 'great' values of life are called 'great', and what precisely constitutes their greatness. We do naturally assume that some values are 'greater' than others. They are, I suppose, generally speaking, those values

[Reprinted from *A Study in Aesthetics*. London: George Allen & Unwin, Ltd., 1931. Pp. 237–243. Footnotes have been renumbered.]

which, positively regarded, are the fulfilments of tendencies which are not only marked and strong, but profound and lofty and broad and far-reaching in the complexity of their implications. Great values are, probably, the fulfilments of those tendencies which are most important on the highest emergent plane with which we are acquainted,[1] the intricate life of man. Animal passions are strong, and strength is one character of greatness. But more than strength is needed. Greatness cannot be conceived without also thinking of the wide system of implications, seen or hidden, of the fine organisation of a questing spirit, which reveals the universality of man's nature, which marks him off from the local animal, which reveals "the piece of work" that he is when he is most man. It must be, approximately, for these reasons that the spectacles of human love, hate, mortality, courage, romance, religious experience, or of the strife of man with himself, or his fellows, or nature, are spectacles which, as we say, penetrate to 'the roots of our being'.

That greatness in art consists at least in expression of the great values of life, is seen in the odd examples we mentioned; it is seen in extracts from larger works, as well as in whole and complete works. This quality of greatness may even be realised in the very simplest cases: we may realise something of it in viewing the massive pylons, crude and yet imposing, of an ancient Egyptian Temple. We may get it even in the contemplation of some simple sense datum, such as a patch of colour. It may be that a patch of grey-white may express death to me, carrying with it the flavour of all mortality. Or a patch of blue may express the infinite distances of blue skies, of cosmic sublimity. It may be that even in the apprehension of such extremely simple objects as these there is satisfied in some measure that longing for greatness of which Longinus speaks. "Nature . . . from the first implanted in our souls an invincible yearning for all that is great, all that is diviner than ourselves. . . . And that is why nature prompts us to admire, not the clearness and usefulness of a little stream, but the

---

[1] It does not follow that there may not exist in the universe values higher and greater than these, or that the values cognised for example in great tragedy or through religion are not superhuman values. We are concerned with 'greater' and not with 'greatest'.

Nile, the Danube, the Rhine, and, far beyond all, the Ocean."
Our minds yearn for these 'Ocean'-experiences, and we are glad
when we get them.

But though greatness, in the sense of expression of what we call
the great values of life, can certainly be found in extremely
simple aesthetic objects, and although such expression technically
satisfies the conditions of aesthetic expressiveness, this is certainly
not all, or even most, of what we mean when we speak of artistic
'greatness'. For one thing, as we know, the expressiveness of such
simple data is relatively 'subjective' and private, and lacking in
community. Again, an *extract* from a work of art may exhibit
greatness of quality, but to say, "This extract has 'greatness' *in* it"
is very different from saying, 'This is a great work of art.' Mr.
Lascelles Abercrombie has this in mind when he distinguishes
between great "moments" of poetry, or "great poetry"; and *a*
"great poem".[2] In *moments* of poetic experience we get "the
accent or tone of greatness: it is matter so concentrated and
organised as to effect an unusual richness and intensity of impression". In the great poem, on the other hand, there is more than
this. "When we have some notable range and variety of richly
compacted experience brought wholly into the final harmony of
complex impression given us by a completed poem, with its
perfect system of significances uniting into one significance, then
we may expect to feel ourselves in the presence of great poetry;
and the greater the range, the richer the harmony of its total
significance, and the more evident our sense of its greatness. A
similar effect may be given by a *series* of poems, when some
connection of theme, in idea or mood, some relatedness in the
kind of harmony effected over things, enables our minds to fuse
the several impressions into one inclusive impression; but the
effect can hardly be so decisive as when our minds are, without
interruption, dominated by the single form of *one* poem." [3]

In the extract from the poem or in the simple sense datum
which appears to express something great, or profound, or mysterious, or momentous, there is, as has been said, complexity of

[2] *The Idea of Great Poetry,* p. 60.
[3] Ibid., p. 72.

implication. Nevertheless, in such cases, their complexity and the depth of their penetration are rather implicit than explicit. It is not explicit in the body nor is it worked out in any detail. No one would dream of calling 'great' a simple patch of colour—to take an extreme example which verges on absurdity—even though it appeared genuinely expressive to him of great value. And the extract contains suggestions and possibilities, rather than anything else. But we want more than this in art; we want more than a flavour; we want a greatness made explicit, expressed, embodied in a body, and worked out in some detail.

A considerable complexity of embodiment is, then, required in works of art which are to be called 'great'. The great works of the great poets, Sophocles, Dante, Milton, Shakespeare, are organised embodiments of a large variety of human experience. And, being organisations of considerable complexity of human experience, they require for their development a certain space of 'canvas', a certain length. Perhaps I may be allowed once more to quote a short passage from Mr. Abercrombie, for he puts the matter, as usual, with charming concreteness.

"Length", he says,[4] "in itself is nothing; but the plain fact is that a long poem, if it really is a poem (as for example *The Iliad* or *The Divine Comedy, Paradise Lost* or *Hamlet,* are poems), enables a remarkable range, not merely of experiences, but of *kinds* of experience, to be collected into single finality of harmonious impression: a vast plenty of things has been accepted as a single version of the ideal world, as a unity of significance. As far as unity is concerned, no less than as far as splendour of imagination is concerned, a sonnet by Wordsworth may be just as unmistakably an aspect of the ideal world; and it is a marvel, the range of matter in, for example, the sonnet to Toussaint l'Ouverture. But as for greatness, think for an instant of *The Iliad* as a whole, or *The Divine Comedy.* The thing simply is, that Homer and Dante can achieve an inclusive moment of final unity out of a whole series of moments as remarkable as that single one of Wordsworth's: obviously, then, irrespective of poetic quality as such, that final intricate harmony of theirs will be far richer, and

[4] *The Idea of Great Poetry,* pp. 72–74.

so greater, than his—though by means of a unity far less direct
than his, and a form less immediately impressive and therefore,
no doubt, less lovely."

The character of complexity, of width and comprehensiveness,
is a character of greatness which is of course not confined to the
arts. In the realm of thought, we call him great who has the grasp
of a wide and complex field of knowledge, and who has so
organised his knowledge that any particular proposition readily
falls into place in the system of the whole. Of the man of affairs
who, in his realm, is also called great, the same is true: he too has
capacity for comprehension of the complex, and he too has
insight into the bearing of the whole upon this or that problem
of practice. All real greatness seems to imply this grasp of the
complex, with a sense of proportion and relevance.

The difference between thought and practice, on the one hand,
and art on the other, is the difference between thought-and-prac-
tice-ends, and art-ends. The special situation upon which the
complex system of knowledge must converge is a *knowledge*-situa-
tion, a problem, say, to be solved and understood. So knowledge
of the system of practice converges upon some problem of *practice*. The situation upon which the systematised aesthetic complex must converge, on the other hand, is an embodied *value*-situ-
ation. It is an embodied value to be savoured and enjoyed.

And further, in 'great' art, the embodied value to be savoured
is what we have called a 'great' value, or group of great values.
The thinker, or the man of affairs, must in one sense possess 'a
sense of values', for he has, as we have said, a sense of proportion;
and what is that but a sense of values? But it is a sense of values
relevant to facts to be *understood,* or *acted* upon, whereas in the
case of the work of art the complexity apprehended is relevant to
enjoyment or *appreciation* of value. In great art it is relevant to
enjoyment or appreciation of great value or values. So that,
whilst greatness of intellect, or of practicality, implies only great
power of grasping the complex, with a sense of proportion and
relevance, and has in itself nothing to do with capacity to discern
and to savour and enjoy and appreciate what we have called the
'great' values as such, the greatness of the great artist does involve
possession of *both* these powers. What, for example, has a great

physicist or a great mathematician or a great strategist to do with the appreciation of mortality or love or mystic rapture? (The physicist, or mathematician, or strategist, *qua* these things, I mean, not *qua* human beings or as possible artists.) The answer is, He has nothing to do with them. But appreciation of these values is just the artist's very province, so far as they are embodied. The function of art is expression of content in a body. The content, we have seen, is a content of values, and the content of great art, of great values. We may conclude then, that when great value or values are embodied in and through the complex whole of a work of art, then the work is great. And the greater the values, and the more of great values we have, provided they are united into one coherent meaning, the greater is the work.

This account, if at all true, ought to hold good of all art. It is far more difficult, as has been said, to work out and to illustrate in such cases as music and architecture; and to prove that it really works in these cases we should require to refer to a long series of experiments which have not, as far as I know, been made. We have therefore to fall back on a certain dogmatism, on a certain body of educated opinion, which says that in art these things are so. In some of Bach's Chorales and in some of his great Passion music, as well as in some of Beethoven's later work (to cite but two names), our intuition tells us that there is embodied this range and comprehensiveness of experience convergent upon, and making vivid and real, some of the profoundest values of human life. We cannot prove it; we can only say that our intuitions, our deepest feelings, our whole *being* of body-and-mind, tell us that it is so. If anyone says us nay, we have no very clear answer to give in reply. But lack of science need not unduly depress us here. Our present impotence at least does not *prove* us wrong. And we have on our side the prestige of the greatest and most distinguished minds.

Cleanth Brooks and
Robert Penn Warren

Joyce Kilmer's "Trees"

This poem has been very greatly admired by a large number of people. But it is a bad poem.

First, let us look at it merely on the technical side, especially in regard to the use Kilmer makes of his imagery. Now the poet, in a poem of twelve lines, makes only one fundamental comparison on which the other comparisons are based; this is the same method used by Housman in "To an Athlete Dying Young." In "Trees" this fundamental comparison is not definitely stated but is constantly implied. The comparison is that of the tree to a human being. If the tree is compared to a human being, the reader has a right to expect a consistent use to be made of the aspects of the human being which appear in the poem. But look at stanza two:

> A tree whose hungry mouth is pressed
> Against the earth's sweet flowing breast.

Here the tree is metaphorically treated as a sucking babe and the earth, therefore, as the mother—a perfectly good comparison that has been made for centuries—the earth as the "great mother," the "giver of life," and so on.

But the third stanza introduces a confusion:

> A tree that looks to God all day,
> And lifts her leafy arms to pray.

Here the tree is no longer a sucking babe, but, without warning, is old enough to indulge in religious devotions. But that is not

[Reprinted from *Understanding Poetry*. New York: Holt, Rinehart, and Winston, 1960. Pp. 288–289.]

260

the worst part of the confusion. Remember that the tree is a human being and that in the first stanza the *mouth* of that human being was the *root* of the tree. But now, if the branches are "leafy arms," the tree is a strangely deformed human being.

The fourth and fifth stanzas maintain the same anatomical arrangement for the tree as does the third, but they make other unexpected changes: the tree that wears a "nest of robins in her hair" must be a grown-up person, a girl with jewels in her hair; the tree with snow on its bosom is a chaste and pure girl, for so the *associations* of snow with purity and chastity tell the reader; and the tree that "lives with rain" is a chaste and pure young woman who, although vain enough to wear jewels, is yet withdrawn from the complications of human relationships and lives alone with "nature," that is, rain, or might be said to be nunlike, an implication consonant with the religious tone of the poem.

Now it would be quite legitimate for the poet to use any one of the thoughts he wishes to convey about the tree (1. the tree as a babe nursed by mother earth, 2. the tree as a devout person praying all day, 3. the tree as a girl with jewels in her hair, or 4. the tree as a chaste woman alone with nature and God) and to create a metaphor for it, but the trouble is that he tries to convey all of these features by a single basic comparison to a person, and therefore presents a picture thoroughly confused.

For a moment it may seem possible to defend the poem by appealing to the title, "Trees," pointing out that no over-all consistency is called for: one tree is like the babe nursing at its mother's breast; another tree is a girl lifting her arms to pray, and so on. But this defense is probably more damaging than the charge it seeks to meet; for the poem provides no real basis for seeing one tree as babe and another as a devout young woman.

David Hume

Of the Standard of Taste

The great variety of Taste, as well as of opinion, which pre-
vails in the world, is too obvious not to have fallen under every
one's observation. Men of the most confined knowledge are able
to remark a difference of taste in the narrow circle of their
acquaintance, even where the persons have been educated under
the same government, and have early imbibed the same prejudices. But those, who can enlarge their view to contemplate
distant nations and remote ages, are still more surprized at the
great inconsistence and contrariety. We are apt to call *barbarous*
whatever departs widely from our own taste and apprehension:
But soon find the epithet of reproach retorted on us. And the
highest arrogance and self-conceit is at last startled, on observing
an equal assurance on all sides, and scruples, amidst such a
contest of sentiment, to pronounce positively in its own favour.

As this variety of taste is obvious to the most careless enquirer;
so will it be found, on examination, to be still greater in reality
than in appearance. The sentiments of men often differ with
regard to beauty and deformity of all kinds, even while their
general discourse is the same. There are certain terms in every
language, which import blame, and others praise; and all men,
who use the same tongue, must agree in their application of
them. Every voice is united in applauding elegance, propriety,
simplicity, spirit in writing; and in blaming fustian, affectation,
coldness, and a false brilliancy: But when critics come to particulars, this seeming unanimity vanishes; and it is found, that they
had affixed a very different meaning to their expressions. In all

[Reprinted from *Essays: Moral, Political, and Literary*. London:
Longmans, and Green, 1875. Pp. 266, 268–281.]

matters of opinion and science, the case is opposite: The difference among men is there oftener found to lie in generals than in particulars; and to be less in reality than in appearance. An explanation of the terms commonly ends the controversy; and the disputants are surprized to find, that they had been quarrelling, while at bottom they agreed in their judgment.

* * * *

It is natural for us to seek a *Standard of Taste;* a rule, by which the various sentiments of men may be reconciled; at least, a decision, afforded, confirming one sentiment, and condemning another.

There is a species of philosophy, which cuts off all hopes of success in such an attempt, and represents the impossibility of ever attaining any standard of taste. The difference, it is said, is very wide between judgment and sentiment. All sentiment is right; because sentiment has a reference to nothing beyond itself, and is always real, wherever a man is conscious of it. But all determinations of the understanding are not right; because they have a reference to something beyond themselves, to wit, real matter of fact; and are not always conformable to that standard. Among a thousand different opinions which different men may entertain of the same subject, there is one, and but one, that is just and true; and the only difficulty is to fix and ascertain it. On the contrary, a thousand different sentiments, excited by the same object, are all right: Because no sentiment represents what is really in the object. It only marks a certain conformity or relation between the object and the organs or faculties of the mind; and if that conformity did not really exist, the sentiment could never possibly have being. Beauty is no quality in things themselves: It exists merely in the mind which contemplates them; and each mind perceives a different beauty. One person may even perceive deformity, where another is sensible of beauty; and every individual ought to acquiesce in his own sentiment, without pretending to regulate those of others. To seek the real beauty, or real deformity, is as fruitless an enquiry, as to pretend to ascertain the real sweet or real bitter. According to the disposition of the organs, the same object may be both sweet and bitter; and the

proverb has justly determined it to be fruitless to dispute concerning tastes. It is very natural, and even quite necessary, to
extend this axiom to mental, as well as bodily taste; and thus
common sense, which is so often at variance with philosophy,
especially with the sceptical kind, is found, in one instance at
least, to agree in pronouncing the same decision.

But though this axiom, by passing into a proverb, seems to
have attained the sanction of common sense; there is certainly a
species of common sense which opposes it, at least serves to
modify and restrain it. Whoever would assert an equality of
genius and elegance between OGILBY and MILTON, or BUNYAN
and ADDISON, would be thought to defend no less an extravagance, than if he had maintained a mole-hill to be as high as
TENERIFFE, or a pond as extensive as the ocean. Though there
may be found persons, who give the preference to the former
authors; no one pays attention to such a taste; and we pronounce
without scruple the sentiment of these pretended critics to be
absurd and ridiculous. The principle of the natural equality of
tastes is then totally forgot, and while we admit it on some
occasions, where the objects seem near an equality, it appears an
extravagant paradox, or rather a palpable absurdity, where objects so disproportioned are compared together.

It is evident that none of the rules of composition are fixed by
reasonings *a priori,* or can be esteemed abstract conclusions of the
understanding, from comparing those habitudes and relations of
ideas, which are eternal and immutable. Their foundation is the
same with that of all the practical sciences, experience; nor are
they any thing but general observations, concerning what has
been universally found to please in all countries and in all ages.
Many of the beauties of poetry and even of eloquence are
founded on falsehood and fiction, on hyperboles, metaphors, and
an abuse or perversion of terms from their natural meaning. To
check the sallies of the imagination, and to reduce every expression to geometrical truth and exactness, would be the most contrary to the laws of criticism; because it would produce a work,
which, by universal experience, has been found the most insipid
and disagreeable. But though poetry can never submit to exact
truth, it must be confined by rules of art, discovered to the author

either by genius or observation. If some negligent or irregular writers have pleased, they have not pleased by their transgressions of rule or order, but in spite of these transgressions: They have possessed other beauties, which were conformable to just criticism; and the force of these beauties has been able to overpower censure, and give the mind a satisfaction superior to the disgust arising from the blemishes. ARIOSTO pleases; but not by his monstrous and improbable fictions, by his bizarre mixture of the serious and comic styles, by the want of coherence in his stories, or by the continual interruptions of his narration. He charms by the force and clearness of his expression, by the readiness and variety of his inventions, and by his natural pictures of the passions, especially those of the gay and amorous kind: And however his faults may diminish our satisfaction, they are not able entirely to destroy it. Did our pleasure really arise from those parts of his poem, which we denominate faults, this would be no objection to criticism in general: It would only be an objection to those particular rules of criticism, which would establish such circumstances to be faults, and would represent them as universally blameable. If they are found to please, they cannot be faults; let the pleasure, which they produce, be ever so unexpected and unaccountable.

But though all the general rules of art are founded only on experience and on the observation of the common sentiments of human nature, we must not imagine, that, on every occasion, the feelings of men will be conformable to these rules. Those finer emotions of the mind are of a very tender and delicate nature, and require the concurrence of many favourable circumstances to make them play with facility and exactness, according to their general and established principles. The least exterior hindrance to such small springs, or the least internal disorder, disturbs their motion, and confounds the operation of the whole machine. When we would make an experiment of this nature, and would try the force of any beauty or deformity, we must choose with care a proper time and place, and bring the fancy to a suitable situation and disposition. A perfect serenity of mind, a recollection of thought, a due attention to the object; if any of these circumstances be wanting, our experiment will be fallacious, and we shall be unable to judge of the catholic and universal beauty. The relation, which nature has placed between the form and the sentiment, will at least be more obscure; and it will require greater accuracy to trace and discern it. We shall be able to ascertain its influence not so much from the operation of each particular beauty, as from the durable admiration, which attends those works, that have survived all the caprices of mode and fashion, all the mistakes of ignorance and envy.

The same HOMER, who pleased at ATHENS and ROME two thousand years ago, is still admired at PARIS and at LONDON. All the changes of climate, government, religion, and language, have not been able to obscure his glory. Authority or prejudice may give a temporary vogue to a bad poet or orator; but his reputation will never be durable or general. When his compositions are examined by posterity or by foreigners, the enchantment is dissipated, and his faults appear in their true colours. On the contrary, a real genius, the longer his works endure, and the more wide they are spread, the more sincere is the admiration which he meets with. Envy and jealousy have too much place in a narrow circle; and even familiar acquaintance with his person may diminish the applause due to his performances: But when these obstructions are removed, the beauties, which are naturally fitted to excite agreeable sentiments, immediately display their energy; and while the world endures, they maintain their authority over the minds of men.

It appears then, that, amidst all the variety and caprice of taste, there are certain general principles of approbation or blame, whose influence a careful eye may trace in all operations of the mind. Some particular forms or qualities, from the original structure of the internal fabric, are calculated to please, and others to displease; and if they fail of their effect in any particular instance, it is from some apparent defect or imperfection in the organ. A man in a fever would not insist on his palate as able to decide concerning flavours; nor would one, affected with the jaundice, pretend to give a verdict with regard to colours. In each creature, there is a sound and a defective state; and the former alone can be supposed to afford us a true standard of taste and sentiment. If, in the sound state of the organ, there be an entire or a considerable uniformity of sentiment among men, we may thence derive an idea of the perfect beauty; in like manner as the appearance of objects in day-light, to the eye of a man in health, is denominated their true and real colour, even while colour is allowed to be merely a phantasm of the senses.

Many and frequent are the defects in the internal organs, which prevent or weaken the influence of those general principles, on which depends our sentiment of beauty or deformity. Though some objects, by the structure of the mind, be naturally calculated to give pleasure, it is not to be expected, that in every individual the pleasure will be equally felt. Particular incidents and situations occur, which either throw a false light on the objects, or hinder the true from conveying to the imagination the proper sentiment and perception.

One obvious cause, why many feel not the proper sentiment of beauty, is the want of that *delicacy* of imagination, which is requisite to convey a sensibility of those finer emotions. This delicacy every one pretends to: Every one talks of it; and would reduce every kind of taste or sentiment to its standard. But as our intention in this essay is to mingle some light of the understanding with the feelings of sentiment, it will be proper to give a more accurate definition of delicacy, than has hitherto been attempted. And not to draw our philosophy from too profound a source, we shall have recourse to a noted story in DON QUIXOTE.

It is with good reason, says SANCHO to the squire with the great nose, that I pretend to have a judgment in wine: This is a quality hereditary in our family. Two of my kinsmen were once called to give their opinion of a hogshead, which was supposed to be excellent, being old and of a good vintage. One of them tastes it; considers it; and after mature reflection pronounces the wine to be good, were it not for a small taste of leather, which he perceived in it. The other, after using the same precautions, gives also his verdict in favour of the wine; but with the reserve of a taste of iron, which he could easily distinguish. You cannot imagine how much they were both ridiculed for their judgment. But who laughed in the end? On emptying the hogshead, there was found at the bottom, an old key with a leathern thong tied to it.

The great resemblance between mental and bodily taste will easily teach us to apply this story. Though it be certain, that beauty and deformity, more than sweet and bitter, are not qualities in objects, but belong entirely to the sentiment, internal or external; it must be allowed, that there are certain qualities in objects, which are fitted by nature to produce those particular feelings. Now as these qualities may be found in a small degree, or may be mixed and confounded with each other, it often happens, that the taste is not affected with such minute qualities, or is not able to distinguish all the particular flavours, amidst the disorder, in which they are presented. Where the organs are so fine, as to allow nothing to escape them; and at the same time so exact as to perceive every ingredient in the composition: This we call delicacy of taste, whether we employ these terms in the literal or metaphorical sense. Here then the general rules of beauty are of use; being drawn from established models, and from the observation of what pleases or displeases, when presented singly and in a high degree: And if the same qualities, in a continued composition and in a smaller degree, affect not the organs with a sensible delight or uneasiness, we exclude the person from all pretensions to this delicacy. To produce these general rules or avowed patterns of composition is like finding the key with the leathern thong; which justified the verdict of SANCHO's kinsmen, and confounded those pretended judges who had condemned them. Though the hogshead had never been emptied, the taste of the one was still equally delicate, and that of the other equally dull and languid: But it would have been more difficult to have proved the superiority of the former, to the conviction of every by-stander. In like manner, though the beauties of writing had never been methodized, or reduced to general principles; though no excellent models had ever been acknowledged; the different degrees of taste would still have subsisted, and the judgment of one man been preferable to that of another; but it would not have been so easy to silence the bad critic, who might always insist upon his particular sentiment, and refuse to submit to his antagonist. But when we show him an avowed principle of art; when we illustrate this principle by examples, whose operation, from his own particular taste, he acknowledges to be conformable to the principle; when we prove, that the same principle may be applied to the present case, where he did not perceive or feel its influence: He must conclude, upon the whole, that the fault lies in himself, and that he wants the delicacy, which is requisite to make him sensible of every beauty and every blemish, in any composition or discourse.

It is acknowledged to be the perfection of every sense or faculty, to perceive with exactness its most minute objects, and allow nothing to escape its notice and observation. The smaller the objects are, which become sensible to the eye, the finer is that organ, and the more elaborate its make and composition. A good palate is not tried by strong flavours; but by a mixture of small ingredients, where we are still sensible of each part, notwithstanding its minuteness and its confusion with the rest. In like manner, a quick and acute perception of beauty and deformity must be the perfection of our mental taste; nor can a man be satisfied with himself while he suspects, that any excellence or blemish in a discourse has passed him unobserved. In this case, the perfection of the man, and the perfection of the sense or feeling, are found to be united. A very delicate palate, on many occasions, may be a great inconvenience both to a man himself and to his friends: But a delicate taste of wit or beauty must always be a desirable quality; because it is the source of all the finest and most innocent enjoyments, of which human nature is susceptible. In this decision the sentiments of all mankind are agreed. Wherever you can ascertain a delicacy of taste, it is sure to meet with approbation; and the best way of ascertaining it is to appeal to those models and principles, which have been established by the uniform consent and experience of nations and ages.

But though there be naturally a wide difference in point of delicacy between one person and another, nothing tends further to encrease and improve this talent, than *practice* in a particular art, and the frequent survey or contemplation of a particular species of beauty. When objects of any kind are first presented to the eye or imagination, the sentiment, which attends them, is obscure and confused; and the mind is, in a great measure, incapable of pronouncing concerning their merits or defects. The taste cannot perceive the several excellences of the performance; much less distinguish the particular character of each excellency, and ascertain its quality and degree. If it pronounce the whole in general to be beautiful or deformed, it is the utmost that can be expected; and even this judgment, a person, so unpractised, will be apt to deliver with great hesitation and reserve. But allow him to acquire experience in those objects, his feeling becomes more exact and nice: He not only perceives the beauties and defects of each part, but marks the distinguishing species of each quality, and assigns it suitable praise or blame. A clear and distinct sentiment attends him through the whole survey of the objects; and he discerns that very degree and kind of approbation or displeasure, which each part is naturally fitted to produce. The mist dissipates, which seemed formerly to hang over the object: The organ acquires greater perfection in its operations; and can pronounce, without danger of mistake, concerning the merits of every performance. In a word, the same address and dexterity, which practice gives to the execution of any work, is also acquired by the same means, in the judging of it.

So advantageous is practice to the discernment of beauty, that, before we can give judgment on any work of importance, it will even be requisite, that that very individual performance be more than once perused by us, and be surveyed in different lights with attention and deliberation. There is a flutter or hurry of thought which attends the first perusal of any piece, and which confounds the genuine sentiment of beauty. The relation of the parts is not discerned: The true characters of style are little distinguished: The several perfections and defects seem wrapped up in a species of confusion, and present themselves indistinctly to the imagination. Not to mention, that there is a species of beauty, which, as it is florid and superficial, pleases at first; but being found incompatible with a just expression either of reason or passion, soon palls upon the taste, and is then rejected with disdain, at least rated at a much lower value.

It is impossible to continue in the practice of contemplating any order of beauty, without being frequently obliged to form *comparisons* between the several species and degrees of excellence, and estimating their proportion to each other. A man, who has had no opportunity of comparing the different kinds of beauty, is indeed totally unqualified to pronounce an opinion with regard to any object presented to him. By comparison alone we fix the epithets of praise or blame, and learn how to assign the due degree of each. The coarsest daubing contains a certain lustre of colours and exactness of imitation, which are so far beauties, and would affect the mind of a peasant or Indian with the highest admiration. The most vulgar ballads are not entirely destitute of harmony or nature; and none but a person, familiarized to superior beauties, would pronounce their numbers harsh, or narration uninteresting. A great inferiority of beauty gives pain to a person conversant in the highest excellence of the kind, and is for that reason pronounced a deformity: As the most finished object, with which we are acquainted, is naturally supposed to have reached the pinnacle of perfection, and to be entitled to the highest applause. One accustomed to see, and examine, and weigh the several performances, admired in different ages and nations, can only rate the merits of a work exhibited to his view, and assign its proper rank among the productions of genius.

But to enable a critic the more fully to execute this undertaking, he must preserve his mind free from all *prejudice,* and allow nothing to enter into his consideration, but the very object which is submitted to his examination. We may observe, that every work of art, in order to produce its due effect on the mind, must be surveyed in a certain point of view, and cannot be fully relished by persons, whose situation, real or imaginary, is not conformable to that which is required by the performance. An orator addresses himself to a particular audience, and must have a regard to their particular genius, interests, opinions, passions, and prejudices; otherwise he hopes in vain to govern their resolutions, and inflame their affections. Should they even have entertained some prepossessions against him, however unreasonable, he must not overlook this disadvantage; but, before he enters upon the subject, must endeavour to conciliate their affection, and acquire their good graces. A critic of a different age or nation, who should peruse this discourse, must have all these circumstances in his eye, and must place himself in the same situation as the audience, in order to form a true judgment of the oration. In like manner, when any work is addressed to the public, though I should have a friendship or enmity with the author, I must depart from this situation; and considering myself as a man in general, forget, if possible, my individual being and my peculiar circumstances. A person influenced by prejudice, complies not with this condition; but obstinately maintains his natural position, without placing himself in that point of view, which the performance supposes. If the work be addressed to persons of a different age or nation, he makes no allowance for their peculiar views and prejudices; but, full of the manners of his own age and country, rashly condemns what seemed admirable in the eyes of those for whom alone the discourse was calculated. If the work be executed for the public, he never sufficiently enlarges his comprehension, or forgets his interest as a friend or enemy, as a rival or commentator. By this means, his sentiments are perverted; nor have the same beauties and blemishes the same influence upon him, as if he had imposed a proper violence on his imagination, and had forgotten himself for a moment. So far his taste evidently departs from the true standard; and of consequence loses all credit and authority.

It is well known, that in all questions, submitted to the understanding, prejudice is destructive of sound judgment, and perverts all operations of the intellectual faculties: It is no less contrary to good taste; nor has it less influence to corrupt our sentiment of beauty. It belongs to *good sense* to check its influence in both cases; and in this respect, as well as in many others, reason, if not an essential part of taste, is at least requisite to the operations of this latter faculty. In all the nobler productions of genius, there is a mutual relation and correspondence of parts; nor can either the beauties or blemishes be perceived by him, whose thought is not capacious enough to comprehend all those parts, and compare them with each other, in order to perceive the consistence and uniformity of the whole. Every work of art has also a certain end or purpose, for which it is calculated; and is to be deemed more or less perfect, as it is more or less fitted to attain this end. The object of eloquence is to persuade, of history to instruct, of poetry to please by means of the passions and the imagination. These ends we must carry constantly in our view, when we peruse any performance; and we must be able to judge how far the means employed are adapted to their respective purposes. Besides, every kind of composition, even the most poetical, is nothing but a chain of propositions and reasonings; not always, indeed, the justest and most exact, but still plausible and specious, however disguised by the colouring of the imagination. The persons introduced in tragedy and epic poetry, must be represented as reasoning, and thinking, and concluding, and acting, suitably to their character and circumstances; and without judgment, as well as taste and invention, a poet can never hope to succeed in so delicate an undertaking. Not to mention, that the same excellence of faculties which contributes to the improvement of reason, the same clearness of conception, the same exactness of distinction, the same vivacity of apprehension, are essential to the operations of true taste, and are its infallible concomitants. It seldom, or never happens, that a man of sense, who has experience in any art, cannot judge of its beauty; and it is no less rare to meet with a man who has a just taste without a sound understanding.

Thus, though the principles of taste be universal, and, nearly, if not entirely the same in all men; yet few are qualified to give judgment on any work of art, or establish their own sentiment as the standard of beauty. The organs of internal sensation are seldom so perfect as to allow the general principles their full play, and produce a feeling correspondent to those principles. They either labour under some defect, or are vitiated by some disorder; and by that means, excite a sentiment, which may be pronounced erroneous. When the critic has no delicacy, he judges without any distinction, and is only affected by the grosser and more palpable qualities of the object: The finer touches pass unnoticed and disregarded. Where he is not aided by practice, his verdict is attended with confusion and hesitation. Where no comparison has been employed, the most frivolous beauties, such as rather merit the name of defects, are the object of his admiration. Where he lies under the influence of prejudice, all his natural sentiments are perverted. Where good sense is wanting, he is not qualified to discern the beauties of design and reasoning, which are the highest and most excellent. Under some or other of these imperfections, the generality of men labour; and hence a true judge in the finer arts is observed, even during the most polished ages, to be so rare a character: Strong sense, united to delicate sentiment, improved by practice, perfected by comparison, and cleared of all prejudice, can alone entitle critics to this valuable character; and the joint verdict of such, wherever they are to be found, is the true standard of taste and beauty.

But where are such critics to be found? By what marks are they to be known? How distinguish them from pretenders? These questions are embarrassing; and seem to throw us back into the same uncertainty, from which, during the course of this essay, we have endeavoured to extricate ourselves.

But if we consider the matter aright, these are questions of fact, not of sentiment. Whether any particular person be endowed with good sense and a delicate imagination, free from prejudice, may often be the subject of dispute, and be liable to great discussion and enquiry: But that such a character is valuable and estimable will be agreed in by all mankind. Where these doubts occur, men can do no more than in other disputable questions, which are submitted to the understanding: They must produce the best arguments, that their invention suggests to them; they must acknowledge a true and decisive standard to exist somewhere, to wit, real existence and matter of fact; and they must have indulgence to such as differ from them in their appeals to this standard. It is sufficient for our present purpose, if we have proved, that the taste of all individuals is not upon an equal footing, and that some men in general, however difficult to be particularly pitched upon, will be acknowledged by universal sentiment to have a preference above others. . . .

Though men of delicate taste be rare, they are easily to be distinguished in society, by the soundness of their understanding and the superiority of their faculties above the rest of mankind. The ascendant, which they acquire, gives a prevalence to that lively approbation, with which they receive any productions of genius, and renders it generally predominant. Many men, when left to themselves, have but a faint and dubious perception of beauty, who yet are capable of relishing any fine stroke, which is pointed out to them. Every convert to the admiration of the real poet or orator is the cause of some new conversion. And though prejudices may prevail for a time, they never unite in celebrating any rival to the true genius, but yield at last to the force of nature and just sentiment. Thus, though a civilized nation may easily be mistaken in the choice of their admired philosopher, they never have been found long to err, in their affection for a favorite epic or tragic author.

But notwithstanding all our endeavours to fix a standard of taste, and reconcile the discordant apprehensions of men, there still remain two sources of variation, which are not sufficient indeed to confound all the boundaries of beauty and deformity, but will often serve to produce a difference in the degrees of our approbation or blame. The one is the different humours of particular men; the other, the particular manners and opinions of our age and country. The general principles of taste are uniform in human nature: Where men vary in their judgments, some defect or perversion in the faculties may commonly be remarked; proceeding either from prejudice, from want of practice, or want of delicacy; and there is just reason for approving one taste, and condemning another. But where there is such a diversity in the internal frame or external situation as is entirely blameless on both sides, and leaves no room to give one the preference above the other; in that case a certain degree of diversity in judgment is unavoidable, and we seek in vain for a standard, by which we can reconcile the contrary sentiments.

A young man, whose passions are warm, will be more sensibly touched with amorous and tender images, than a man more advanced in years, who takes pleasure in wise, philosophical reflections concerning the conduct of life and moderation of the passions. At twenty, Ovid may be the favourite author; Horace at forty; and perhaps Tacitus at fifty. Vainly would we, in such cases, endeavour to enter into the sentiments of others, and divest ourselves of those propensities, which are natural to us. We choose our favourite author as we do our friend, from a conformity of humour and disposition. Mirth or passion, sentiment or reflection; whichever of these most predominates in our temper, it gives us a peculiar sympathy with the writer who resembles us.

One person is more pleased with the sublime; another with the tender; a third with raillery. One has a strong sensibility to blemishes, and is extremely studious of correctness: Another has a more lively feeling of beauties, and pardons twenty absurdities and defects for one elevated or pathetic stroke. The ear of this man is entirely turned towards conciseness and energy; that man is delighted with a copious, rich, and harmonious expression. Simplicity is affected by one; ornament by another. Comedy, tragedy, satire, odes, have each its partizans, who prefer that particular species of writing to all others. It is plainly an error in a critic, to confine his approbation to one species or style of writing, and condemn all the rest. But it is almost impossible not to feel a predilection for that which suits our particular turn and disposition. Such preferences are innocent and unavoidable, and can never reasonably be the object of dispute, because there is no standard, by which they can be decided. . . .

Morris Weitz

Criticism without Evaluation

I can put the philosophical problem of criticism best in this way. In their discussions about art, people are always saying things like "This is good," "This is great," "This is better than that," etc.; but when they ask themselves in their reflective moments or are asked by others in their disputative moments precisely what it is that these statements are about or how one could show them to be true, they find it exceedingly difficult to offer any satisfactory answer.

What crystallizes the problem for them is the fact that they encounter no similar difficulty in their other remarks. They can assert with no fear of engendering insoluble disputes many salient things about art, for example, about the specific character and functioning of the images, metaphors, and metrics of a given poem. Stated succinctly, then, the problem is this: What is the difference between, for example, "This is an image" and "This is a good image"?

Aestheticians call this the problem of the status of the key terms of the critic's vocabulary, or the problem of standards or criteria in art. And they note with genuine concern how many of our contemporary professional critics have come to consider this problem of the validation of aesthetic judgments as the central, crucial one in their craft, having written about it in such a way as to link the future of the critical enterprise to a specific solution of the problem. From each other, but especially from philosophers, these critics demand an answer which will render their statements about the aesthetic values of works of art objectively true or false.

[Reprinted from *The Philosophical Review*, 61: 59–65 (1952). Footnote renumbered.]

Now, if this sketch is at all consonant with your own thoughts on the philosophical problem of criticism, and if any of you share in the manifest anxieties over it, then I ought to confess at the very beginning that this paper will offer you no comfort whatsoever since it has no solution to propose that can establish the requisite parallels between the evaluative and the descriptive claims about art. Rather my hope is that before we are finished we shall see that no solution is needed in order to retain that which is essential in criticism.

As much as I may agree with some of you in your understandable antipathies to the value theories of the logical positivists, it seems to me that we must accept at least two related, fundamental points that they have succeeded in making, which together constitute a prolegomenon to any future philosophy of criticism. These two points are, first, that aesthetic judgments, like "This poem is great," are not factual reports on the properties of works of art or, at any rate, that no one has yet shown that they are; and, secondly, that consequently, these judgments are not objectively true or false in the sense desired by those who are anxious over the problem of criticism.

It does not, of course, in the least follow that, therefore, all aesthetic evaluations are emotive or persuasive definitions in character, which is an entirely separate consideration; and, if anyone should persist in maintaining that they are, simply because they are not factual reports, he would be indulging in a *non sequitur,* the enormity of which is a blight upon a good deal of our prevalent thinking about evaluation.

One rather expansive example will suffice, I think, to establish the thesis that aesthetic evaluations are not true or false in the requisite sense. Let us begin, paradigmatically, with two readers of a poem, disputing over its aesthetic worth. On the simplest level of argument, the first (A) may say to the second (B) : "This poem is good." B, faced with a number of alternatives, asks, "Why is it good?" to which A replies: "Well, it has good imagery, good metaphor, fine language, and an important theme." This may be all that is required, and B concludes, "Yes, what you say is true. This poem is good."

It is easy to see what has happened here. A has persuaded B to change his opinion about the poem through a simple reference to some of the constituents of it. Although this pattern of disputation may strike us as rather simplified, we can quickly assure ourselves that it occurs again and again in ordinary as well as professional criticism. People are constantly changing each other's evaluations by reference to some of the constituents of works of art which one of the disputants has distorted or overlooked.

Any such resolution of disagreement into agreement should not mislead us into concluding either that the imagery, metaphors, language, and theme are good; or that the total goodness of the poem is identical with the goodness of its constituents. Neither of these has been proved or even discussed. Instead, they are simply taken for granted by both disputants. Thus, the fact of agreement, either in two's or even in total human universality, some sociologists notwithstanding, is no argument for the truth or falsity of aesthetic judgments.

Suppose—to bring out another point with our example—that, when A says, "This poem is good because of its good imagery, metaphors, etc.," B replies instead, "I disagree. This is a bad poem; the imagery is strained, the language is precious, the metaphors are forced, and the theme is trivial." Now, our first inclination might be to suppose that with these remarks B has shifted the dispute from one of evaluation to one of fact, for surely everyone knows what a strained image is, or a forced metaphor, or precious language, or a trivial theme. But I think that any persistent attempt to state the difference between a strained image and one that is not, or between a trivial theme and an important one, will bring us right back to our starting point rather than to any solution. "What is a strained image?" is like "What is a good image?" not like "What is an image?" In other words, "strained," "precious," and "trivial" are in the same category as "good," "bad," and "great."

The dispute may take a different turn. A says, "This poem is good." B asks, "Why?" A replies, "Because it has good imagery, metaphor, language, and theme." B may now counter with "So what if it does?" to which A replies, "But that is what makes a good poem." A's move here could be a powerful one, for what he has proposed is a definition of good poetry, and in a manner which is disguised, perhaps even to himself, in an attempt to persuade his opponent. If A is successful, i.e., if B accepts the move, B will resolve the dispute with his "I agree. This is a good poem." But here, too, the resolution of the argument through the use of a persuasive definition does not in the least support the claim that "This is a good poem" is a factual report, either true or false, on anything in the poem in the way that the images, language, metaphors, and themes are there. We can see that this is the case by considering B's alternative to A's definition. If B returns a rejective, "I disagree. Good poetry, whatever it is, is certainly not the same as good imagery, metaphor, language, and theme," A has no further recourse. He and B have reached a final disagreement, and it is useless to continue the argument any further.

Now, what this whole example adds up to is that no evaluative judgment in artistic criticism can be interpreted as a factual report on constituents of works of art and that there are no objective standards or criteria in evaluative criticism, at least in so far as these latter depend upon the truth of the report.

No doubt many of you will feel that whatever plausibility the analysis possesses thus far depends entirely upon the nature of the example. Any two readers of poetry, it will be remarked, who argue aesthetic worth in such a manner deserve to come to their nihilistic end. There may be a good deal of cogency in this observation and, therefore, before we capitulate to the axiology of positivism, perhaps we ought to try to formulate a more acceptable theory of aesthetic validation.

Many distinguished contemporary readers of poetry are agreed that the necessary condition of good poetry (and of any work of art) is what they call the fact of integration: that any constituent, be it an image, an allusion, a specific metrical pattern, shall relate effectively in a contributory manner to every other constituent of the work. Integrated constituents enhance the aesthetic values of each other and, consequently, the whole poem. This means that no constituent, an image, for example, can be isolated from the entirety of the poem, to be probed for its aesthetic goodness. Whatever value it may have will derive from its relations to the other constituents. The difference, then, between good poetry and bad is the difference between the presence of integration and its absence, where by the latter is meant the detrimental working against each other of the constituents. Thus, Shelley's poem, "Death," is rejected by at least two critics because "Here . . . we have a case in which the specific feeling stimulated by the jigging rhythm, tends to contradict the response suggested by the ideas, images, etc. of the poem. The poem is an unsuccessful poem because the parts do not work together—they are not properly related." [1]

There are some among these readers of poetry who, if they could refute positivism and because of their specific solution of the problem of poetic belief, consider the factor of integration as the total necessary and sufficient condition of good poetry. But, be that as it may, there are at any rate many people who would say that "This poem is good" means (at least) "This poem has integrated imagery, metaphor, language, and theme, etc."

Logically speaking, on this view, the evaluative judgments of criticism purport to be about certain second-order properties of the first-order constituents of poetry, namely, the properties of integration, or its absence, of the various images, metaphors, etc. Aesthetic goodness, badness, greatness, in all their degrees, are second-order properties of the relations among the various constituents of poetry. Therefore, aesthetic judgments, when they are about these properties, are objective, verifiable, testable and, of course, true or false in the requisite sense. And, as for disputation, it is completely resolvable through reference to the work of art. Thus, if one critic declares a certain poem to be bad because, let us say, the final stanza is read as mere addendum to the rest of the poem, then a second critic, on this view, can refute him by showing that the stanza in question functions to integrate the total poem, for example, that it serves to complete a metaphor, begun in the first few lines and unfolded through the entire poem, including the final stanza. The second critic has proved the first to be aesthetically wrong by showing that the poem, because it is integrated, is a good one.

We all know, I think, that this organic theory, as it is now called, has become an important one in modern aesthetics, being

---

[1] C. Brooks and R. P. Warren, *Understanding Poetry*, pp. 219–220.

championed in artistic creation as well as in criticism, and in all the arts along with their associated bodies of criticism. It would seem to me that if any theory of criticism is credible at all in contemporary aesthetics, then the organic is that theory. But, unfortunately, we are once again confronted with the problem: Is it possible, i.e., can it withstand the positivist analysis? As much as I should like to deny it, it seems to me that the following brief dialogue suffices to show that it cannot; that, philosophically, it is no more secure than any other view.

Critic: "This poem is good."

Positivist: "Why?"

Critic: "Because all of its constituents work together successfully. It is integrated."

Positivist: "But why is good poetry integrated poetry?"

This, to my mind, is the crucial question, the one that sustains the positivist thesis of the nonfactual character of critical evaluations. Integration is a fact, lack of it is a fact, but that it is either basic to or identical with good poetry (or art) is not a fact, or at least no one has shown that it is. The searching critic, seeking validation of his theory, must ask himself about the status of his definition of a good poem as an integrated one: Is it a self-evident truth? Obviously not, since the denial of the definition is not self-contradiction. Is it an empirical truth? Then what is the fact to which it corresponds? Is it merely a stipulation or a recommendation? But, if that is all that it is, the definition loses all of its requisite effectiveness in dealing with the problem of validation. As matters now stand, philosophically speaking, the only recourse of the critic is to admit that he is employing the definition either in a persuasive sense or, what is more likely, as a working postulate which he accepts as basic in his critical practice, but which has none of the characteristics of the objective doctrine that he desires.

It is not hard to see that the same sort of difficulty confronts any other definition, however traditional and respectable in the history of criticism. What has been said of the criterion of integration can also be said of the criteria of profundity, truth, universality, social significance, freshness, scope, maturity, etc., even if these could be rendered less vague and more applicable to works of art than they are at present. That good art is profound art, or universal art, for example, is no more a necessary or empirical truth than that it is integrated art.

Once more we have reached our negative goal; and, again, may I remind you that there is no devil's advocacy in this recitation of the facts in the present crisis of criticism. Rather, my advocacy is that we begin where we must, with the stunning attack by positivism on the possibility of evaluative criticism. To many of you who share in this conviction regarding the cogency of the positivist analysis, it may now seem like the end: no objective evaluation, no criticism. Until recently, I would have agreed with you; but the more I have thought about the problem and have been able to comprehend what has been occurring lately in at least one prolific quarter of professional criticism, the less inclined I am to take such a hopeless view of the situation. As a matter of fact, it may be no exaggeration to say that we are instead at the very beginning of a new and extremely fruitful stage in the history of criticism, one which we can properly refer to as criticism without evaluation. If some of the recent examples of this new approach may serve as signs of things to come, then we may be able to formulate, in terms of them, a constructive program for artistic criticism which would be rooted in the affirmation of the nonfactual character of aesthetic judgments and which would be subject to none of the pervasive anxieties over evaluation.

It is in the specific area of literary criticism that one can discern most clearly the basic ideas of this new approach to a criticism which is primarily nonevaluative; and where the evaluations, such as they are, seem to function in the separate critical essays only as final addenda or interspersed interjections. Most of this criticism, quite rightly, although for somewhat different reasons from those enumerated here, has become designated as the "New Criticism." Whatever their supposed shortcomings or exaggerations, and quite independently of some of their specific doctrines regarding the nature of poetry, what is fundamental in a number of the essays of these "new critics" is their insight into the possibility of extremely illuminating nonevaluative criticism. Working on the assumption that the fundamental obligation of the critics is to provide readers, including themselves, with as

complete and intelligent a reading of the work of art—conceived
as a work of art and not as something else, like a social tract or a
metaphysical discourse—as they can, they have come to interpret
their primary function to be the explication of the various constituents of the work of art before them. And because they have
correctly understood the organic character of these constituents,
they have stressed in their critical exegeses the functional roles of
the various constituents. It is never a particular image which is
isolated from a particular poem that is their critical concern, but
the functioning of that image in relation to the rest of the poem.
The same with metaphor, metrics, theme, etc. To explicate the
interrelated roles of the various constituents of works of art and
to communicate this explication to the reader in as clear, compre-
hensive, and concrete a fashion as he can—that is the primary
task of the "new critic," no matter whether he fulfills this task in
the criticism of literature or painting or music, etc. And it is
indeed with a sense of tremendous satisfaction that the aesthetician can turn to a number of critical essays in all of the arts today
and see the partial realization of the same sort of program of
explication that has developed in literary criticism. In their
persistent desire to get as close as they can to the actual, concrete
character of the painting or building or motion picture under
scrutiny, many critics have forsaken the traditional rhapsodical
vocabularies associated with the gasping theories of art appreciation and have supplanted them with precise, denotative terms
which can function effectively in the communication between the
critic and his public. To read any of these critics on a particular
work of art is to get near to the work in a way that we have never
been able to before. When, for example, we read one of these
"new critics" on a particular poem, let us say, and grasp and,
more important, test what he is saying about the functional
character of the imagery, metaphors, metrics, or, especially, the
depth meanings and symbols within the poem, whether that
poem be one of Donne's or Keats's or Eliot's, then it seems to me
that in the mutual comprehension of the explication, we have
completed the whole of the critical transaction. What would it
add to our appreciation, i.e., our reading, to be told, by him or
us, that the poem is also good or bad or great? I submit, nothing.